Pocket Rough Guide

ROME

W9-CEN-034

this third edition updated by

NATASHA FOGES

Contents

<< SWISS GUARDS AT THE VATICAN
< PONTE SANT'ANGELO WITH CASTEL SANT'ANGELO IN THE BACKGROUND

INTRODUCTION TO
ROME

When most people think of Rome they imagine sights and monuments: the Colosseum, Forum, the Vatican and St Peter's. Yet it is much more than an open-air museum: the city has constantly reinvented itself over the years, and with its unpretentious outlook, vibrant people, culture and food it has a modern and irresistible edge. As a historic place, it is special enough, but as a contemporary European capital, it is unique.

TREVI FOUNTAIN

Best places for the perfect Roman pizza

There are loads of great pizzerias in Rome that serve up traditional thin, crispy pizzas with the usual accompaniments of *supplí* and *fiori di zucca*. Most are open evenings only; if you want a lunchtime slice of pizza – *pizza al taglio* – try *Lo Zozzone* (see p.47), *Pizzarium* (see p.153) or *Il Forno di Campo de'Fiori* (see p.57). **THESE ARE OUR OTHER FAVOURITES** > Da Francesco p.48 > La Montecarlo p.48 > Alle Carette p.100 > Da Remo p.120

Rome's eras crowd in on top of one another to a remarkable degree: there are medieval churches atop ancient basilicas and palaces, houses and apartment blocks that incorporate fragments of Roman columns and inscriptions, and roads and piazzas that follow the lines of ancient amphitheatres and stadiums. It's not an easy place to absorb on one visit, and you need to take things slowly, even if you only have a couple of days here. Most of the sights can be approached from a number of directions, and part of the allure of Rome is stumbling across things by accident, gradually piecing the city together, rather than marching around to a timetable. It's best to decide on a few key attractions (check out our ideas in "Best of Rome") and see where your feet take you. Above all, don't be afraid to just wander.

You'd certainly be mad to risk your blood pressure in any kind of vehicle, and the best way of getting around the city centre is to walk. The same goes for the ancient sites, and probably the Vatican and Trastevere quarter too – although for these last two you might want to jump on a bus or a tram going across the river. Keep public transport for longer hops – down to Testaccio, Ostiense or EUR, or to the catacombs and the Via Appia Antica, and of course for trips outside the city: to Ostia Antica, Tivoli or nearby beaches.

AL FRESCO EATING BY THE PANTHEON

However you get around, the atmosphere is like no other city – a monumental, busy capital and yet an appealingly relaxed one, with a centre that has yet to be consumed by chainstores and multinational hotels. Above all, there has perhaps never been a better time to visit. Rome has recently been hauled into the twenty-first century: museums, churches and other buildings that had been "in restoration" as long as anyone can remember have reopened, and some of the city's historic collections have been re-housed. Plus, the city's cultural life has been enhanced, with frequent open-air concerts and a flourishing film festival in October. Transport, too, is being tackled, with the construction of a third metro line, although it may be some time before this is finished.

Whether all this will irrevocably alter the character of the city remains to be seen – the enhanced crowds of visitors, spurred on by the growth of cheap flights in recent years, are certainly having a go. But it's a resilient place, with a character like no other, and for now at least there's definitely no place like Rome.

When to visit

You can enjoy Rome at any time of year. However, you should, if you can, avoid coming in July and especially August, when it can be uncomfortably hot and most Romans are on holiday – indeed in August you may find many of the restaurants recommended in this book closed. May, June and September are the most comfortable months weather-wise – warm but not unbearably so, and not too humid. April and October can be nice too – the city is less crowded, outside Easter, and days can still be warm and sunny. The winter months can be a good time to visit, but bear in mind that the weather is unpredictable and while you'll find everything pleasantly uncrowded, a lot of attractions will have reduced opening hours.

ROME AT A GLANCE

>>EATING

Food is one of the highlights of any trip to Rome. You won't really eat badly anywhere: there are lots of good choices in the centro storico; the **Ghetto** and **Testaccio** have a large number of places serving traditional Roman food, while the densest concentration of restaurants of all kinds can be found in **Trastevere**. There's also an abundance of good, honest **pizzerias**, churning out thin, crispy pizza from wood-fired ovens. Be wary of restaurants adjacent to some major monuments. Note that many places are closed during August.

>>DRINKING

Many Roman bars are traditionally daytime haunts, but nowadays there are also plenty of bars and pubs conducive to an evening's drinking, and the city's old-fashioned wine bars or *enoteche* have also become more popular in recent years. The Milanese tradition of *aperitivi* has taken off in bars throughout the city; many places put on a free buffet at around 6–7pm to attract pre-dinner drinkers. Wherever you are, you can drink late – most places are open until at least 1am – but **Campo de' Fiori** and the **centro storico** near Piazza Navona, and the nightlife districts of **Trastevere** and **Testaccio**, are the liveliest areas in the city centre.

>>SHOPPING

Fashion straight from the catwalk is well represented on the streets close to the Spanish Steps – Via Condotti, Via Borgognona and Via del Babuino – where you'll find the flagship stores of Prada, Valentino and the like. **Via del Corso** caters to young fashion and cheap clothing. There are lots of small, independent boutiques around **Campo de' Fiori** and in **Monti**, and antique shops line **Via dei Coronari** and the streets around. Food is freshest and best in the markets on Campo de' Fiori and Testaccio. The **Porta Portese** flea market every Sunday morning is a quintessentially Roman experience.

>>NIGHTLIFE

There's a concentration of clubs in **Ostiense** and **Testaccio** (especially lively in summer), while **Trastevere**, and the **centro storico** from the Jewish Ghetto to the Pantheon, are good for bars, with the odd backstreet club. The **San Lorenzo** and **Pigneto** areas near Termini have plenty of laid-back, studenty hangouts, often with live music. More alternative places are run as private clubs – usually known as *centri sociali*, where entry will be free but you may be stung for a membership fee. Festivals take place throughout the summer with concerts of every sort, many of them free.

OUR RECOMMENDATIONS FOR WHERE TO EAT, DRINK AND SHOP ARE LISTED AT THE END OF EACH PLACES CHAPTER

Day One in Rome

1 Capitoline Hill > p.62. Rome began here, and the two museums that flank the elegant square are among the city's key sights.

2 Roman Forum > p.70. Some of the most ruined ruins you'll see, but also the most atmospheric.

3 Colosseum > p.68. The most recognizable and perhaps the greatest ancient Roman monument of them all.

Lunch > p.102. Enjoying the good, traditional Roman food at *Valentino*, it's hard to believe you're just a few minutes from the Colosseum.

4 Trevi Fountain > p.81. No trip to the city could be complete without a visit to this fountain.

5 Piazza di Spagna > p.74. The Spanish Steps, Keats-Shelley House and the square itself are among the city's most compelling attractions.

6 Ara Pacis > p.80. Enclosed in an impressive purpose-built structure, this amazing frieze displays the imperial family during the time of Augustus.

7 Galleria Borghese > p.133. The Bernini sculptures here are the pure essence of Rome (be sure to book in advance).

Dinner > p.129. A meal in lively Trastevere is a must – and you can't go wrong with a slap-up dinner at *La Gensola*.

Ice cream > p.86. *San Crispino* serves arguably the city's best ice cream.

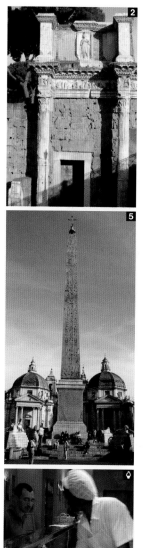

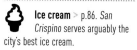

Day Two in Rome

1 St Peter's > p.144. It would be a pity to leave Rome without seeing the city's greatest Baroque attraction.

2 Vatican Museums > p.146. So much more than the Sistine Chapel – this staggering complex of museums is not to be missed.

Lunch > p.153. *Dal Toscano*, a long-established Tuscan restaurant close by the Vatican walls, is a good place to recover from museum fatigue.

3 Piazza Navona > p.40. One of the centro storico's loveliest open spaces, and close to the church of San Luigi dei Francesi and Palazzo Altemps.

4 Campo de' Fiori > p.52. Wander through Campo de' Fiori – many people's favourite Roman square – and explore the surrounding streets, full of shops and cafés.

5 The Pantheon > p.38. Rome's most intact ancient sight, and near one of the city's great churches, Santa Maria sopra Minerva.

6 The Ghetto > p.55. Stroll through the crumbling old Jewish quarter, an ancient part of the city centre.

Dinner > p.58. *Piperno* is the best of the Ghetto's restaurants, with fantastic Roman-Jewish cooking served in lovely surroundings.

Ice cream > p.57. *Alberto Pica* is one of the longest running and best of Rome's many *gelaterie*.

Budget Rome

Rome's piazzas, fountains and other public structures are a fantastic free spectacle, and many of its churches are packed with sumptuous art. Here are some suggestions for how to spend a great day in Rome without spending a penny on anything, apart from food and drink.

1 Vittoriano > p.61. Free to clamber up the steps and enjoy the views – though you pay for the lifts to the very top.

2 Trevi Fountain > p.81. The only cost is the coins you decide to chuck in.

3 Spanish Steps > p.75. All you need is energy to climb to the top and enjoy the views.

Lunch > p.57. *Il Forno di Campo de´ Fiori* is renowned for its pizza by the slice.

4 Palazzo Farnese > p.54. Tours of the fantastic Carracci ceiling cost only €5, if you can time it right and book in advance.

5 St Peter's > p.144. There's no entry fee for this or any other Roman church.

6 Vatican Museums > p.146. Free on the last Sunday of the month – perhaps the world's greatest sightseeing bargain.

Dinner > p.152. Head up to *Mondo Arancina* for some of the city's best *arancini* –just €2 a pop.

Ice cream > p.152 *Fatamorgana* serves huge portions of delicious ice cream.

Secret Rome

You could spend several days seeing Rome's most obvious sights, and you'd have a wonderful time – mostly with lots of other people. Here are some suggestions for having a great day out in the city, while avoiding the crowds.

1 Piazza dei Cavalieri di Malta > p.111. Peer through the ornate keyhole and you'll be rewarded with a special view – best enjoyed at sunset. Well worth the trek up the Aventine Hill.

5 Santi Quattro Coronati > p.105. The frescoes in the chapel of St Sylvester here are really something special.

6 Museo Storico della Liberazione > p.108. Housed in the wartime headquarters of the Gestapo, this is one of Rome's most moving museums.

Dinner > p.109. Close by San Giovanni, *Charly's Sauciere* is a long-established French food outpost that is little known by

2 Rooms of St Ignatius > p.51. Take in the small museum next door to the Gesù; it incorporates the rooms where St Ignatius stayed and a fantastic trompe l'oeil painting by Andrea Pozzo.

3 Galleria Colonna > p.81. Only open on a Saturday morning, and partly because of this an undiscovered treasure among the city's great family palace-galleries.

Lunch > p.87. Tucked away around the corner from the Trevi Fountain, *Colline Emiliane* does delicious Emilian food.

4 Casa de Chirico > p.75. Don't miss this "house" museum, left just as it was when the artist lived and worked here.

11

BEST OF ROME

Museums and galleries

1 Vatican Museums Home to the largest, richest, most diverse and most dazzling collections in the world. **> p.146**

2 Capitoline Museums Two amazing galleries – one displaying Roman sculpture, the other Roman sculpture and Italian art. **> p.62**

3 Galleria Borghese Fabulous Bernini sculpture and one of Rome's best picture galleries, housed in the Borghese family villa. **> p.133**

4 Museo Nazionale Romano You'll find the finest art collection in this museum's two main locations: Palazzo Altemps and Palazzo Massimo. **> p.44 & p.97**

5 Galleria Doria Pamphilj Private art collection that's intimately exhibited. **> p.34**

Viewpoints

1 St Peter's It's worth the climb up the dome to see this classic panorama.
> p.144

2 Vittorio Emanuele Monument

Many people's favourite view of Rome, because you can't see the Vittoriano monument itself. > **p.61**

3 Janiculum Hill
Of all Rome's hills, this one, to the west of the city centre, gives the fullest panorama of Rome. > **p.127**

4 Spanish Steps
Tourist Central, but ignore the crowds – the whole of Rome's centre is spread out before you. > **p.75**

5 Aventine Hill
The best views of the Vatican are from the top of Aventine Hill on the other side of the river. > **p.110**

Eating out

1 Roman specialities Sample traditional "poor" cuisine at *Checchino dal 1887*; the oxtail stew is a classic. > **p.120**

2 Eating alfresco Dining outdoors at *Dar Filettaro a Santa Barbara* gives you a great view of the evening *passeggiata*. > **p.58**

3 Pizza With a thin, crispy base and the freshest of toppings, the pizza at *Da Remo* is irresistible. > **p.120**

4 Backstreet trattorias
Unassuming, tucked-away trattorias can be full of surprises; old-timer *Da Tonino* is a gem. > **p.48**

5 Fine dining For a blow-the budget meal, Rome's clutch of Michelin-starred restaurants won't disappoint. *Oliver Glowig* is the foodies' favourite. **P.139**

Shopping

1 Campo de' Fiori This long-standing fruit and veg market takes place every morning except Sunday; in the surrounding streets you'll find countless independent boutiques. > **p.52**

2 Via del Corso This narrow street, lined with all the mid-range chains, is jam-packed with shoppers at weekends. **> p.34**

3 Via Condotti Lined with eye-wateringly expensive boutiques, this is the main spine of Rome's designer shopping quarter. **> p.74**

4 Via dei Coronari Rome's antiques alley, lined with shops selling everything from Renaissance chests to 1960s Italian coffeepots. **> p.43**

5 Monti Browse Monti's independent boutiques for cool clothes and chic homewares. **> p.99**

Palaces

1 Palazzo Farnese Perhaps the city's most elegant palace, now the French embassy, whose Carracci murals are one of the city's must-sees. **> p.54**

2 Villa Farnesina This Trastevere mansion was home to the banker Agostino Chigi, who employed Raphael to do the decorating. **> p.126**

3 Palazzo Spada The home of one Cardinal Spada is perhaps best known for its ingenious Borromini trompe l'oeil tunnel. **> p.53**

4 Palazzo Barberini The Barberini family's palace is one of the most sumptuous in Rome, and it also houses remarkable collections of art. **> p.83**

5 Palazzo del Quirinale The residence of the Italian president, today open once a week. **> p.84**

Churches

1 Santa Maria Maggiore One of the great Roman basilicas, and a treasure trove of art and history. **> p.91**

2 Santa Maria sopra Minerva
Rome's only Gothic church is also rich in Renaissance art, fronted by Bernini's endearing Elephant Statue.. > **p.35**

4 San Pietro in Vincoli A beautifully plain church, home to one of Michelangelo's greatest sculptures. > **p.94**

3 St Peter's Basilica Italy's largest church is stuffed with masterpieces, most notably Michelangelo's *Pietà* and Bernini's baldacchino. > **p.144**

5 San Clemente This ancient Roman church is the best place to appreciate the city's multi layered history. > **p.106**

Ancient Rome

1 Colosseum The most photographed of Rome's monuments – it has provided the blueprint for virtually all sports stadiums since. **> p.68**

2 The Pantheon An amazing building even in its time, but all the more incredible now, given how completely it has survived. > **p.38**

3 The Roman Forum Political, economic and religious hub of ancient Rome, the Forum is a must-see. > **p.70**

4 Ostia Antica The ruins of Rome's ancient port are some of the most atmospheric you will find anywhere. > **p.160**

5 Ara Pacis The gleaming marble walls were sculpted in 13 BC to celebrate the subjugation of Spain and Gaul. > **p.80**

Baroque Rome

1 Palazzo Barberini Check out Pietro da Cortona's ceiling, gushingly appropriate for the main patrons of the Baroque movement. **> p.83**

2 Santa Maria della Vittoria The daring statue of the *Ecstasy of St Theresa* by Bernini is perhaps the city's most dramatic piece of Baroque art. **> p.84**

3 San Carlo alle Quattro Fontane With four lovely fountains outside, this church is a masterpiece in Baroque design. **> p.83**

4 The Gesù As the centre of the Jesuit movement, this church set the benchmark for all Baroque churches to come. **> p.50**

5 St Peter's Square Bernini's colonnaded piazza is pure, theatrical Baroque – as is the church itself. **> p.141**

Outdoor Rome

1 Villa Borghese Rome's largest and most central open space, and by any standards a beautiful and diverse city park. > **p.132**

3 Janiculum Hill Some of the best views of the city are from this hill just above Trastevere. **> p.127**

2 Tivoli Tivoli's two Renaissance gardens are among the region's most compelling sights, and are just forty-five minutes from the city centre. **> p.154**

4 Via Appia Antica Though relatively close to the city centre, the Via Appia Antica feels like real countryside and is full of intriguing sights from ancient times. **> p.116**

5 Villa Celimontana Just above the Colosseum, this little park is a good venue for both shady picnics and regular summer jazz concerts. **> p.104**

The centro storico

The heart of Rome is the centro storico ("historic centre"), which makes up most of the triangular knob of land that bulges into a bend in the Tiber. This area, known in ancient Roman times as the Campus Martius, was outside the ancient city centre and mostly given over to barracks and sporting arenas, together with several temples, including the Pantheon. Later it became the heart of the Renaissance city, and nowadays it's the part of the town that is densest in interest, a knot of narrow streets and alleys that hold some of the best of Rome's churches and monuments and its most vivacious street- and nightlife. Whichever direction you wander in there's something to see; indeed its appeal is that even the most aimless ambling leads you past some memorably beautiful and historic spots.

VIA DEL CORSO

MAP P.36–37, POCKET MAP F13–15

Running north–south from Piazza del Popolo to Piazza Venezia, **Via del Corso** divides the city centre in two: the western side gives onto the dense streets of the centro storico and to the east, the swish shopping streets that converge on Piazza di Spagna. Named after the races that used to take place along here during Renaissance times, it is also Rome's main shopping street.

GALLERIA DORIA PAMPHILJ

Via del Corso 305. Daily 10am–5pm; €10.50, including audio guide in English; ☎ 06 679 7323, ⓦ doriapamphilj.it. MAP P.36–37, POCKET MAP F15

The Palazzo Doria Pamphilj is among the city's finest Rococo palaces; the Doria-Pamphilj have long been one of Rome's most illustrious families, and still own the building and live in part of it. They were prodigious collectors of art, and, inside, the **Galleria Doria Pamphilj** constitutes one of Rome's best late Renaissance art collections, its paintings mounted in the style of the time, crammed in floor-to-ceiling, around the main courtyard. There are many highlights: a rare Italian work by Bruegel the Elder, a highly realistic portrait of an old man, the fabulously ugly *Moneylenders and their Clients* by Quentin Matsys, and a Hans Memling *Deposition*, as well as several paintings by Caravaggio – the magnificent *Rest on the Flight into Egypt*, *John the Baptist* and *Repentant Magdalene* – in the series of rooms on the right, alongside *Salome with the head of St John*, by Titian. Across the courtyard look out for the gallery's most famous works: a badly cracked bust of Innocent X by Bernini, which the sculptor apparently replaced in a week with the more famous version down the hall, next door to Velázquez's famous painting of the same man. All in all, it is a marvellous collection of work, displayed in a wonderfully appropriate setting.

GALLERIA DORIA PAMPHILJ

PALAZZO CIPOLLA

Via del Corso 320 ☎ 06 678 6209. Tues–Sun 10am–8pm. Tickets from €10. MAP P.36–37, POCKET MAP F15

Run by a cultural foundation, **Palazzo Cipolla** is a major exhibition space offering a dose of culture on shop-heavy Via del Corso. Its high-profile international shows are always worth a look.

SANT'IGNAZIO

Via del Caravita 8a. Mon–Sat 7.30am–7pm, Sun 9am–7pm. MAP P.36–37, POCKET MAP F15

The Jesuit church of **Sant'Ignazio** was dedicated to the founder of the Society of Jesus after his death and canonization. It's worth visiting for its Baroque ceiling by Andrea Pozzo, showing St Ignatius being welcomed into paradise by Christ and the Virgin, a spectacular work that creates the illusion of looking at the sky through open colonnades. Pozzo also painted the ingenious false dome in the crossing (a real dome was planned but was deemed too expensive). Stand on the disc in nave's centre to get the full effect of this trompe l'oeil masterpiece.

SANTA MARIA SOPRA MINERVA

Piazza della Minerva 42. Mon–Fri 8am–7pm, Sat & Sun 8am–12.30pm & 3–7pm. MAP P.36–37, POCKET MAP E15

Piazza della Minerva is home to the medieval church of **Santa Maria sopra Minerva**, Rome's only Gothic church, and one of the city's art-treasure churches, with the Carafa chapel, in the south transept, home to Filippino Lippi's fresco of the *Assumption*. The children visible in the foreground are portraits of the future Medici popes, Leo X and Clement VII – both of whose tombs lie either side of the main altar. Look also at the figure of *Christ Bearing the Cross*, just in front, a serene work that Michelangelo completed for the church in 1521. Outside, the diminutive **Elephant Statue** is Bernini's most endearing piece of work: a cheery elephant trumpeting under the weight of the obelisk he carries on his back – a reference to Pope Alexander VII and supposed to illustrate the fact that strength should support wisdom.

The centro storico

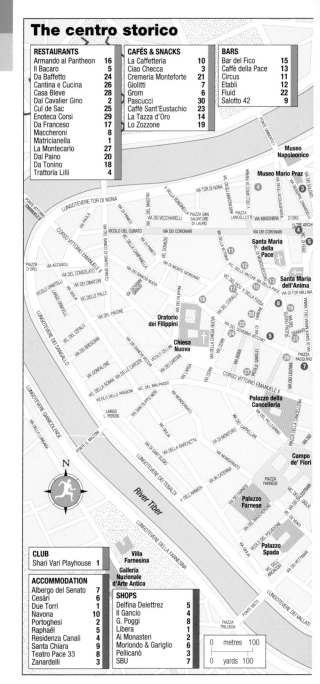

RESTAURANTS

Armando al Pantheon	16
Il Bacaro	5
Da Baffetto	24
Cantina e Cucina	26
Casa Bleve	28
Dal Cavalier Gino	2
Cul de Sac	25
Enoteca Corsi	29
Da Francesco	17
Maccheroni	8
Matricianella	1
La Montecarlo	27
Dal Paino	20
Da Tonino	18
Trattoria Lilli	4

CAFÉS & SNACKS

La Caffettiera	10
Ciao Checca	3
Cremeria Monteforte	21
Giolitti	7
Grom	6
Pascucci	30
Caffè Sant'Eustachio	23
La Tazza d'Oro	14
Lo Zozzone	19

BARS

Bar del Fico	15
Caffè della Pace	13
Circus	11
Etabli	12
Fluid	22
Salotto 42	9

CLUB

Shari Vari Playhouse	1

ACCOMMODATION

Albergo del Senato	7
Cesàri	6
Due Torri	1
Navona	10
Portoghesi	2
Raphaël	5
Residenza Canali	4
Santa Chiara	9
Teatro Pace 33	8
Zanardelli	3

SHOPS

Delfina Delettrez	5
Il Gancio	4
G. Poggi	8
Libera	1
Ai Monasteri	2
Moriondo & Gariglio	6
Pellicanò	3
SBU	7

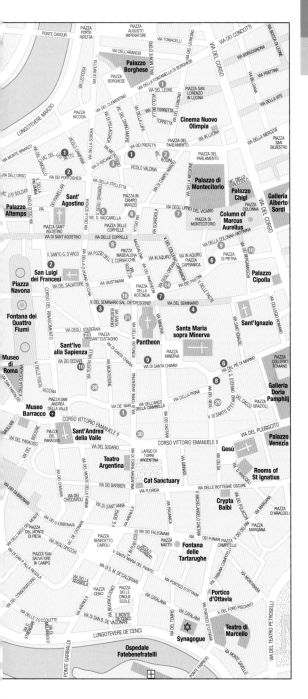

THE PANTHEON

Piazza della Rotonda. Mon–Sat
8.30am–7.30pm, Sun 9am–6pm; free. MAP
P.36–37, POCKET MAP E15

One of the centro storico's
busiest sights, the **Pantheon**
is the most complete ancient
Roman structure in the city,
and along with the Colosseum,
visually the most impressive.
Though originally a temple
that formed part of Marcus
Agrippa's redesign of the
Campus Martius in around
27 BC – hence the inscription
– the building was rebuilt by
the emperor Hadrian and
finished around the year 125
AD. Since consecrated as
a church, it's a formidable
architectural achievement
even now, and inside you get
the best impression of the
engineering expertise of the
time: the diameter is precisely
equal to its height (43m),
the hole in the centre of the
dome – from which shafts of
sunlight descend to illuminate
the musty interior – a full 9m
across. Most impressively,
there are no visible arches or
vaults to hold the whole thing
up; instead they're sunk into
the concrete of the walls of
the building. It would have
been richly decorated, the
coffered ceiling heavily
stuccoed and the niches filled
with the statues of gods. Now,
apart from the sheer size of
the place, the main object of
interest is the tomb of Raphael,
between the second and third
chapel on the left, with an
inscription by the humanist
cardinal Pietro Bembo: "Living,
great Nature feared he might
outvie Her works, and dying,
fears herself may die." The same
kind of sentiments might well
have been reserved for the
Pantheon itself.

SAN LUIGI DEI FRANCESI

Piazza San Luigi dei Francesi. Mon–Wed &
Fri –Sun 8.30am–12.30pm & 4–7pm, Thurs
10am–12.30pm. MAP P.36–37, POCKET MAP E14

The French national church of
San Luigi dei Francesi is worth
a visit, mainly for the works by
Caravaggio it numbers amongst
its collection. In the last chapel
on the left are three paintings:
The Calling of St Matthew,
in which Christ points to
Matthew, who is illuminated by
a shaft of sunlight; *St Matthew*

and the Angel, showing the visit of an angel as the apostle writes his Gospel; and *The Martyrdom of St Matthew*. Caravaggio's first public commission, these paintings were actually rejected at first, partly on grounds of indecorum, and it took considerable reworking by the artist before they were finally accepted. These days they are considered to be among the artist's greatest ever works, especially *The Calling of St Matthew*, which manifests the simple, taut drama, as well as the low-life subject matter, for which Caravaggio became so well known.

SANT'AGOSTINO

Piazza di Sant'Agostino. Daily 7.45am–noon & 4–7.30pm. MAP P.36–37, POCKET MAP D14

The Renaissance facade of the church of **Sant'Agostino** is not much to look at from the outside, but a handful of art treasures might draw you in – this was the church of Rome's creative community in the sixteenth century and as such drew wealthy patrons and well-connected artists. Just inside the door, the serene statue of the *Madonna del Parto*, by Sansovino is traditionally invoked during pregnancy, and is accordingly surrounded by photos of newborn babes and their blissful parents. Further into the church, Raphael's vibrant fresco of *Isaiah* is on the third pillar on the left, beneath which is another work by Sansovino – a craggy *St Anne, Virgin and Child*. But the biggest crowds gather around the first chapel on the left, where the *Madonna di Loreto*, painted in 1605 by Caravaggio, is a characteristic work of what was at the time almost revolutionary realism,

COLUMN OF MARCUS AURELIUS

scruffy clothes contrasting with the pale, delicate feet and skin of Mary.

PIAZZA DI MONTECITORIO AND PIAZZA COLONNA

MAP P.36–37, POCKET MAP E14–15

On the northern edge of the centro storico, **Piazza Montecitorio** takes its name from the bulky Palazzo di Montecitorio on its northern side, home since 1871 to the lower house of the Italian parliament (open first Sun of each month 10am–6pm; free). Just beyond, Piazza Colonna, flanked on its north side by the late sixteenth-century Palazzo Chigi, official residence of the prime minister, hosts the **Column of Marcus Aurelius,** erected between 180 and 190 AD to commemorate military victories in northern Europe, and – like the column of Trajan which inspired it – decorated with reliefs depicting scenes from the campaigns.

SANT'IVO ALLA SAPIENZA

Corso del Rinascimento 40. Sun 9am–noon; closed July & Aug. MAP P.36–37, POCKET MAP E15

Between the Pantheon and Piazza Navona, the Palazzo della Sapienza cradles the church of **Sant'Ivo alla Sapienza** – from the outside at least, one of Rome's most impressive churches, with a playful facade designed by Carlo Borromini. Each of the two small towers is topped with the weird, blancmange-like groupings that are the symbol of the Chigi family and the central cupola spirals helter-skelter fashion to its zenith, crowned with flames that are supposed to represent the sting of the Barberini bee, their family symbol. Inside, too, it's very cleverly designed, impressively light and spacious given the small space the church is squeezed into, rising to the tall parabolic cupola.

PIAZZA NAVONA

MAP P.36–37, POCKET MAP D14–15

The western half of the centro storico focuses on **Piazza Navona**, Rome's most famous square. Lined with cafés and restaurants and often thronged with tourists, street artists and pigeons, the best time to come is at night, when the flavour of the place is at its most vibrant, with crowds hanging out around the fountains watching the buskers and street artists or enjoying the scene while nursing a pricey drink at a table outside one of the bars. The square takes its shape from the first-century AD Stadium of Domitian, the principal venue of the athletic events and later chariot races that took place in the Campus Martius, and until the mid-fifteenth century the ruins of the arena were still here, overgrown and disused. It was given a facelift

in the mid-seventeenth century by Pope Innocent X, who built most of the grandiose palaces that surround it and commissioned Borromini to redesign the church of **Sant'Agnese in Agone** (Tues–Sat 9.30am–12.30pm & 3.30–7pm, Sun 9am–1pm & 4–8pm) on the piazza's western side. One of three fountains that punctuate Piazza Navona, the **Fontana dei Quattro Fiumi** is a masterpiece by Bernini, built in 1651. Each figure represents one of what were considered at the time to be the four great rivers of the world – the Nile, Danube, Ganges and Plate – though only the horse, symbolizing the Danube, was actually carved by Bernini himself. The fountain is topped with an Egyptian obelisk, brought here by Pope Innocent X from the Circus of Maxentius.

PIAZZA PASQUINO

MAP P.36–37, POCKET MAP D15

Just off Piazza Navona, it's easy to miss the battered marble torso of Pasquino, in the corner of the small triangular space of Piazza Pasquino. This is perhaps the best known of Rome's "talking statues" of the Middle Ages and the

Renaissance, upon which anonymous comments on the affairs of the day would be attached. These comments had a serious as well as a humorous intent, and gave us the word "pasquinade". The statue is still normally covered with rants, poems and pontifications of all kinds.

MUSEO DI ROMA

Piazza San Pantaleo 10. Tues–Sun 10am–8pm; €8.50, €11 with Museo Barracco ☎ 060608, 🌐 www.museodiroma.it. MAP P.36–37, POCKET MAP D15

The eighteenth-century Palazzo Braschi is the home of the **Museo di Roma**, which has a permanent collection relating to Rome's history from the Middle Ages to the present day. The large museum is only sporadically interesting; the building is probably the main event, particularly the magnificent Sala Nobile where you go in, the main staircase and some of the renovated rooms. But some of the paintings are absorbing, showing the city during different eras. Frescoes from demolished palaces are highlights.

MUSEO BARRACCO

Corso Vittorio Emanuele II 166. Tues–Sun: June–Sept 1–7pm, Oct–May 10am–4pm. €6.50, €11 with Museo di Roma. MAP P.36–37, POCKET MAP D15

The Piccola Farnesina palace, built by Antonio Sangallo the Younger, holds the **Museo Barracco**, a high-quality collection of ancient sculpture that was donated to the city in 1904 by one Baron Barracco. It contains ancient Egyptian and Hellenistic pieces, ceramics and statuary from the Greek classical period and later Roman items, most notably a small figure of Neptune from the first century BC and

an odd column-sculpture of a very graphically depicted hermaphrodite. The two charming busts of young Roman boys date from the first century AD.

SANT'ANDREA DELLA VALLE

Piazza Vidoni 6. Daily 7.30am–12.30pm & 4.30–7.30pm. MAP P.36–37, POCKET MAP E16

This church sports the city's second-tallest dome (after St Peter's) built by Carlo Maderno, and of being the setting for the first scene of Puccini's *Tosca*. Inside, it's one of the most Baroque of Rome's churches and your attention is drawn not only to the dome, decorated with paintings of the *Glory of Paradise* by Giovanni Lanfranco, but also to a marvellous set of frescoes in the apse by his contemporary, Domenichino, illustrating the life of St Andrew. In a side chapel on the right, you may, if you've been in Rome a while, recognize some copies of not only Michelangelo's *Pietà* (the original is in St Peter's), but also of his figures of *Leah* and *Rachel*, from the tomb of his patron, Julius II, in the church of San Pietro in Vincoli (see p.94).

SANT'ANDREA DELLA VALLE

PALAZZO DELLA CANCELLERIA

Piazza della Cancelleria. MAP P.36–37, POCKET MAP D15

The grand **Palazzo della Cancelleria** was the seat of the papal government that once ran the city. The Renaissance architect Bramante is thought to have had a hand in its design and it is a well-proportioned edifice, exuding a cool poise quite at odds with the rather grimy nature of its location. You can't get in to see the interior, but you can stroll into the marvellously proportioned, multi-tiered courtyard, which is a treat enough in itself, although **San Lorenzo in Damaso** (daily 7.30am–noon & 4.30–8pm), one of the oldest churches in Rome, also forms part of the complex. It was rebuilt with the palace and has since been greatly restored, most recently at the end of the nineteenth century, and has a painting by Federico Zuccaro, *The Coronation of the Virgin*, over the altar, and a twelfth-century icon of the Virgin Mary in a chapel.

VIA DEL GOVERNO VECCHIO

MAP P.36–37, POCKET MAP D15

Via del Governo Vecchio leads west from Piazza Pasquino through one of Rome's liveliest quarters, the narrow streets noisy at night and holding some of the city's most vigorous restaurants and bars. A little way down on the left, the delightfully small **Piazza dell'Orologio** is named after the quaint clocktower that is its main feature – part of the Oratorio dei Filippini, designed by Borromini, which is part of the Chiesa Nuova complex (see below). The followers of St Philip Neri attended musical gatherings here, gifting the language forever with the musical term "oratorio".

CHIESA NUOVA

Via del Governo Vecchio 134. Daily 7.30am–noon & 4.30–7.30pm. MAP P.36–37, POCKET MAP C15

The **Chiesa Nuova** was founded by St Philip Neri, who tended the poor and sick in the streets around here for most of his life, and commissioned this church in 1577. Neri died in 1595 and was canonized in 1622, and this large church, as well as being his last resting-place (he lies in the chapel to the left of the apse), is his principal memorial. Inside, its main features include three

paintings by Rubens hung at the high altar, centring on the *Virgin with Angels*, and Pietro da Cortona's ceiling paintings, showing the *Ascension of the Virgin* in the apse and, above the nave, the construction of the church and Neri's famous "vision of fire" of 1544, when a globe of fire entered his mouth and dilated his heart – a physical event which apparently affected his health thereafter.

VIA DEI CORONARI

MAP P.36–37, POCKET MAP F13–15

Running from the Tiber to the top end of Piazza Navona, this is the fulcrum of Rome's **antiques** trade. Although the prices are as high as you might expect in such a location, there is a huge number of shops (Via dei Coronari itself consists of virtually nothing else), selling a large variety of stuff. A browse makes for one of the city's most absorbing bits of sightseeing.

SANTA MARIA DELL'ANIMA

Via di Santa Maria dell'Anima 66. Daily 7.30am–1pm & 2–6pm. MAP P.36–37, POCKET MAP D14

Just off Via dei Coronari, this church takes its name from the statue of the Virgin on its facade, between two pleading souls in purgatory. It's another darkly cosy Roman church, wide and squat and crammed into an impossibly small space. Nowadays it's the German national church in Rome, a richly decorated affair, almost square in shape, with a protruding main sanctuary flanked by Renaissance tombs. The one on the right, a beautiful, rather sad concoction, is that of the last non-Italian pope before John Paul II, the Dutchman Hadrian VI, who died in 1523, while at the far end, above the altar, you can just make out a dark and glowing *Virgin with Saints* by Giulio Romano.

SANTA MARIA DELLA PACE

Via Arco della Pace 5. Mon, Wed, Sat 9am–noon; cloister open Mon–Fri 10am–8pm, Sat & Sun 10am–9pm. MAP P.36–37, POCKET MAP D14

The church of **Santa Maria della Pace** dates from the late fifteenth century, although its facade and portico were added a couple of hundred years later by Pietro da Cortona. Inside, you can see Raphael's frescoes of various sibyls above the Chigi chapel (first on the right), executed in the early sixteenth century, although the opening times are erratic. If the church is closed, look in on the attached **chiostro del Bramante**, finished in 1504, a beautifully proportioned two-tiered cloister that nowadays holds temporary art exhibitions and a small café where you can grab a coffee and a spot of lunch (entry ticket to exhibition not required).

ANTIQUES SHOP ON VIA DEI CORONARI

PALAZZO ALTEMPS

Piazza di Sant'Apollinare 46. Tues–Sun 9am–7.45pm. €7, includes Palazzo Massimo, Terme di Diocleziano, Crypta Balbi, valid 3 days. MAP P.36–37, POCKET MAP D14

Just across the street from the north end of Piazza Navona, the beautifully restored fifteenth-century Palazzo Altemps now houses the cream of the **Museo Nazionale Romano**'s aristocratic collections of Roman statues. Among treasures too many to mention, there are two, almost identical renderings of Apollo the Lyrist, a magnificent statue of Athena taming a serpent, and, in the far corner of the courtyard, a shameless Dionysus with a satyr and panther. Upstairs, the **Painted Views Room**, so-called for the bucolic scenes on its walls, has a fine statue of Hermes; the Cupboard Room, next door, named for its fresco of a display of wedding gifts against a floral background, has a wonderful statue of a warrior at rest, the *Ludovisi Ares*, restored by Bernini in 1622, and a sensitive portrayal of *Orestes and Electra*, from the first century AD by a sculptor called Menelaus – his name is carved at the base of one of the figures. Beyond, one room retains a frieze telling the story of Moses as a cartoon strip, with each scene enacted by nude figures as if on an unfurled tapestry, while in the room itself there is a colossal head of Hera, and – what some consider the highlight of the entire collection – the famous Ludovisi throne: an original fifth-century BC Greek work embellished with a delicate relief portraying the birth of Aphrodite. There's also the Fireplace Salon, whose huge fireplace, embellished with caryatids and lurking ibex – the symbol of the Altemps family – looks onto the *Suicide of Galatian*, apparently commissioned by Julius Caesar to adorn his Quirinal estate and an incredible sarcophagus depicting a battle in graphic, almost visceral sculptural detail. Without question, one of Rome's best collections of classical art.

PALAZZO ALTEMPS

Shops

DELFINA DELETTREZ

Via del Governo Vecchio 67. Mon 3.30–7.30pm, Tues–Sat 10.30am–2pm, & 3–7.30pm. MAP P.36–37, POCKET MAP D15

Delettrez, a fourth-generation Fendi, lives up to her fashion pedigree with her line of glamorous jewellery with a retro edge, sold from her bijou shop on trendy Via del Governo Vecchio.

IL GANCIO

Via del Seminario 82/83. Daily 10.30am–7.30pm. MAP P.36–37, POCKET MAP E15

High-quality leather bags, purses and shoes, all made right here on the premises.

G. POGGI

Via del Gesù 74/75. Mon–Sat 9am–2pm & 3–7.30pm. MAP P.36–37, POCKET MAP F15

This long-established store in the heart of centro storico, caters to all your artistic needs, with paper, paint, brushes and more basic stationery items.

LIBERA

Via dei Prefetti 23. Mon–Sat 10am–1.30pm & 3.30–7.30pm. MAP P.36–37, POCKET MAP E14

Run by a non-profit organization marketing its own brand of anti-mafia pasta, biscuits and wine – all made on ex-mafia land – Libera is great for unusual souvenirs.

AI MONASTERI

Corso Rinascimento 72. Mon–Wed, Fri & Sat 10am–7pm, Thurs 10am–1pm. MAP P.36–37, POCKET MAP D14

Cakes, spirits, toiletries and other items, all made by monks.

MORIONDO & GARIGLIO

Via Pie di Marmo 21/22. Daily 9am–7.30pm. MAP P.36–37, POCKET MAP F15

A short walk from the Pantheon, this is the city centre's most sumptuous and refined hand-made chocolate shop – great for exquisitely wrapped gifts.

PELLICANÒ

Via del Seminario 93. Daily 10am–7pm. MAP P.36–37, POCKET MAP E15

Ezio Pellicano only sells one thing: ties, made by Ezio himself or his daughter. You can buy any of the hundreds you see on display, or you can choose from one of the many rolls of material and have your own made up in a couple of days.

SBU

Via di San Pantaleo 68–69. Mon–Sat 10am–7.30pm. MAP P.36–37, POCKET MAP D15

The bafflingly named Strategic Business Unit has a great selection of hip menswear – mainly Italian, with the odd Japanese import – including their popular own-brand jeans. There's a small womens-wear section too, plus cool, affordable jewellery.

ENOTECA CORSI

ENOTECA CORSI

Via del Gesù 87/88 ☎ 06 679 0821. Mon-Wed & Sat noon-3pm, Thurs & Fri noon-3pm & 8-11pm. MAP P.36-37, POCKET MAP F15

Tucked away between Piazza Venezia and the Pantheon, this is an old-fashioned, inexpensive Roman trattoria and wine shop where you eat what they've cooked that morning.

DA FRANCESCO

Piazza del Fico 29 ☎ 06 686 4009. Daily 12.30-3.30pm & 7pm-midnight. MAP P.36-37, POCKET MAP D15

Not just pizzas in this full-on place in Rome's trendy heart – though they're tasty enough – but good *antipasti*, *primi* and *secondi* too. The service can be slapdash, but the food and atmosphere are second to none

MACCHERONI

Piazza delle Coppelle 44 ☎ 06 6830 7895. Daily 1-3pm & 7.30-11.30pm. MAP P.36-37, POCKET MAP E14

A friendly restaurant set in the heart of the centro storico. Inside is spartan yet comfy, while the outside tables make the most of the pretty street. The basic Italian fare is affordably priced and cheerfully served.

MATRICIANELLA

Via del Leone ☎ 06 683 2100. Mon-Sat 12.30-3pm & 7.30-11pm. MAP P.36-37, POCKET MAP E13

This old favourite is one of the best places to try real Roman food, with deep-fried dishes like *filetti di baccali* and various vegetable *fritti*, classic Roman pasta dishes such as *cacio e pepe*, and a great wine list.

LA MONTECARLO

Vicolo Savelli 13 ☎ 06 686 1877. Tues-Sun 12.30-3pm & 6.30pm-1am. MAP P.36-37, POCKET MAP D15

This hectic pizzeria not far from Piazza Navona is owned by the daughter of the owner of Da Baffetto (see p.47) and serves similar crisp, blistered pizza, along with good pasta dishes. Tables outside in summer but be prepared to queue.

DAL PAINO

Via di Parione 34A-35 ☎ 06 6813 5140. Mon, Tues & Thurs-Sun noon-3pm & 7pm-midnight. MAP P.36-37, POCKET MAP D15

Perfectly cooked, thin and crispy Roman-style pizza, at half the price of the offerings in nearby Piazza Navona. There's a large, shady terrace and a no-frills little dining room.

DA TONINO

Via del Governo Vecchio 18/19 ☎ 06 333 587 0779. Mon-Sat 12.30-3.30pm & 7-11pm. MAP P.36-37, POCKET MAP C15

Basic Roman food, delicious and always freshly cooked, at this unmarked centro storico favourite. The pasta dishes are around €8; among the *secondi* try the *straccetti* (strips of beef with rocket). The few tables fill up fast, so come early or expect to queue. No credit cards.

TRATTORIA LILLI

Via Tor di Nona 73 ☎ 06 686 1916. Tues–Sat
12.30–3pm & 7.30–11pm, Sun 12.30–3pm.
MAP P.36–37, POCKET MAP D14

One of the city centre's most
untouristed trattorias, with a
great menu of classic Roman
staples, well prepared and
served with gritty Roman
directness. Starters go for
€9–10, mains for €9–12, and
litres of house wine for €9.
Tables outside, though you may
need to book.

Bars

BAR DEL FICO

Piazza del Fico 26. Daily 8am–2am. MAP
P.36–37, POCKET MAP D15

This super little place has a
vibrant terrace on which you
can sip your (rather expensive)
drink and feel at the heart of
Rome's urban buzz.

CAFFÈ DELLA PACE

Via della Pace 5. ☎ 06 686 1216. Mon
3pm–2am, Tues–Sat 9pm–2am.
MAP P.36–37, POCKET MAP D15

The summer bar, with outside
tables full of Rome's beautiful
people. Quietest during the
day, when you can enjoy the
nineteenth-century interior
– marble, mirrors, mahogany
and plants – in peace. Though
under threat of closure at the
time of writing, its legion of
fans have pledged to keep it
open.

CIRCUS

Via della Vetrina 15 ☎ 06 9761 9258. Daily
10am–2am. MAP P.36–37, POCKET MAP D14

Drop by this cool backstreet
bar for its generous *aperitivo*
buffet (6.30–9pm; €5), or come
for a cocktail late on in the
snug back-lit bar. There are dj
sets at weekends, and a popular
brunch on Sundays.

ETABLI

Vicolo delle Vacche 9 ☎ 06 9761 6694.
Mon–Wed & Sun noon–1am, Thurs–Sat
noon–2am. MAP P.36–37, POCKET MAP D14

Lounge-style bar-restaurant in
the heart of the centro storico's
drinking triangle. Comfy sofas
and a laid-back vibe.

FLUID

Via del Governo Vecchio 46–47 ☎ 06 683 2361.
Daily 6pm–2am. MAP P.36–37, POCKET MAP D15

With a cavernous interior,
shimmering bar and clubby
atmosphere, *Fluid* is a fun
place to kick off a night out.
Its popular *aperitivo* buffet
(€8.50 including a drink) offers
generous helpings of salads,
rice dishes and pastas.

SALOTTO 42

Piazza di Pietra 42 ☎ 06 678 5804, ⓦ www
.salotto42.it. Tues–Sun 7pm–2am. MAP P.36–37,
POCKET MAP F14

This cosy café (with squishy
sofas, a great lunchtime buffet
and lots of art and design
books to flick through)
transforms into a glamorous
cocktail bar after dark, with
great music, expertly mixed
drinks (around €10) and a
polished clientele.

Clubs

SHARI VARI PLAYHOUSE

Via di Torre Argentina 78 ☎ 06 6880 6936,
ⓦ www.sharivari.it. Daily 7pm–4am. MAP
P.36–37, POCKET MAP E15

Full of glammed-up Romans,
Shari Vari is one of the city's
newest and best clubs. Full
of cosy nooks and on various
different levels, it's great
for people-watching, and
the music's not bad either;
Saturday's club tunes draw
the crowds, but Tuesday's
electronica and Sunday's jazz
nights are fun too.

Campo de' Fiori, the Ghetto and around

This southern slice of Rome's historic core lies between busy Corso Vittorio Emanuele II and the river. It's an appealing area for a wander, with cramped, cobbled streets opening out onto picturesque little piazzas. More of a working quarter than the neighbouring centro storico, it is less monumental, with more functional buildings and shops, as evidenced by its main square, Campo de' Fiori, whose fruit-and-veg stalls and down-to-earth bars form a marked contrast to the pavement artists and sleek cafés of Piazza Navona. To the east it merges into the narrow streets and scrabbly Roman ruins of the old Jewish Ghetto, an atmospheric neighbourhood that huddles up close to the city's giant synagogue, while just north of here lies the major traffic intersection and ancient Roman site of Largo di Torre Argentina.

LARGO DI TORRE ARGENTINA

MAP P.52–53, POCKET MAP E16

The busy traffic hub of **Largo di Torre Argentina** holds the ruins of four Republican-era temples, now home to a thriving colony of cats; down the steps on the southwestern corner you can visit the somewhat pungent **cat sanctuary** (daily noon–6pm; Ⓦwww.romancats.com), which tends to the 250 cats that live in the excavations. On the far side of the square, the Teatro Argentina was, in 1816, the venue for the first performance of Rossini's *Barber of Seville*, not a success at all on the night: Rossini was apparently booed into taking refuge in a nearby pastry shop. Built in 1731, it is today one of the city's most prestigious theatres, and is thought to stand over the spot in Pompey's theatre where Caesar was assassinated.

A PROWLING CAT AT LARGO DI TORRE ARGENTINA

THE GESÙ

Piazza del Gesù. Daily 6.45am–12.45pm & 4–7.30pm. MAP P.52–53, POCKET MAP F16

The church of the **Gesù** was the first Jesuit church to be built in Rome, and has since served as the model for Jesuit churches everywhere – its wide single-aisled nave and short transepts edging out under a huge dome were ideal

for the large congregations the movement wanted to draw. Today it's still a well-patronized church, notable not only for its size (the glitzy tomb of the order's founder, St Ignatius, is topped by a huge globe of lapis lazuli representing the earth) but also for the staggering richness of its interior. Opposite, the tomb of the Jesuit missionary, St Francis Xavier, holds a reliquary containing the saint's severed arm (the rest of his body is in Goa), while the ceiling's ingenious trompe l'oeil, the *Triumph of the Name of Jesus* by Baciccia, oozes out of its

frame in a tangle of writhing bodies, flowing drapery and stucco angels stuck like limpets – the Baroque at its most fervent.

Occupying part of the first floor of the Jesuit headquarters are the **Rooms of St Ignatius** (Mon–Sat 4–6pm, Sun 10am–noon; free), where the saint lived from 1544 until his death in 1556. There are bits and pieces of furniture and memorabilia, but the true draw is the corridor just outside, decorated by Andrea Pozzo in 1680 – a superb exercise in perspective, giving an illusion of a grand hall in what is a relatively small space.

ACCOMMODATION

Argentina Residenza	3
Campo de' Fiori	2
Fortyseven	5
Residenza Farnese	4
Teatro di Pompeo	1

CAFÉS & SNACKS

Alberto Pica	16
Barnum Café	3
Il Forno Di Campo de' Fiori	6
Forno Roscioli	10

RESTAURANTS

Al Bric	4
Ar Galletto	7
Dar Filettaro a Santa Barbara	8
Grappolo d'Oro Zampanò	5
Nonna Betta	17
Piperno	18
Roscioli	12
Da Sergio	13

BARS

L'Angolo Divino	11
Il Goccetto	3
Jerry Thomas Project	2
Latte Più	14
Open Baladin	15
Vinaietto	9

SHOPS

Beppe e i suoi Formaggi	3
Ibiz	2
Loco	1

CRYPTA BALBI

Via delle Botteghe Oscure 31 ☎ 06 3996 7700. Tues–Sun 9am–7.45pm. €7. MAP P.52-53, POCKET MAP F16

This corner plot is the site of a **Roman theatre**, the remains of which later became incorporated in a number of medieval houses. An exhibition takes you through the evolution of the site, with lots of English explanation, but you have to take one of the hourly tours to see the site proper, and try to glean what you can from the various arches, latrines, column bases and supporting walls that make up the cellar of the current building. The real interest is in the close dissection of one city block over two thousand years. On Sundays at 3pm there are visits to parts of the site currently under excavation.

CAMPO DE' FIORI

MAP P.52-53, POCKET MAP D16

In many ways Rome's most appealing square, **Campo de' Fiori** is home to a lively fruit and vegetable market (Mon–Sat 8am–2pm), flanked by restaurants and cafés, and busy pretty much all day and night; it's one of the best places in town for an early-evening *aperitivo*, but a rough late-night crowd means it's worth avoiding later on, at weekends especially.

No one really knows how the square came by its name, which means "field of flowers", but one theory holds that it was derived from the Roman Campus Martius, which used to cover most of this part of town; another claims it is after Flora, the mistress of Pompey, whose theatre used to stand on what

Campo de' Fiori and the Ghetto

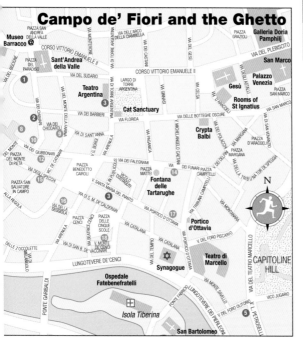

is now the northeast corner of the square – a huge complex by all accounts, which stretched right over to Largo Argentina, and where Julius Caesar was famously stabbed on the Ides of March, 44 BC. Later, Campo de' Fiori was the site of the city's cattle market and public executions, the most notorious of which is commemorated by the statue of a hooded Giordano Bruno in the middle of the square. Bruno was a late sixteenth-century freethinker who was denounced to the Inquisition; when he refused to renounce his philosophical beliefs, he was burned at the stake.

PALAZZO SPADA

Piazza Capo di Ferro 13 ☎ 06 686 1158, ⓦ www.galleriaborghese.it. Tues–Sun 8.30am–7.30pm. €5. MAP P.52–53, POCKET MAP D16

The Renaissance **Palazzo Spada** houses a **gallery** of paintings collected by Cardinal Bernardino Spada and his brother Virgilio in the seventeenth century. However, the main feature is the building itself: its facade is frilled with stucco adornments, and off the small courtyard is a crafty trompe l'oeil by Borromini – a tunnel whose nine-metre length is multiplied about four times through the architect's tricks with perspective. Inside, the gallery's four rooms aren't spectacularly interesting unless you're a connoisseur of seventeenth- and eighteenth-century Italian painting; of special note, though, are two portraits of Cardinal Bernardino by Reni and Guercino.

PALAZZO FARNESE

Piazza Farnese. Mon, Wed & Fri afternoon visits (45min) in English; €5; book several weeks in advance through ⓦ www.inventer rome.com. MAP P.52–53, POCKET MAP D16

Just south of Campo de' Fiori, **Piazza Farnese** is a quite different square, with great fountains spurting out of carved lilies – the Farnese emblem – into marble tubs brought from the Baths of Caracalla, and the sober bulk of the Palazzo Farnese itself. Commissioned in 1514 by Alessandro Farnese – later Paul III – from Antonio di Sangallo the Younger, the building was worked on after the architect's death by Michelangelo, who added the top tier of windows and cornice. It now houses the French Embassy and holds what has been called the greatest of all Baroque ceiling paintings, Annibale Carracci's *Loves of the Gods*, completed in 1603. Centring on the *Marriage of Bacchus and Ariadne*, this is supposed to represent the binding of the Aldobrandini and Farnese families, and is an erotic hotchpotch of cavorting flesh. Carracci did the main

plan and the central painting himself, but left the rest to his brother and cousin, Agostino and Ludovico, and various assistants such as Guido Reni and Guercino, who went on to become some of the most sought-after artists of the seventeenth century. It's a fantastic piece of work, perhaps only eclipsed in Rome by the Sistine Chapel itself; sadly, Carracci, disillusioned by the work, and bitter about the relative pittance that he was paid for it, didn't paint much afterwards, and died penniless a few years later.

VIA GIULIA

MAP P.52–53, POCKET MAP B14–D17

Via Giulia, running parallel to the Tiber, was built by Julius II to connect Ponte Sisto with the Vatican. The street was conceived as the centre of papal Rome, and Julius commissioned Bramante to line it with imposing palaces. Bramante didn't get very far, but the street became a popular residence for wealthier Roman families, and is still lined with elegant *palazzi*; it makes for a

VIA GIULIA

9am–6pm) through the ancient fish market, leading to the adjacent **Teatro di Marcello** (see p.65).

FONTANA DELLE TARTARUGHE

MAP P.52–53, POCKET MAP E16

A sheltered enclave between Via Portico d'Ottavia and Via delle Botteghe Oscure, Piazza Mattei might be recognizable from its role as a set in the 1990s film, *The Talented Mr Ripley*. But it's best known as the site of one of the city's most charming fountains, the **Fontana delle Tartarughe**, or Turtle Fountain, a late sixteenth-century creation restored by Bernini, who apparently added the turtles.

THE SYNAGOGUE

Lungotevere Cenci ☎ 06 6840 0661, ⓦ www .museoebraico.roma.it. Synagogue: Mon–Thurs 9am–6pm, Fri & Sun 9am–12.30pm. Museum: mid-June to mid-Sept Sun–Thurs 10am–6.15pm, Fri 10am–3.15pm; mid-Sept to mid-June Sun–Thurs 10am–4.15pm, Fri 9am–1.15pm; closed Jewish holidays. €11.
MAP P.52–53, POCKET MAP E17

The Ghetto's principal Jewish sight is the huge **Synagogue**, built in 1904. There are hourly guided tours of the building in English, and you should also visit the **Museo Ebraico**, which has a well-presented collection of artefacts relating to Jewish ritual, the history of the Jews in Rome and of course the war years. The interior of the building is impressive, rising to a high, rainbow-hued dome, and the tours (20min) are excellent, giving a good background on the building and the persecution of Rome's Jewish community through history. Hour-long tours of the Ghetto in English are also organized (book through the museum; €8).

pleasant wander, with features like the playful Fontana del Mascherone to tickle your interest along the way.

VIA PORTICO D'OTTAVIA

MAP P.52–53, POCKET MAP E17

Cross Via Arenula into the Ghetto and the contrast with stately Via Giulia can be felt immediately: this crumbling area of narrow, confusing switchback streets and alleys with a lingering sense of age is one of Rome's most atmospheric. The city's Jewish population stretches as far back as the second century BC, though nowadays a handful of kosher restaurants, butchers and the like are pretty much all that remains to mark this out from any other quarter.

The Ghetto's main artery, **Via Portico d'Ottavia**, leads down to the **Portico d'Ottavia**, a second-century BC gate, rebuilt by Augustus and dedicated to his sister in 23 BC. There's a walkway (summer daily 9am–7pm, winter daily

ISOLA TIBERINA

MAP P.52–53, POCKET MAP E17

Almost opposite the Synagogue, the Ponte Fabricio crosses the Tiber to the Isola Tiberina. Built in 62 BC, it's the only classical bridge to remain intact without help from the restorers. The island is a calm respite from the city centre, and is mostly given over to Rome's oldest hospital, that of the **Fatebenefratelli**, founded in 1548 – appropriately, it would seem, as the island was originally home to a third-century BC temple of Aesculapius, the Roman god of healing. The tenth-century church of **San Bartolomeo** (Mon–Sat 9am–1pm & 3.30–5.30pm, Sun 9am–1pm & 6.30–8pm) stands on the temple's original site and is worth a peep inside for its ancient columns, probably rescued from the temple, and an ancient wellhead on the altar steps, carved with figures relating to the founding of the church, including St Bartholomew himself. The saint also features in the painting above the altar, hands tied above his head, on the point of being skinned alive – his famous and gruesome mode of martyrdom.

PIAZZA BOCCA DELLA VERITÀ

MAP P.52–53, POCKET MAP F18

Piazza Bocca della Verità has as its focus two of the city's better-preserved Roman temples – the Temple of Portunus and the Temple of Hercules Victor, the latter long known as the Tempio Rotondo because of its circular shape. Both date from the end of the second century BC, and are fine examples of republican-era places of worship. You can visit Tempio Rotondo on a guided tour (Italian only; first and third Sun of the month at 11am; €5.50; book on ☎ 06 3996 7700). The feature that gives the square its name, however, is the **Bocca della Verità** (Mouth of Truth), an ancient Roman drain cover in the shape of an enormous face that in medieval times would apparently swallow the hand of anyone who hadn't told the truth. It was particularly popular with husbands anxious to test the fidelity of their wives; now it is one of the city's biggest tour-bus attractions.

The piazza's church, **Santa Maria in Cosmedin** (daily 9.30am–5.50pm, until 4.50pm in winter) is a typically Roman medieval basilica with a huge marble altar and a colourful Cosmati-work mosaic floor – one of the city's finest.

Shops

BEPPE E I SUOI FORMAGGI

Via di Santa Maria del Pianto 9A/11.
Tues–Sat 8.30am–10.30pm. MAP P.52–53,
POCKET MAP E16

This excellent shop is presided over by renowned cheese maker Beppe, and specializes in cheeses from Piemonte and Sardinia. You can also pick up chutneys, jams, chocolates and wine. The attached cheese-centric restaurant is great too.

IBIZ

Via dei Chiavari 39. Mon–Sat 10am–7.30pm.
MAP P.52–53, POCKET MAP D16

Great leather bags, purses and rucksacks in exciting contemporary designs made on the premises.

LOCO

Via dei Baullari 22. Mon 3.30–7.30pm, Tues–Sat 10.30am–7.30pm, Sun 11am–7pm (except Feb, Aug & Sept). MAP P.52–53, POCKET MAP D16

Pricey, eccentrically designed shoes, the like of which you won't find anywhere else.

Cafés and snacks

ALBERTO PICA

Via della Seggiola 12. Daily 9am–1.30am. MAP P.52–53, POCKET MAP E17

Gelato has been in the Pica family for generations, and it shows: this *gelateria* has a great choice of flavours, and the ice cream is sublime.

BARNUM CAFÉ

Via del Pellegrino 87. Mon 8.30am–9.30pm, Tues–Sat 8.30am–2am. MAP P.52–53, POCKET MAP D15

This friendly circus-themed café with free wi-fi is great for breakfast, coffee or lunch. After dark, it's a relaxing bar with great cocktails and light meals.

FORNO ROSCIOLI

Via Chiavari 34. Mon–Sat 7am–8pm. MAP P.52–53, POCKET MAP D16

Not to be confused with the posher *Roscioli* round the corner (see p.58), this is a top-notch pizza *al taglio* place, with hefty slices costing a few euros. There are also a few hot dishes at lunch (gnocchi in pesto sauce €6), and tasty cakes.

IL FORNO DI CAMPO DE' FIORI

Campo de' Fiori 22. Mon–Sat 7.30am–2.30pm & 5–8pm. MAP P.52–53, POCKET MAP D16

The *pizza bianca* here (just drizzled with olive oil on top) is a Roman legend, and their *pizza rossa* (with a smear of tomato sauce) follows close behind.

Restaurants

AL BRIC

Via del Pellegrino 51/52 ☎ 06 686 8986.
Tues–Sun 7.30pm–midnight. MAP P.52–53, POCKET MAP D15

Al Bric takes its wine and food seriously: expect a hushed atmosphere, giant wine list and high prices. The food is varied, with influences from all over Italy. Pastas around €15, mains €17–27.

ALBERTO PICA

GRAPPOLO D'ORO ZAMPANÒ

in a traditional trattoria atmosphere.

NONNA BETTA

Via del Portico d'Ottavia 16 ☎ 06 6880 6263. Mon & Wed-Fri noon–11pm, Sat & Sun noon–4pm & 6–11pm. MAP P.52–53, POCKET MAP E17

The best kosher restaurant in the Ghetto serves all the classes of *cucina Romana*, including fantastic deep-fried artichokes.

PIPERNO

Monte de' Cenci 9 ☎ 06 6880 6629. Tues–Sat 12.45–2.20pm & 7.45–10.20pm, Sun 12.45–2.20pm. MAP P.52–53, POCKET MAP E17

Tucked away on a hard-to-find piazza, *Piperno* is the best of the area's Roman-Jewish restaurants. It's not cheap, but it's a lovely space and there's outside seating in the summer. *Antipasti* and *primi* go for around €15, and *secondi* for €15–25.

AR GALLETTO

Piazza Farnese 104 ☎ 06 686 1714. Daily 12.30–3pm & 7.30–11pm. MAP P.52–53, POCKET MAP D16

This popular old-timer has had a chic overhaul, with bottle-lined rooms and coffee-coloured walls, as well as tables outside on one of Rome's stateliest piazzas. The menu offers fairly pricey staples of Roman cuisine and is also strong on fish dishes.

DAR FILETTARO A SANTA BARBARA

Largo dei Librari 88 ☎ 06 686 4018. Mon–Sat 5–10.40pm. MAP P.52–53, POCKET MAP D16

A fish-and-chip shop without the chips. Paper-covered Formica tables (outdoors in summer), cheap wine, beer and fried cod. A timeless Roman speciality, though the service can be offhand.

GRAPPOLO D'ORO ZAMPANÒ

Piazza della Cancelleria 80 ☎ 06 689 7080. Mon, Tues & Thurs–Sun 12.30–3pm & 7–11.30pm, Wed 7–11.30pm. MAP P.52–53, POCKET MAP D16

Curiously untouched by the hordes in nearby Campo de' Fiori, this restaurant serves imaginative Roman cuisine

ROSCIOLI

Via dei Giubbonari 21–22 ☎ 06 687 5287. Mon–Sat 12.30–4pm & 7pm–midnight; open last three Sats in Dec. MAP P.52–53, POCKET MAP E16

Is it a deli, a wine bar, or fully fledged restaurant? Actually it's all three, and you can either just have wine and cheese or go for the full menu, which has great pasta dishes and *secondi* at lunch time and in the evening. It's pricey, and the service can be snooty, but the food is terrific. *Roscioli* also has its own bakery nearby (see p.57).

DA SERGIO

Vicolo delle Grotte 27 ☎ 06 686 4293. Mon–Sat 12.30am–3.30pm & 6pm–midnight. MAP P.52–53, POCKET MAP D16

Towards the river from Campo de' Fiori, this cosy trattoria has a limited menu and the feel of old Rome. Inexpensive, and with outdoor seating in summer.

Bars

L'ANGOLO DIVINO

Via dei Balestrari 12. Tues–Sat 10.30am–3pm & 5pm–1.30am, Mon & Sun 5pm–1.30am; closed one week in Aug. MAP P.52–53, POCKET MAP D16

Quite a peaceful haven after lively Campo de' Fiori, this place a large selection of wine, and a menu of simple, typical wine-bar food – bread, cheese and cold cuts – as well as more substantial dishes in the evening, such as smoked goose with mashed potato (€15).

IL GOCCETTO

Via dei Banchi Vecchi 14. Mon–Sat 11.30–2pm & 6.30pm–midnight. MAP P.36–37, POCKET MAP C15

This family-run wine bar and shop, patronized by devoted regulars, is an atmospheric place for a drink, with wood-clad walls and a cosy feel. There is an extensive menu of wines by the glass and a selection of light appetizers, deli meats and cheeses.

JERRY THOMAS PROJECT

Vicolo Cellini 30 ☎ 06 9684 5937 or ☎ 370 114 6287, ⓦ www.thejerrythomasproject.it. Tues–Sat 10pm–4am. MAP P.52–53, POCKET MAP C15

Dedicated to Jerry Thomas, the author of the first guide to cocktail-making (published in 1862), this is a hole-in-the-wall speakeasy with a fantastic cocktail menu – a rarity in Rome. Officially you need a password to gain entry, but you might get in without; as space is tight, though, booking is always a good idea. Cash only.

LATTE PIÙ

Via dei Funari 21/A ☎ 06 686 8668. Mon–Wed 11am–4pm, Thurs–Sat 11am–4pm & 7pm–2am. MAP P.52–53, POCKET MAP E16

Laid-back café by day (good lunch deals and free wi-fi), cool wine-bar by night, the newest branch of this small Roman chain has funky pop decor and a twinkling mirrored bar.

OPEN BALADIN

Via degli Specchi. Daily noon–2am. MAP P.36–37, POCKET MAP D16

Central Rome's ultimate *birreria*, owned by the Baladin brewing company, has a stark, modern interior and literally hundreds of mainly artisanal Italian beers to choose from, forty of them on tap.

VINAIETTO

Via Monti della Farina 38. Mon–Sat 10am–3pm & 6.30–11pm. MAP P.52–53, POCKET MAP E16

This hole-in-the-wall *enoteca* has just a handful of tables, so most of its regulars drink their wine outside on the cobbles. Though mainly a wine shop, the enthusiastic owners offer a range of wines to drink by the glass – and it's far less expensive than nearby Campo de' Fiori.

ROSCIOLI

Piazza Venezia and the Capitoline Hill

For many people the modern centre of Rome is Piazza Venezia – not so much a square as a road junction, close to both the medieval and Renaissance centre of Rome and the city's ancient ruins, and the best landmarked space in Rome, the great white bulk of the Vittorio Emanuele monument marking it out from anywhere else in the city. Behind lie the Piazza del Campidoglio and the Capitoline Hill, one of the first settled of Rome's seven hills.

PALAZZO VENEZIA

Via del Plebiscito 118. Tues–Sun 8.30am–7.30pm. €4. MAP P.61, POCKET MAP F16

Forming the western side of the piazza, **Palazzo Venezia** was built for the Venetian Pope Paul II in the mid-fifteenth century and was for a long time the embassy of the Venetian Republic. More famously, Mussolini moved in here while in power, occupying the vast Sala del Mappamondo and making his declamatory speeches to the huge crowds below from the small balcony, although this is only viewable if you're attending one of the exhibitions held here. Most of the rest of the building is home to the **Museo Nazionale del Palazzo di Venezia** – which has a lot of fifteenth-century devotional works from central and northern Italy, some beautifully displayed bronzes and rooms full of weapons and ceramic jars from an ancient monastic pharmacy. You can also walk out to the palace's upper **loggia** for a view over the palm-filled courtyard – the gardens are some of the prettiest in Rome.

SAN MARCO

Piazza di San Marco 52. Tues–Sat 9am–12.30pm & 4–6pm, Sun 9am–1pm & 4–8pm. MAP P.61, POCKET MAP F16

Adjacent to the Palazzo Venezia on its southern side, the church of **San Marco** is one of the oldest basilicas in Rome. Originally founded in 336 AD on the spot where the apostle is said to have lived, it was rebuilt in 833 and added to by various Renaissance and eighteenth-century popes including Pope Paul II. The apse mosaic dates from the ninth century and shows Pope Gregory IV offering his church to Christ above a graceful semicircle of sheep.

PRIESTS WALKING THROUGH PIAZZA VENEZIA

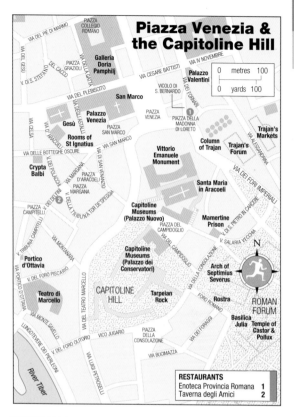

Piazza Venezia & the Capitoline Hill

RESTAURANTS

Enoteca Provincia Romana	1
Taverna degli Amici	2

VITTORIO EMANUELE MONUMENT

Daily 9.30am–5.30pm (4.30pm in winter); free. Lifts to terrace: Mon–Thurs 9.30am–6.30pm, Fri–Sun 9.30am–7.30pm; €7. Museum: daily 9.30am–6.30pm; closed first Monday of the month; €5. MAP P.61, POCKET MAP F16–G16

The rest of the buildings on Piazza Venezia pale into insignificance beside the marble monstrosity rearing up across the street– the **Vittorio Emanuele Monument** or "Vittoriano", erected at the turn of the nineteenth century to commemorate Italian Unification. Variously likened in the past to a typewriter, and, by American GIs, to a wedding cake, there are things to see inside, not least the large **Museo del Risorgimento**, one of the best of many you will see in Italy. But it's the outside that's best, centring on the tomb of the unknown soldier and an enormous equestrian statue of Vittorio Emanuele II, on a plinth friezed with figures representing the major Italian cities. Clamber up and down the sweeping terraces and take the lifts from behind the monument to the top, which give perhaps the most fabulous views in Rome – partly because it's the one place in Rome from which you can't see the Vittoriano.

PALAZZO VALENTINI

Via IV Novembre 119/A ☎ 06 32 810.
ⓦ www.palazzovalentini.it. Mon & Wed–Sun
9.30am–5.30pm; visit by guided tour only (1hr
30min). €10. MAP P.61, POCKET MAP G15

Book at least two weeks in
advance for a tour of this
absorbing attraction: the
excavated remains of two
ancient Roman houses in the
depths of a municipal office
building, brought to life by
technological trickery. Viewed
through a glass floor, the houses
offer a fascinating glimpse into
the lives of a patrician Roman
family around the third century,
whose lavish home was in the
heart of the ancient city. Sound
and light effects transform the
site, painting the faded walls,
embellishing the floor with
pristine mosaics and filling
the bathing pool with water. A
good place to visit before you
hit the ancient sights (especially
if you have kids in tow).

THE CAPITOLINE HILL

MAP P.61, POCKET MAP F17

The real pity about the Vittorio
Emanuele Monument is that
it obscures the view of the
Capitoline Hill behind – once,
in the days of imperial Rome,
the spiritual and political centre
of the Roman Empire. Its name
derives from its position as the
"caput mundi" or "head of the
world", and its influence and
importance resonates to this
day – words like "capitol" and
"capital" all derive from here, as
does the word "money", which
comes from the temple to Juno
Moneta that once stood nearby
and housed the Roman mint.

THE CAPITOLINE MUSEUMS

Tues–Sun 9am–8pm ☎ 060608, ⓦ www
.museicapitolini.org. €9.50, €11.50 for joint
ticket with Centrale Montemartini (see p.000);
valid 7 days. MAP P.61, POCKET MAP F16–F17

If you see no other museums of
ancient sculpture in Rome, try
to at least see the **Capitoline
Museums**, which are perhaps
the most venerable of all the
city's collections. They're
divided into two parts – the
Palazzo dei Conservatori and
the Palazzo Nuovo – and you
should try to see both rather
than choosing one. Tickets are
valid for a day so you can fit in
each museum with a break in
between, perhaps for a stroll
around the Roman Forum.

The **Palazzo dei Conservatori**
is the larger, more varied
collection, with some ancient
sculpture as well as later pieces
and an art gallery. Inside, the
centrepiece of the first floor,

VITTORIO EMANUELE MONUMENT

the Sala degli Orazi e Curiazi, is appropriately decorated with giant, late sixteenth-century frescoes depicting legendary tales from the early days of Rome. Check out the corner room, which contains the so-called *Spinario*, a Roman statue of a boy picking a thorn out of his foot, and, next door, the sacred symbol of Rome, the Etruscan bronze she-wolf nursing the mythic founders of the city. Move on to the airy new wing, where an equestrian statue of Marcus Aurelius, formerly in the square outside, takes centre stage, alongside a giant bronze statue of Constantine – or at least its head, hand and orb – and a rippling bronze of Hercules.

The second-floor *pinacoteca* holds Renaissance paintings from the fourteenth to the late seventeenth centuries – highlights include a couple of portraits by Van Dyck and a *Portrait of a Crossbowman* by Lorenzo Lotto, a pair of paintings by Tintoretto – a *Flagellation* and *Christ Crowned with Thorns*, and a fine early

work by Ludovico Carracci, *Head of a Boy*. There's also a vast picture by Guercino, depicting the *Burial of Santa Petronilla* (an early Roman martyr who was the supposed daughter of St Peter), and two paintings by Caravaggio, one a replica of the young *John the Baptist,* which hangs in the Palazzo Doria-Pamphilj (see p.34), the other an early work known as *The Fortune-Teller*.

The **Palazzo Nuovo** across the square – also accessible by way of an underpass – has some of the best of the city's Roman sculpture crammed into half a dozen or so rooms. Among them are the remarkable statue of a *Dying Gaul*, a *Satyr Resting*, the inspiration for Hawthorne's book *The Marble Faun*, and the red marble *Laughing Silenus* – along with busts of Roman emperors and other famous names: a young Augustus, a cruel Caracalla, and the centrepiece, a life-sized portrait of Helena, the mother of Constantine. Also, don't miss the coy *Capitoline Venus*, housed in a room on its own.

THE SHE-WOLF

SANTA MARIA IN ARACOELI

Scala dell'Arcicapitolina 12. May–Sept 9am–6.30pm; Oct–April 9.30am–5.30pm. MAP P.61, POCKET MAP G16

The church of **Santa Maria in Aracoeli** crowns the highest point on the Capitoline Hill and is built on the ruins of a temple to Juno. Reached by a flight of 124 steps up the steep **Aracoeli staircase**, erected in 1348, or more easily from a side entrance accessible from the Vittoriano or Piazza del Campidoglio, the church is one of Rome's most ancient basilicas, known for its role as keeper of the so-called "Santo Bambino", a small statue of the Christ Child, carved from the wood of a Gethsemane olive tree. The statue is said to have miraculous healing powers and was traditionally called out to the sickbeds of the ill and dying all over the city, its coach commanding instant right of way through the heavy Rome traffic. The Bambino was stolen in 1994, but a copy now stands in its place, in a small chapel to the left of the high altar. Take a look also at the frescoes by Pinturicchio in a chapel on the right, recording the life of St Bernardino.

PIAZZA DEL CAMPIDOGLIO

MAP P.61, POCKET MAP F16–G16

Next door to the Aracoeli staircase, the smoothly rising ramp of the Cordonata leads to **Piazza del Campidoglio**, one of Rome's most perfectly proportioned squares, designed by Michelangelo in the last years of his life for Pope Paul III. Michelangelo died before his plan was completed, but his designs were faithfully executed – balancing the piazza, redesigning the facade of the Palazzo dei Conservatori and projecting an identical building across the way, the Palazzo Nuovo. These buildings are home to the Capitoline Museums (see p.62); both are angled slightly to focus on Palazzo Senatorio, Rome's town hall. In the centre of the square Michelangelo placed an equestrian statue of Emperor Marcus Aurelius (now a copy), which had previously stood outside San Giovanni in Laterano; early Christians had refrained from melting it down because they believed it to be of Constantine (the first Roman emperor to follow Christianity).

THE SHE-WOLF AND TARPEIAN ROCK

MAP P.61, POCKET MAP F17

Just off the Piazza del Campidoglio, the statue of Romulus and Remus suckling the **she-wolf** provides one of Rome's most enduring images. Beyond is the **Tarpeian Rock**, from which traitors were thrown in ancient times – and which now gives excellent views over the Forum.

THE MAMERTINE PRISON

April–Oct 9am–7pm; Nov–March 9am–5pm. €10. MAP P.61, POCKET MAP G16

Steps lead down from the Tarpeian Rock to little **San Pietro in Carcere** – a low-vaulted church that lies above the ancient **Mamertine Prison**, where spies, vanquished soldiers and other enemies of the Roman state were incarcerated, and where St Peter himself was held. It's now part of a multimedia-assisted tour, taking in the depths of the jail, including the column to which St Peter was chained, along with the spring the saint is said to have used to baptize his guards and other prisoners. At the top of the staircase, hollowed out of the stone, is an imprint claimed to be of St Peter's head as he tumbled down the stairs. The tour also takes in further excavations and a film on the saint's life, and finishes with a brief bit of evangelizing in the church.

TEATRO DI MARCELLO

Via del Teatro di Marcello. Daily: summer 9am–7pm, winter 9am–6pm. Free. MAP P.61, POCKET MAP F17

Close to the Capitoline Hill, the **Teatro di Marcello** was begun by Julius Caesar and finished by Augustus. It became a fortified palace in Renaissance times, the property of the powerful Orsini family. Forming the backdrop for summer concerts, it also provides a neat cut-through to the Jewish Ghetto (see p.50) just beyond.

TEATRO DI MARCELLO

Restaurants

ENOTECA PROVINCIA ROMANA

Foro Traiano 82 ☎ 06 6994 0273. Mon & Sun 12.30–3pm, Tues–Sat 12.30–3pm & 6.30–11pm. MAP P.61, POCKET MAP G16

Perfectly sited for lunch after a mooch round the Forum, the menu here centres on local ingredients, offering light meals, pastas, and meat and fish *secondi*; a full meal costs around €30. Stop by for the evening *aperitivo* buffet (from 6.30pm) to enjoy the view of Trajan's Column without the crowds.

TAVERNA DEGLI AMICI

Piazza Margana 36/37 ☎ 06 6992 0637. Tues–Sun noon–3pm & 7.30–11pm. MAP P.61, POCKET MAP F16

This long-standing place is great for a post-Capitoline Hill lunch, with tables outside on this little square. Lots of Roman classics, at moderate prices – starters for around €12, mains for €15–20.

Ancient Rome

There are remnants of ancient Rome all over the city, but the most famous and concentrated collection of sights – the Forum and Colosseum together with the Palatine Hill – stretches southeast from the Capitoline Hill. You can spend a good half-day, perhaps longer, picking your way through the rubble of what was once the core of the ancient world. The most obvious place to start is the original, Republican-period Forum, the political and commercial heart of the ancient city. You can then visit the later Imperial Forums that lie across Via dei Fori Imperiali before heading up the legendary Palatine Hill, once home to the city's most powerful citizens and now an appealingly tranquil spot. Just beyond the Forum, the Colosseum is Rome's most iconic monument, a beautiful construction seemingly at odds with its violent past.

TRAJAN'S MARKETS

Visiting the Forum, Palatine and Colosseum

A **joint ticket** to the Colosseum, Forum and Palatine Hill costs €12 (valid two days from first use). **Queues**, to the Colosseum especially, can be a problem: while they do move quickly, they're rarely less than 100m long. The **RomaPass** and **Archeologia Card** (see p.183) allow you to use a different queue, or you can prebook online through CoopCulture (€2 booking fee; ☏ 06 3996 7700, ⊙ www.coopculture.it) and skip the line. Failing that, the Palatine ticket office on Via di San Gregorio generally has a shorter wait. There are **tours** of the Colosseum daily (10.15am, 10.45am, 11.15am, 11.45am, 12.30pm, 1.45pm & 3pm; €5; 45min), as well as a night tour in the summer months (€20; 1hr). Tours of the Forum (Mon–Thurs 1.30pm & 3pm, Fri–Sun noon, 1.30pm & 3pm; 1hr) and the Palatine (Mon–Thurs 12.30pm, Fri–Sun 11am, 12.30pm & 1pm; 1hr) cost €5 each. Audio and video guides are also available for each site.

For a bite to eat after sightseeing, head to the restaurants around Monti (see p.100) or San Giovanni (see p.109).

IMPERIAL FORUMS

MAP P.68–69, POCKET MAP F5

The original Roman Forum was the centre of republican-era Rome but the rise of the empire, and Rome's increased importance as a world power, led to the extensions of the **Imperial Forums** nearby. Julius Caesar began the expansion in around 50 BC, and work was continued after his assassination by his nephew and successor Augustus, and later by the Flavian emperors – Vespasian, Nerva and finally Trajan. The remains litter the sides of Via dei Fori Imperiali, and are now in large part open to the public.

TRAJAN'S MARKETS

Via IV Novembre 94 ⓦ www.mercatiditraiano .it. Tues–Sun 9am–7pm. €9.50. MAP P.68–69, POCKET MAP F5

Trajan's Markets are the most exciting city-centre ruins to be recently excavated, the result of years of restoration work. The museum starts with the airy Great Hall; beyond is the Great Hemicycle section, with displays of important finds from the various forums, as well as the Via Biberatica, an ancient street lined with the well-preserved remains of shops and bars. Outside, the **Forum of Trajan** holds the **Column of Trajan**, erected to celebrate the emperor's victories in Dacia and covered top to bottom with reliefs commemorating the highlights of the campaign.

THE COLUMN OF TRAJAN

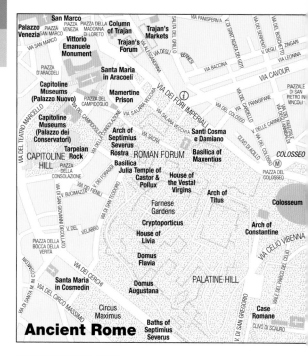

San Marco
Palazzo Venezia
PIAZZA SAN MARCO
PIAZZA VENEZIA
PIAZZA DELLA MADONNA DI LORETO
Column of Trajan
Vittorio Emanuele Monument
Trajan's Markets
Trajan's Forum
VIA SAN MARCO
PIAZZA D'ARACELI
Santa Maria in Aracoeli
Capitoline Museums (Palazzo Nuovo)
Mamertine Prison
Capitoline Museums (Palazzo dei Conservatori)
PIAZZA DEL CAMPIDOGLIO
VIA DEI FORI IMPERIALI
Santi Cosma e Damiano
Tarpeian Rock
Arch of Septimius Severus
Rostra
ROMAN FORUM
Basilica of Maxentius
COLOSSEO
CAPITOLINE HILL
PIAZZA DELLA CONSOLAZIONE
Basilica Julia
Temple of Castor & Pollux
House of the Vestal Virgins
PIAZZA DEL COLOSSEO
Arch of Titus
Colosseum
Farnese Gardens
Cryptoporticus
Arch of Constantine
House of Livia
Domus Flavia
Santa Maria in Cosmedin
Domus Augustana
PALATINE HILL
Case Romane
Circus Maximus
Baths of Septimius Severus

Ancient Rome

SANTI COSMA E DAMIANO

Via dei Fori Imperiali 1. Fri–Sun 9am–1pm & 3–7pm. MAP P.68–69, POCKET MAP F6

Across the road from the Forum of Augustus, the vestibule of the church of **Santi Cosma e Damiano** was originally created from the Temple of Romulus in the Forum, which you can look down into from the nave of the church. Turn around, and you'll see the mosaics in the apse, showing the naturalistic figures of the two saints being presented to Christ by St Peter and St Paul, flanked by St Felix on the left and St Theodore on the right. Outside, the cloister is wonderfully peaceful compared to the busy roads around. For a €1 donation you can also visit the massive eighteenth-century Neapolitan **presepio** or Christmas crib

(Fri–Sun 10am–1pm & 3–6pm; closed Aug), displayed in a room in the corner, a huge piece of work with literally hundreds of figures spread amongst the ruins of ancient Rome.

THE COLOSSEUM

Piazza del Colosseo. Daily 8.30am–1hr before sunset ☎ 06 3996 7700. €12 joint ticket with the Palatine and Roman Forum. MAP P.63–69, POCKET MAP G6

The **Colosseum** is perhaps Rome's most awe-inspiring ancient monument: an enormous amphitheatre that, despite the depredations of nearly 2000 years still stands relatively intact. You'll not be alone in appreciating it, and during summer visits can be a chore. But go late in the evening or early morning before the tour buses arrive,

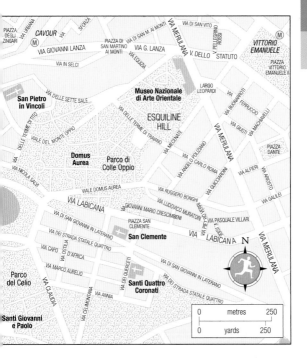

PIAZZA DEGLI ZINGARI · PIAZZA URBANA · CAVOUR Ⓜ · VIA CAVOUR · VIA SFORZA · VIA GIOVANNI LANZA · PIAZZA DI SAN MARTINO AI MONTI · VIA DI SAN M. AI MONTI · VIA G. LANZA · VIA DI SAN VITO · VIA MERULANA · VIA DI S. VITO · V. DELLO STATUTO · VIA PELLETTIERI · ROSSI · VITTORIO EMANUELE Ⓜ · PIAZZA VITTORIO EMANUELE II · VIA IN SELCI · VIA EQUIZIA · LARGO LEOPARDI · VIA DELLE SETTE SALE · San Pietro in Vincoli · Museo Nazionale di Arte Orientale · VIA BUONARROTI · VIA FERRUCCIO · ESQUILINE HILL · VIA DELLE TERME DI TRAIANO · VIA MERULANA · VIA GIUSTI · VIA MACHIAVELLI · VIA DELLE TERME DI TITO · VIALE DEL MONTE OPPIO · Domus Aurea · Parco di Colle Oppio · VIA MECENATE · VIA ANGELO POLIZIANO · VIA CARLO ROMA · VIA MERULANA · PIAZZA DANTE · VIA NICOLA SALVI · VIALE DOMUS AUREA · VIA RUGGERO BONGHI · VIA GUICCIARDINI · VIA ALFIERI · VIA ARIOSTO · VIA LABICANA · VIA GIOVANNI MARIO CRESCIMBENI · VIA LUDOVICO MURATORI · VIA PASQUALE VILLARI · VIA GALILEI · VIA DI SAN GIOVANNI IN LATERANO · PIAZZA SAN CLEMENTE · San Clemente · VIA LABICANA · N · VIA MERULANA · VIA DEI STRADA STATALE QUATTRO · VIA CAPO D'AFRICA · VIA OSTILIA · VIA DI SAN GIOVANNI IN LATERANO · VIA MARCO AURELIO · VIA DEI QUERCETI · Santi Quattro Coronati · VIA DEI STRADA STATALE QUATTRO · Parco del Celio · VIA CLAUDIA · VIA CELIMONTANA · VIA ANNIA · Santi Giovanni e Paolo

| 0 | metres | 250 |
| 0 | yards | 250 |

and the arena can seem more like the marvel it really is.

Originally known as the Flavian Amphitheatre (the name Colosseum is a much later invention), it was begun around 72 AD by the Emperor Vespasian, who was anxious to extinguish the memory of Nero, and so chose the site of Nero's Domus Aurea for the stadium. Inside, 60,000 people could be seated, with 10,000 or so standing. The seating was allocated on a strict basis, with the emperor and his attendants occupying the best seats in the house, and the social class of the spectators diminishing nearer the top. There was a labyrinth below that was covered with a wooden floor and punctuated at various places with trap doors and lifts to raise and lower the

animals that were to take part in the games. The floor was covered with canvas to make it waterproof and the canvas was covered with several centimetres of sand to absorb blood; in fact, our word "arena" is derived from the Latin word for sand. Once inside, you can wander around most of the lower level, and a larger section of the upper level, though even here you are still only about halfway up the original structure. You can gaze down into the innards of the arena, but there's been no original arena floor since its excavation in the nineteenth century. The lower floor contains a decent bookshop and a space for regular temporary exhibitions; an area by the lifts is given over to a display of fragments of masonry from the Colosseum.

THE ROMAN FORUM

Largo della Salara Vecchia 5/6 ☎ 06 3996
7700. Daily 8.30am–1hr before sunset. €12
joint ticket with Colosseum and Palatine.
MAP P.70–71, POCKET MAP F6–G6

The two or so hectares that
make up the **Forum** were once
the heart of the Mediterranean
world, and although the glories
of ancient Rome are hard to
glimpse here now, there's a
symbolic allure to the place that
makes it one of the world's most
compelling (not to mention
most ruined) sets of ruins
anywhere in the world.

Originally an Etruscan
burial ground, the Forum
was developed in the seventh
century BC and expanded over
the centuries to incorporate
public spaces and temples.
Its importance waned after
the fourth century, when it
became pastureland. Stone and
marble relics were taken for use
elsewhere in the Middle Ages,
and the Forum lay barren until
the eighteenth century, when
archeologists began excavating.
You need an imagination and a
little history to fully appreciate
the place, but the public spaces
are easy enough to discern,
especially the spinal **Via Sacra**,
ancient Rome's best-known
street, along which victorious
emperors and generals would
ride in procession to give thanks
at the Capitoline's Temple of
Juno. A little beyond, the large
cube-shaped building is the
Curia, built on the orders of
Julius Caesar as part of his
programme for expanding the
Forum, although what you
see now is a third-century AD
reconstruction; you can peek
inside on weekday mornings.
The Senate met here, and
inside three wide stairs rise to
the left and right, on which
about 300 senators could sit
with their folding chairs. In the
centre is the speaker's platform,
with a porphyry statue of a
togaed figure. Nearby, the
Arch of Septimius Severus
was constructed in the early
third century AD by his sons
Caracalla and Geta to mark
their father's victories in what
is now Iran. The friezes on it
recall Severus and in particular
Caracalla, who ruled Rome with
undisciplined terror for seven

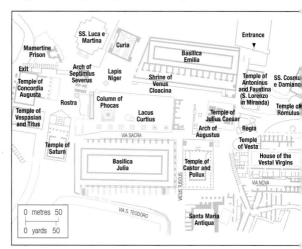

years. To the left of the arch, the low brown wall is the **Rostra,** from which important speeches were made (it was from here that Mark Anthony most likely spoke about Caesar after his death). Left of the Rostra are the long stairs of the **Basilica Julia,** built by Julius Caesar in the 50s BC after he returned from the Gallic wars, and, a bit further along, rails mark the site of the **Lacus Curtius** – the spot where, according to legend, a chasm opened during the earliest days and the soothsayers determined that it would only be closed once Rome had sacrificed its most valuable possession into it. Marcus Curtius, a Roman soldier who declared that Rome's most valuable possession was a loyal citizen, hurled himself and his horse into the void and it duly closed. Further on, to the right, the enormous pile of rubble topped by three graceful Corinthian columns is the **Temple of Castor and Pollux,** dedicated in 484 BC to the divine twins, or Dioscuri, who appeared miraculously to ensure victory for the Romans

in a key battle. Beyond here, the **House of the Vestal Virgins** is a second-century AD reconstruction of a building originally built by Nero: four floors of rooms around a central courtyard, still with its pool in the centre and fringed by the statues or inscribed pedestals of the women themselves, with the round Temple of Vesta at the near end.

Almost opposite, a shady walkway to the left leads up to the **Basilica of Maxentius** – in terms of size and ingenuity, probably the Forum's most impressive remains. Begun by Maxentius, it was continued by his co-emperor and rival, Constantine, after he had defeated Maxentius at the Battle of Ponte Milvio in 312 AD. Back on the Via Sacra, the hill climbs more steeply to the **Arch of Titus**, built by Titus's brother, Domitian, after the emperor's death in 81 AD to commemorate his triumphant return after victories in Judea in 70 AD. It's a long-standing tradition that Jews don't pass under this arch.

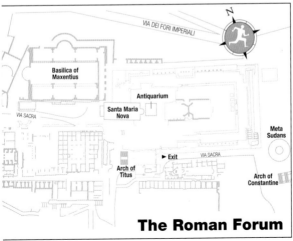

The Roman Forum

THE ARCH OF CONSTANTINE

Via di San Gregorio. MAP P.68-69, POCKET MAP G6
Just west of the Colosseum, the huge **Arch of Constantine** was placed here in the early decades of the fourth century AD after Constantine had consolidated his power as sole emperor. The arch demonstrates the deterioration of the arts during the late stages of the Roman Empire – most of the sculptural decoration here had to be removed from other monuments, and the builders were probably quite ignorant of the significance of the pieces they borrowed: the round medallions are taken from a temple dedicated to the Emperor Hadrian's lover, Antinous, and show Antinous and Hadrian engaged in a hunt. The other pieces, removed from the Forum of Trajan, show Dacian prisoners captured in Trajan's war there.

THE PALATINE HILL

Via di San Gregorio 30 ☎ 06 3996 7700. Daily 8.30am–1hr before sunset. €12 joint ticket with Colosseum and Roman Forum. MAP P.68-69, POCKET MAP G7
Rising above the Roman Forum, the **Palatine** is supposedly where the city of Rome was

founded, and is home to some of its most ancient remnants. In a way it's a more pleasant site to tour than the Forum, a good place to have a picnic and relax after the rigours of the ruins below. In the days of the Republic, the Palatine was the most desirable address in Rome (the word "palace" is derived from Palatine), and the big names continued to colonize it during the Imperial era, trying to outdo each other with ever larger and more magnificent dwellings.

Following the main path up from the Forum, the **Domus Flavia** was one of the most splendid residences, although it's now almost completely ruined. To the left, the top level of the gargantuan **Domus Augustana** spreads to the far brink of the hill – not the home of Augustus as its name suggests, but the private house of any emperor. You can look down from here on its vast central courtyard with fountains and wander to the brink of the deep trench of the Stadium, on the far side of which the ruins of the **Baths of Septimius Severus** cling to the side of the hill, the terrace giving good views over the Colosseum and the churches of the Celian Hill opposite. Nearby, the **Museo Palatino** contains a vast assortment of statuary, pottery, terracotta antefixes and architectural fragments. Walking in the opposite direction from the Domus Flavia, steps lead down to the **Cryptoporticus**, a long passage built by Nero to link his Domus Aurea with the Palatine, and decorated along part of its length with well-preserved Roman stucco-work. You can go either way along the passage.

A left turn leads to the **Casa di Livia**, originally believed to have been the residence of Livia. West of here, the newly restored **Casa di Augusto** (Mon, Wed, Sat & Sun: April –Oct 8.30am–1.30pm, Nov– March 11am–4/5pm) holds beautiful frescoes in striking shades of blue, red and ochre, dating back to 30 BC and considered to be among the most magnificent examples of Roman wall paintings anywhere. Further south, steps take you to the **Farnese Gardens**, among the first botanical gardens in Europe, laid out in the mid-sixteenth century and now a tidily planted, shady retreat from the exposed heat of the ruins. The terrace at the opposite end looks down on the excavations of an Iron Age village that perhaps marks the real centre of Rome's ancient beginnings.

THE PALATINE HILL

The Tridente, Trevi and Quirinale

The northern part of Rome's city centre is sometimes known as the Tridente, due to the shape of the roads leading down from the apex of Piazza del Popolo – Via del Corso in the centre, Via di Ripetta on the left and Via del Babuino on the right. This was historically the artistic quarter of the capital, to which artists and Grand Tourists would flock, in search of the colourful, exotic city. At the top of the Spanish Steps you can turn left for the Pincio and Villa Borghese, or right for Via Sistina and the Quirinale district, which holds some of the city's most compelling sights, including the enormous Palazzo Barberini, home of some of the best of Rome's art. West of here is the Fontana di Trevi, one of the city's most iconic and popular sights.

PIAZZA DI SPAGNA

MAP P.76–77, POCKET MAP F3

Piazza di Spagna underlines the area's international credentials, taking its name from the Spanish Embassy that has been standing here since the seventeenth century. It's a long, thin straggle of a square, almost entirely enclosed by buildings and centring on the distinctive boat-shaped Fontana della Barcaccia, the last work of Bernini's father, which remembers the great flood of Christmas Day 1598, when a barge from the Tiber was washed up on the slopes of Pincio Hill close by. The square itself is fringed by high-end clothes and jewellery shops and normally thronged with tourists, but for all that it is one of the city's most appealing open spaces and a fitting prelude to a spot of designer shopping on **Via Condotti** and nearby **Via Borgognona**.

KEATS-SHELLEY HOUSE

Piazza di Spagna 26 Ⓦ www
.keats-shelley-house.org. Mon–Sat 10am–1pm & 2–6pm. €5.. MAP P.76–77, POCKET MAP F3

The English poet John Keats lived and died in a house on Piazza di Spagna in 1821 and it now serves as the **Keats-Shelley House**, an archive of English-language literary and historical works and a museum of manuscripts and mementos relating to the Keats circle of the early nineteenth century – namely Keats himself, Shelley and

Mary Shelley, and Byron (who at one time lived across the square). Keats came to Rome to recover his health but spent months in pain here before he finally died, at the age of just 25, confined to the house with his artist friend Joseph Severn. Among many bits of manuscript, letters and the like, you can see the poet's death mask, stored in the room where he died.

CASA DE CHIRICO

Piazza di Spagna 31 ☎ 06 679 6546, ✆ www .fondazionedechirico.org. Tues–Sat & 1st Sun of the month 9am–1pm, 1hr tours, only by appointment at 10am, 11am & noon; €7. MAP P.76–77, POCKET MAP F3

Almost next door to the Keats-Shelley House, the fourth-floor **Casa de Chirico** was the home of the Greek-Italian artist Giorgio de Chirico for thirty years until his death in 1978. It's now a small museum that gives a glimpse into how De Chirico lived, and has a great many of his paintings on display: works from his classic surrealist period, and portraits of himself and his wife, who modelled for him. Upstairs, in keeping with

the untouched nature of the house, De Chirico's bedroom is left with his books and rather uncomfortable-looking single bed, while down the hall, the artist's studio, lit by a skylight in the terrace above, has his brushes and canvases.

THE SPANISH STEPS

MAP P.76–77, POCKET MAP F3

The **Spanish Steps** sweep down in a cascade of balustrades and balconies, the hangout of young hopefuls waiting to be chosen as artists' models during the nineteenth century, and nowadays not much changed in their role as a venue for international posing and flirting late into the summer nights. The Steps, like the square, could in fact just as easily be known as the "French Steps" because of the French church of Trinità dei Monti they lead up to, and because it was largely a French initiative to build them. After a few decades of haggling over the plans, they were finally laid in 1725, to a design by Francesco de Sanctis, and they now form one of the city's most distinctive and deliberately showy attractions.

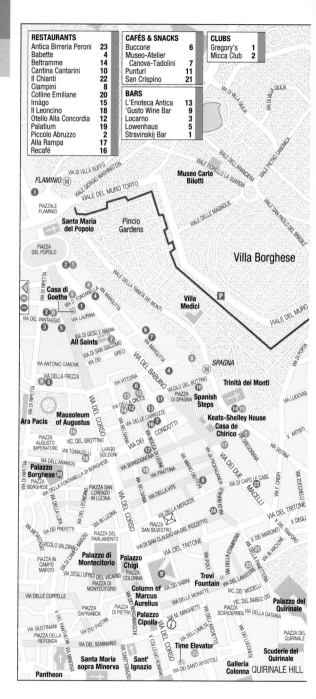

RESTAURANTS		CAFÉS & SNACKS		CLUBS	
Antica Birreria Peroni	23	Buccone	6	Gregory's	1
Babette	4	Museo-Atelier		Micca Club	2
Beltramme	14	Canova-Tadolini	7		
Cantina Cantarini	10	Punturi	11		
Il Chianti	22	San Crispino	21		
Ciampini	8				
Colline Emiliane	20	**BARS**			
Imàgo	15	L'Enoteca Antica	13		
Il Leoncino	18	'Gusto Wine Bar	9		
Otello Alla Concordia	12	Locarno	3		
Palatium	19	Lowenhaus	5		
Piccolo Abruzzo	2	Stravinskij Bar	1		
Alla Rampa	17				
Recafé	16				

FLAMINIO (M)

Museo Carlo Bilotti

PIAZZALE FLAMINIO

Santa Maria del Popolo

Pincio Gardens

PIAZZA DEL POPOLO

Villa Borghese

VIALE DEL MURO TORTO

Casa di Goethe

Villa Medici

VIALE DEL MURO

All Saints

SPAGNA (M)

Trinità dei Monti

Mausoleum of Augustus

Ara Pacis

Spanish Steps

Keats-Shelley House

Casa de Chirico

Palazzo Borghese

Column of Marcus Aurelius

Palazzo di Montecitorio

Palazzo Chigi

Trevi Fountain

Palazzo del Quirinale

Palazzo Cipolla

Time Elevator

Santa Maria sopra Minerva

Sant' Ignazio

Galleria Colonna

Scuderie del Quirinale

QUIRINALE HILL

Pantheon

Tridente, Trevi & Quirinale

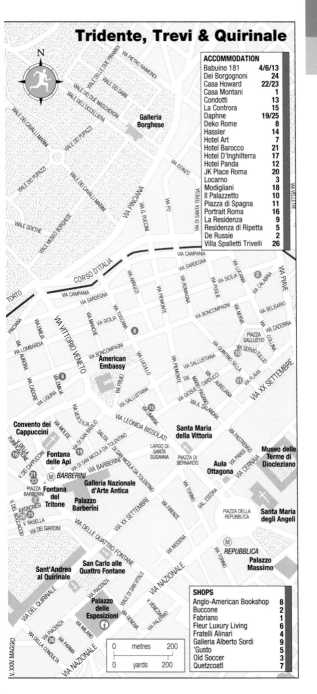

ACCOMMODATION	
Babuino 181	4/6/13
Dei Borgognoni	24
Casa Howard	22/23
Casa Montani	1
Condotti	13
La Controra	15
Daphne	19/25
Deko Rome	8
Hassler	14
Hotel Art	7
Hotel Barocco	21
Hotel D'Inghilterra	17
Hotel Panda	12
JK Place Roma	20
Locarno	3
Modigliani	18
Il Palazzetto	10
Piazza di Spagna	11
Portrait Roma	16
La Residenza	9
Residenza di Ripetta	5
De Russie	2
Villa Spalletti Trivelli	26

SHOPS	
Anglo-American Bookshop	8
Buccone	2
Fabriano	1
Fleur Luxury Living	6
Fratelli Alinari	4
Galleria Alberto Sordi	9
'Gusto	5
Old Soccer	3
Quetzcoatl	7

VIEW FROM PINCIO GARDENS

TRINITÀ DEI MONTI

Piazza della Trinità dei Monti. Tues, Wed & Fri–Sun 6.30am–8pm, Thurs 6.30am–midnight. MAP P.76–77, POCKET MAP F3

Crowning the Spanish Steps, **Trinità dei Monti** is a largely sixteenth-century church designed by Carlo Maderno and paid for by the French. Its rose-coloured Baroque facade overlooks the rest of Rome from its hilltop site, and it's worth clambering up just for the views. While here you may as well pop your head around the door for a couple of impressive works by Daniele da Volterra, notably a soft, beautifully composed fresco of the *Assumption* in the third chapel on the right, whose array of finely realized figures includes a portrait of his teacher Michelangelo, and a superb, ingeniously composed *Deposition* across the nave. The French Baroque painter, Poussin, considered the latter – which was probably painted from a series of cartoons by Michelangelo (he's the greybeard on the right) – as the world's third greatest painting (Raphael's *Transfiguration* was, he thought, the best).

THE PINCIO GARDENS

MAP P.76–77, POCKET MAP E2

The terrace and gardens of the **Pincio**, a short walk from the top of the Spanish Steps, were laid out by Valadier in the early nineteenth century. Fringed with dilapidated busts of classical and Italian heroes, they give fine views over the roofs, domes and TV antennae of central Rome, right across to St Peter's and the Janiculum Hill. The view is the main event here, but there are also plenty of shady benches if you fancy a break, and the quirky nineteenth-century water clock at the back is worth a look. You can also hire bikes, rollerblades and odd little four-wheel carriages for getting around the gardens and the adjacent Villa Borghese (see p.132).

PIAZZA DEL POPOLO

MAP P.76–77, POCKET MAP E2

The oval-shaped expanse of **Piazza del Popolo** is a dignified meeting of roads laid out in 1538 by Pope Paul III to make an impressive entrance to the city; it owes its present symmetry to Valadier, who added the central fountain in 1814. The monumental Porta del Popolo went up in 1655 and was the work of Bernini; the Chigi family symbol of his patron, Alexander VII – a heap of hills surmounted by a star – can clearly be seen above the main gateway. During summer, the steps around the obelisk and fountain, and the cafés on either side of the square, are popular hangouts. But the square's real attraction is the unbroken view it gives all the way back down Via del Corso to the central columns of the Vittorio Emanuele Monument. If you get to choose your first view of the centre of Rome, make it this one.

SANTA MARIA DEL POPOLO

Piazza del Popolo. Mon–Sat 7am–noon & 4–7pm, Sun 7.30am–1.30pm & 4.30–7.30pm. MAP P.76–77, POCKET MAP E2

Santa Maria del Popolo holds some of the best Renaissance art of any Roman church, with frescoes by Pinturicchio in the first chapel of the south aisle, and fine sculpture and mosaics in the Raphael-designed Chigi chapel (second on the left). Designed for the banker Agostino Chigi in 1516, the chapel was not finished until the seventeenth century and most of the work was undertaken by other artists: Michelangelo's protégé, Sebastiano del Piombo, was responsible for the altarpiece, and two of the sculptures in the corner niches, of Daniel and Habakkuk, are by Bernini. The church's star attractions are the two pictures by Caravaggio in the left-hand chapel of the north transept: the *Conversion of St Paul* and the *Crucifixion of St Peter*, whose realism was considered extremely risqué in their time.

VIA DEL BABUINO

MAP P.76–77, POCKET MAP E3–F3

Leading south from Piazza del Popolo to the Piazza di Spagna, **Via del Babuino** and the narrow **Via Margutta** – where the film-maker Federico Fellini once lived – was, in the 1960s, the core of a thriving art community and home to the city's best galleries and a fair number of its artists. High rents forced out all but the most successful, and the neighbourhood now supports a prosperous trade in antiques and designer fashions. Via del Babuino – literally "Street of the Baboon" – derives its name from the statue of Silenus that reclines outside the Tadolini studio about halfway down on the right. In ancient times the wall behind was a focus for satirical graffiti, although it is now coated with graffiti-proof paint. Inside the studio, the **Museo-Atelier Canova-Tadolini** (see p.86) is a café-restaurant, but a highly original one, littered with the sculptural work of four generations of the Tadolini family.

CASA DI GOETHE

Via del Corso 18 ☎ 06 3265 0412, ⓦ www
.casadigoethe.it; Tues–Sun 10am–6pm. €5.
MAP P.76–77, POCKET MAP E3

A short way down Via del
Corso from Piazza del Popolo,
the **Casa di Goethe** is a small
and genuinely engaging
museum, housed in the home
the writer occupied for two
years when travelling in Italy.
He wrote much of his classic
travelogue *Italian Journey*
here – indeed, each room is
decorated with a quote from the
book – and the house has been
restored as a modern exhibition
space and holds books, letters,
prints and drawings, plus a
reconstruction of his study in
Weimar. Among the objects
on display are Piranesi prints
of public spaces in Rome,
watercolours by Goethe himself,
a 1982 Warhol portrait of
Goethe, and drawings by the
German artist **Tischbein**, with
whom he shared the premises.

ARA PACIS

Lungotevere in Augusta ☎ 060608, ⓦ www
.arapacis.it. Tues–Sun 9am–7pm. €8.50. MAP
P.76–77, POCKET MAP E3

Forming the central core of
the largely modern square of
Piazza Augusto Imperatore, just
off Via del Corso, the massive
Mausoleum of Augustus is the
burial place of the emperor
and his family, though these
days it's not much more than
a peaceful ring of cypresses,
circled by paths, flowering
shrubs and the debris of tramps.
On the far side of the square,
the **Ara Pacis Augustae** or
"Altar of Augustan Peace" is
now enclosed in a purpose-built
structure designed by the New
York-based architect Richard
Meier. A marble block enclosed
by sculpted walls, the altar was
built in 13 BC, probably to
celebrate Augustus' victory over
Spain and Gaul and the peace it
heralded. Much of it had been
dug up piecemeal over the years,
but the bulk was uncovered in
the middle of the last century. It
is a superb example of imperial
Roman sculpture, with a frieze
on one side depicting the
imperial family at the height of
its power. It shows Augustus, his
great general Marcus Agrippa
and Augustus' wife Livia,
followed by a victory procession
containing her son (and
Augustus' eventual successor)
Tiberius and niece Antonia and
her husband, Drusus, among
others, while on the opposite
side, the veiled figure is believed
to be Julia, Augustus' daughter.

ARA PACIS

TREVI FOUNTAIN

MAP P.76–77, POCKET MAP G14

One of Rome's more surprising sights, the **Trevi Fountain** is a huge, Baroque gush of water over statues and rocks built onto the backside of a Renaissance palace. There was a Trevi fountain, designed by Alberti, around the corner in Via dei Crociferi, a smaller, more modest affair by all accounts, but Urban VIII decided to upgrade it in line with his other grandiose schemes of the time and employed Bernini, among others, to design an alternative nearby. Work didn't begin until 1732, when Niccolò Salvi won a competition held by Clement XII to design the fountain, and even then it took thirty years to finish the project. It's now, of course, the place you come to chuck in a coin if you want to guarantee your return to Rome, though you might remember Anita Ekberg throwing herself into it in *La Dolce Vita* (you're not encouraged to do the same).

TIME ELEVATOR

Via dei Santissimi Apostoli 20 ☎06 6992 1823, ⌨www.timeelevator.it. Daily 10.30am–7.30pm. €12, 5–12 years €9. MAP P76–77, POCKET MAP F15

Flight-simulator seats and headphones (English audio available) set the stage for a 45min virtual tour of three thousand years of Roman history; one way of priming the kids for the sights they will be seeing, though it probably wouldn't suit toddlers. Shows every 30min.

GALLERIA COLONNA

Piazza dei Santissimi Apostoli 66 ☎06 678 4350, ⌨www.galleriacolonna.it. Sat 9am–1.15pm, closed Aug; €12; free guided tours in English at noon. MAP P76–77, POCKET MAP G15

The **Galleria Colonna** is well worth a visit if you can time it right, not least for its chandelier-decked Great Hall, which glorifies the achievements of the nobleman Marcantonio Colonna – notably his great victory against the Turks at the Battle of Lepanto in 1589. Of the paintings, highlights include two lascivious depictions of Venus and Cupid, facing each other across the room, by Bronzino and Ghirlandaio, a group of landscapes by Dughet (Poussin's brother-in-law), Carracci's early and unusually spontaneous *Bean Eater*, a *Portrait of a Venetian Gentleman,* caught in supremely confident pose by Veronese, and a Tintoretto portrait of an old man. A newly opened wing holds seventeenth-century tapestries and other masterpieces.

PALAZZO BARBERINI

PIAZZA BARBERINI

MAP P.76-77, POCKET MAP F4-G4

At the top of the busy shopping street of Via del Tritone, Piazza Barberini is centred around Bernini's **Fontana del Tritone**, whose god of the sea gushes a high jet of water from a conch shell. Traditionally, this was the Barberini family's quarter of the city, and works by Bernini in their honour – they were the sculptor's greatest patrons – are thick on the ground here. He finished the Tritone fountain in 1644, going on shortly after to design the **Fontana delle Api** (Fountain of the Bees) across the road at the bottom end of Via Veneto – a smaller, quirkier work, with a broad scallop shell studded with bees, the symbol of the Barberinis.

CONVENTO DEI CAPPUCCINI

Via Veneto 27 ☎ 06 8880 3695, ⌨ www .cappuciniviaveneto.it. Daily 9am–7pm; ticket office closes 30min earlier. €6. MAP P.76-77, POCKET MAP G3

The church of **Santa Maria della Concezione**, another Barberini-sponsored creation, holds the **Convento dei Cappuccini**, now an eight-room **museum** exploring the lives of the Capuchin friars. The star exhibit is Caravaggio's *St Francis*

in Meditation; other rooms focus on daily objects that offer a glimpse into the friars' lives, from medicine-making apparatus to a collection of watches they wore as a reminder of their own mortality. What most visitors come to see, however, is the **crypt**, seen at the end of the museum. Erected in the mid-eighteenth century, it holds the bones of 3700 monks and paupers, painstakingly assembled into works of art, and fashioned into chandeliers, shelves and door frames. One of the more macabre and bizarre sights of Rome.

VIA VENETO

MAP P.76-77, POCKET MAP G3

The pricey bars and restaurants lining Via Veneto were once the haunt of Rome's beautiful people, made famous by Fellini's 1960 film *La Dolce Vita*. But they left a long time ago, and the street, despite being home to some of Rome's fanciest hotels, has never quite recovered the cachet it had in the Sixties and Seventies. Nonetheless, its pretty tree-lined aspect, pavement cafés, swanky stores and uniformed hotel bellmen lend it an upmarket European air that is unlike anywhere else in Rome.

PALAZZO BARBERINI

Via delle Quattro Fontane 13. ☎ 06 482 4184.
Tues–Sun 8.30am–7pm; €7; apartment tours
(Sat 11am; €5) and tours in Italian of the
Mithraeum (2nd & 4th Sat of the month at
10am; €5.50) need to be booked in advance.
MAP P.76–77, POCKET MAP G4

The Palazzo Barberini is home to the **Galleria Nazionale d'Arte Antica** – a rich patchwork of mainly Italian art from the early Renaissance to the late Baroque period. It's a splendid collection, highlighted by works by Titian, El Greco and Caravaggio. But perhaps the most impressive feature of the gallery is the building itself, worked on by Bernini, Borromini and Maderno. The first-floor Gran Salone is dominated by Pietro da Cortona's manic fresco of *The Triumph of Divine Providence*, an exuberant Baroque work which almost crawls down the walls to meet you. Of the paintings, be sure to see Caravaggio's *Judith Beheading Holofernes*; Fra' Filippo Lippi's *Madonna and Child*; and Raphael's *Fornarina* – a painting of the daughter of a Trasteveran baker thought to have been his mistress (Raphael's name appears clearly on the woman's bracelet). Look out also for Bronzino's rendering of the marvellously erect *Stefano Colonna* and a portrait of *Henry VIII* by Hans Holbein.

Twice a month, you can visit the **Barberini mithraeum** – discovered in 1936 but dating back to the second century AD – dedicated to the cult of Mithras and containing a fresco telling the Persian god's story.

SAN CARLO ALLE QUATTRO FONTANE

Via del Quirinale 23. Mon–Fri 10am–1pm &
3–6pm, Sat 10am–1pm, Sun noon–1pm.
MAP P.76–77, POCKET MAP G4

The church of **San Carlo alle Quattro Fontane** – next door to the four fountains that give it its name – was Borromini's first real design commission. In it he displays all the ingenuity he later became known for, cramming the church elegantly into a tiny and awkwardly shaped site that apparently covers roughly the same surface area as one of the main piers of St Peter's.

SANT'ANDREA AL QUIRINALE

Via del Quirinale 29. Mon–Sat 8.30am–noon
& 3.30–7pm, Sun 9am–noon & 4–7pm.
MAP P.76–77, POCKET MAP G4

A flamboyant building that Bernini planned as a kind of flat oval shape to fit into its wide but shallow site. Like San Carlo, it's ingenious inside, its wide, elliptical nave cleverly made into a grand space despite its small size. For €2 you can visit the sacristy, with its artful frescoes, where cherubs pull aside painted drapery to let in light from mock windows, and the rooms of St Stanislaus Kostka, where the Polish saint lived (and died) in 1568. Paintings by Andrea Pozzo illustrate the saint's life and culminate in a chapel that focuses on a rather lifelike painted statue of Stanislaus on his deathbed.

FONTANA DEL TRITONE IN PIAZZA BARBERINI

PALAZZO DEL QUIRINALE

Piazza del Quirinale ⓦ www.quirinale.it. Sun 8.30am–noon. €5. MAP P.76–77, POCKET MAP F4

The sixteenth-century **Palazzo del Quirinale** was the official summer residence of the popes until Unification, when it became the royal palace. It's now the home of Italy's president. The main feature of the piazza outside is the huge statue of the Dioscuri, aka Castor and Pollux: massive five-metre-tall Roman copies of classical Greek statues, brought here by Pope Sixtus V in the early sixteenth century. Inside, the palace is well worth a visit if you're in town on a Sunday, with some spectacular rooms glorifying Pope Paul V among others, and a fragment of Melozzo da Forlì's fifteenth-century fresco of Christ, painted for the apse of Santi Apostoli – the rest is in the Vatican (see p.150).

SCUDERIE DEL QUIRINALE

Via XXIV Maggio 16 ☎ 06 3996 7500, ⓦ www .scuderiequirinale.it. Exhibitions around €12. MAP P.76–77, POCKET MAP F4

Set in the old papal stables and strikingly remodelled in the 1990s, this is one of Rome's biggest and best art spaces, putting on prestigious international exhibitions. Don't miss the spectacular view of Rome from the rear staircase.

VIA XX SETTEMBRE

MAP P.76–77, POCKET MAP G4–H3

Via XX Settembre spears out to the Aurelian Wall from Via del Quirinale and was the route by which troops entered the city on September 20, 1870 – the place where they breached the wall is marked with a column. It's not Rome's most appealing thoroughfare by any means, flanked by the deliberately faceless bureaucracies of the national government. However, halfway down, the Fontana dell'Acqua Felice is worth a look: it focuses on a massive, bearded figure of Moses playfully fronted by four basking lions, and marks the end of the Acqua Felice aqueduct.

SANTA MARIA DELLA VITTORIA

Via XX Settembre 17. Daily 8.30am–noon & 3.30–6pm. MAP P.76–77, POCKET MAP G3

Santa Maria della Vittoria's best-known feature is Bernini's sculpture the *Ecstasy of St Theresa of Avila*, the centrepiece of the sepulchral chapel of Cardinal Cornaro. St Theresa is one of the Catholic Church's most enduring mystics, and Bernini's sculpture records the moment when, in 1537, she had a vision of an angel piercing her heart with a dart. It's a very Baroque piece of work in the most populist sense – not only is the event quite literally staged, but St Theresa's ecstasy verges on the worldly as she lies back in groaning submission beneath a mass of dishevelled garments and drapery. The Cornaro cardinals are depicted murmuring and nudging each other as they watch the spectacle from theatre boxes.

Shops

ANGLO-AMERICAN BOOKSHOP

Via della Vite 102. Mon 3.30–7.30pm, Tues–Sat 10.30am–7.30pm; open later on Mon and closes earlier on Sat in summer. MAP P.76–77, POCKET MAP F13

One of the best selections of new English books in Rome, especially good on history and academic books.

BUCCONE

Via di Ripetta 19. Mon–Thurs 9am–8.30pm, Fri & Sat 9am–11.30pm, Sun 11am–7pm. MAP P.76–77, POCKET MAP E3

The centre's best wine shop, this is an atmospheric enoteca with a large selection of wines, spirits and especially grappa.

FABRIANO

Via del Babuino 173. Daily 10am–8pm. MAP P.76–77, POCKET MAP E3

Tridente branch of this chain, specializing in lovely contemporary stationery in rainbow colours, wallets and bags.

FLEUR LUXURY LIVING

Via Bocca di Leone 46. Daily 10.30am–7.30pm. MAP P.76–77, POCKET MAP E3

A stylish concept store, with a tasteful selection of furniture, homeware, high-end womenswear (from the likes of Paul & Joe, Tara Jarmon and Michael Kors), jewellery and cult perfumes. Also, the on-site café serves gourmet teas.

FRATELLI ALINARI

Via Alibert 16a. Mon–Sat 3.30–7.30pm. MAP P.76–77, POCKET MAP F3

If you want to know what Rome's piazzas looked like before *McDonald's* came to town, come here for a fine selection of black-and-white photographs of Rome.

GALLERIA ALBERTO SORDI

Via del Corso. Mon–Fri 8.30am–9pm, Sat 8.30am –10pm, Sun 9.30am–9pm. MAP P.76–77, POCKET MAP F14

This nineteenth-century shopping arcade is home to some great shops and provides a cool escape from the Via del Corso crowds on hot days.

'GUSTO

Piazza Augusto Imperatore 7. Daily 10.30am–8pm. MAP P.76–77, POCKET MAP E3

Everything for the aspirant gourmet: wines, decanters, glasses and all the top-of-the-line kitchen gadgets you could ever hope to find. Also a large selection of cookbooks in English.

OLD SOCCER

Via di Ripetta 30. Daily 10am–8pm. MAP P.76–77, POCKET MAP E3

Old-fashioned Italian football shirts – ironically enough, made in England. Great presents for football-mad friends.

QUETZALCOATL

Via delle Carrozze 26. Daily 10am–7.30pm. MAP P.76–77, POCKET MAP E3

Chocolates here are presented as if they were art; once you taste them, you'll probably feel that they are. Gift boxes of all sizes available.

GALLERIA ALBERTO SORDI

RECAFÉ

or go for dishes like *tonnarelli cacio e pepe* or mains like rabbit or sausage from the hills to the north and south of the city.

PICCOLO ABRUZZO

Via Sicilia 237 ☎ 06 4282 0176. Daily 12.30–3pm & 6.30–11pm. MAP P.76–77, POCKET MAP H2

A five-minute stroll up the unprepossessing Via Sicilia from Via Veneto, this is a great alternative to the glitzy, mob-run places on the *Dolce Vita* street. No menu, just a seemingly endless parade of Abruzzese and other goodies plonked out to your table at regular intervals – all for around €35 a head. Be sure to come hungry.

ALLA RAMPA

Piazza Mignanelli 18 ☎ 06 678 2621. Mon–Sat noon–3pm, 6–11pm. MAP P.76–77, POCKET MAP G13

An unashamedly touristy joint, but with perhaps the best antipasti buffet in town – a snip for €10 – as well as excellent service and decent food. The dining room, a mocked-up piazza, is pretty kitsch but the outside terrace, just off Piazza di Spagna, is large and undeniably appealing.

RECAFÉ

Piazza Augusto Imperatore 9 ☎ 06 6813 4730. Mon 12.15–3pm & 7pm–midnight, Tues–Sun 12.15–midnight. MAP P.76–77, POCKET MAP E13

The entrance on Via del Corso is a Neapolitan café, while on the Piazza Augusta Imperatore side you can enjoy proper Neapolitan pizzas, good pasta and salad dishes and excellent grilled *secondi* for moderate prices – €13 or so for a *primo*, €13–23 for a *secondo*. Neapolitan sweets and *fritti* too. The ambience is chic and the large outside terrace always has a buzz about it.

OTELLO ALLA CONCORDIA

Via della Croce 81 ☎ 06 679 1178. Mon–Sat 12.30–3pm & 7.30–11pm. MAP P.76–77, POCKET MAP E3

This place used to be one of Fellini's favourites – he lived just a few blocks away on Via Margutta – and it remains an elegant yet affordable choice in the heart of Rome. A complete offering of Roman and Italian dishes, but ask for *spaghetti Otello* for a taste of tradition – a delicious combination of fresh tomatoes and basil with garlic.

PALATIUM

Via Frattina 94 ☎ 06 6920 2132. Mon–Sat 11am–11pm. MAP P.76–77, POCKET MAP F13

Cool and sleek, this Spanish Steps-area wine bar-cum-restaurant celebrates the wine and food of the Lazio region around Rome, with a short menu of local specialities and a long list of Lazio wines. You can just settle for a plate of salami or cheese for €5–7,

SANTA MARIA MAGGIORE

Piazza di Santa Maria Maggiore. Daily 7am–7pm. Museum and archeological area daily 9am–6.15pm. €3. MAP P.92–93, POCKET MAP H5

One of the city's four patriarchal basilicas, **Santa Maria Maggiore** includes one of Rome's best-preserved Byzantine interiors. It was originally built during the fifth century after the Virgin Mary appeared to Pope Liberius in a dream on the night of August 4, 352 AD. She told him to erect a church in her honour on the Esquiline Hill – the exact spot would be marked the next morning by newly fallen snow outlining the plan of the church. Despite it being the height of summer, Liberius duly found the miraculous blueprint and the event is commemorated every year on August 5, when at midday Mass white rose petals are showered on the congregation from the ceiling, and at night the fire department operates an artificial snow machine in the piazza in front of the church.

Inside, the **basilica** is fringed on both sides with well-kept mosaics, most of which date from the time of Pope Sixtus III and recount incidents from the Old Testament. The chapel in the right transept holds the elaborate tomb of Sixtus V – another, less famous Sistine chapel, decorated with frescoes and stucco reliefs showing events from his reign. Outside is the tomb of the Bernini family; opposite, the Pauline chapel is home to the tombs of the Borghese pope, Paul V, and his immediate predecessor Clement VIII, as well as that of Pauline Bonaparte, Napoleon's sister. Between the two chapels, the *confessio* contains a kneeling statue of

SANTA MARIA MAGGIORE

Pope Pius IX, and, beneath it, a reliquary that is said to contain fragments of the crib of Christ. It's the mosaics of the arch that really dazzle, a vivid representation of scenes from the life of Christ. The **museum** underneath the basilica sports what is, even by Roman standards, a wide variety of relics, and an **archeological area** holds relics from the Paleochristian basilica (tours hourly 10am–5pm; no tour at 2pm).

SANTA PUDENZIANA

Via Urbana 160. Daily 8.30am–noon & 3–6pm. MAP P.92–93, POCKET MAP H5

This church was for many years believed to have been built on the site where St Peter lived and worshipped and once housed two relics: the chair that St Peter used as his throne and the table at which he said Mass, though both have long gone – to the Vatican and the Lateran Palace respectively. It still has one feature of ancient origin – its superb fifth-century apse **mosaics**, fluid and beautiful works centring on a golden enthroned Christ surrounded by the apostles.

Esquiline, Monti & Termini

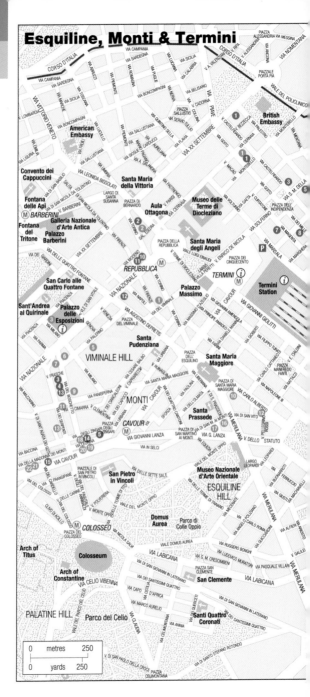

PIAZZA ALESSANDRIA VIA MESSINA

CORSO D'ITALIA

VIA CAMPANIA

VIA SICILIA

PIAZZALE PORTA PIA

VIALE DEL POLICLINICO

VIA LOMBARDIA

American Embassy

British Embassy

Convento dei Cappuccini

Santa Maria della Vittoria

BARBERINI

Fontana delle Api

Galleria Nazionale d'Arte Antica
Palazzo Barberini

Fontana del Tritone

Aula Ottagona

Museo delle Terme di Diocleziano

PIAZZA DI SANTA SUSANNA

PIAZZA DELL' INDIPENDENZA

PIAZZA DELLA REPUBBLICA

Santa Maria degli Angeli

REPUBBLICA

San Carlo alle Quattro Fontane

PIAZZA DEI CINQUECENTO

TERMINI

Termini Station

Sant'Andrea al Quirinale

Palazzo delle Esposizioni

Palazzo Massimo

VIMINALE HILL

Santa Pudenziana

PIAZZA DELL' ESQUILINO

Santa Maria Maggiore

MONTI

CAVOUR

Santa Prassede

San Pietro in Vincoli

Museo Nazionale d'Arte Orientale

ESQUILINE HILL

PIAZZALE DI SAN PIETRO IN VINCOLI

COLOSSEO

Domus Aurea

Parco di Colle Oppio

Arch of Titus

Colosseum

Arch of Constantine

San Clemente

PALATINE HILL

Parco del Celio

Santi Quattro Coronati

| 0 | metres | 250 |
| 0 | yards | 250 |

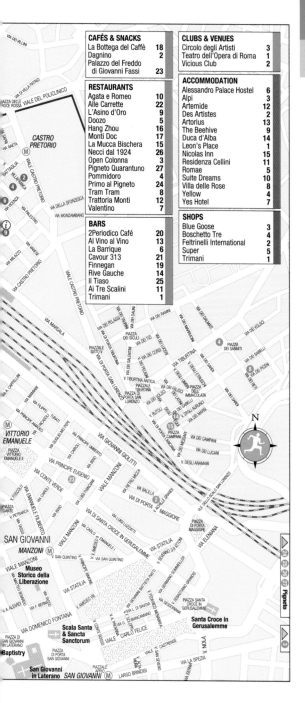

CAFÉS & SNACKS

La Bottega del Caffè	18
Dagnino	2
Palazzo del Freddo di Giovanni Fassi	23

RESTAURANTS

Agata e Romeo	10
Aile Carrette	22
L'Asino d'Oro	9
Doozo	5
Hang Zhou	16
Monti Doc	17
La Mucca Bischera	15
Necci dal 1924	26
Open Colonna	3
Pigneto Quarantuno	27
Pommidoro	4
Primo al Pigneto	24
Tram Tram	8
Trattoria Monti	12
Valentino	7

BARS

2Periodico Café	20
Al Vino al Vino	13
La Barrique	6
Cavour 313	21
Finnegan	19
Rive Gauche	14
Il Tiaso	25
Ai Tre Scalini	11
Trimani	1

CLUBS & VENUES

Circolo degli Artisti	3
Teatro dell'Opera di Roma	1
Vicious Club	2

ACCOMMODATION

Alessandro Palace Hostel	6
Alpi	3
Artemide	12
Des Artistes	2
Artorius	13
The Beehive	9
Duca d'Alba	14
Leon's Place	1
Nicolas Inn	15
Residenza Cellini	11
Romae	5
Suite Dreams	10
Villa delle Rose	8
Yellow	4
Yes Hotel	7

SHOPS

Blue Goose	3
Boschetto Tre	4
Feltrinelli International	2
Super	5
Trimani	1

CHAINS AT SAN PIETRO IN VINCOLI

SAN PIETRO IN VINCOLI

Piazza di San Pietro in Vincoli 4a. Daily 8am–12.30pm & 3–7pm; closes 6pm Oct–March. MAP P.92–93, POCKET MAP G5

San Pietro in Vincoli is one of Rome's most delightfully plain churches. It was built to house an important relic, the two sets of chains (*vincoli*) that bound St Peter when imprisoned in Jerusalem and held him in the Mammertine Prison, which miraculously fused together when they were brought into contact with each other. The chains can still be seen in the *confessio* beneath the high altar, but most people come for the tomb of Pope Julius II at the far end of the southern aisle. The aisle occupied Michelangelo on and off for much of his career and was the cause of many a dispute with Julius and his successors. He reluctantly gave it up to paint the Sistine Chapel – the only statues that he managed to complete are the *Moses*, *Leah* and *Rachel*, which remain here, and two *Dying Slaves*, which are now in the Louvre, Paris. The figures are among the artist's most captivating works, especially *Moses*: because of

a medieval mistranslation of scripture, he is depicted with satyr's horns instead of the "radiance of the Lord" that Exodus tells us shone around his head. Nonetheless this powerful statue is so lifelike that Michelangelo is alleged to have struck its knee with his hammer and shouted "Speak, damn you!"

SANTA PRASSEDE

Via di Santa Prassede 9a. Daily 7.30am–noon & 4–6.30pm. MAP 92–93, POCKET MAP H5

The ninth-century church of **Santa Prassede** occupies an ancient site where it's claimed St Prassede harboured Christians on the run from the Roman persecutions. She apparently collected the blood and remains of the martyrs and placed them in a well where she herself was later buried; a red porphyry disc in the floor of the nave marks the spot. The Byzantine mosaics are the most striking feature, particularly those in the chapel of St Zeno, which make it glitter like a jewel-encrusted box.

MUSEO NAZIONALE D'ARTE ORIENTALE

Via Merulana 248 ☎ 06 469 748. Tues, Wed & Fri 9am–2pm, Thurs, Sat & Sun 9am–7.30pm. €6. MAP P.92–93, POCKET MAP H5

Housed in the imposing Palazzo Brancaccio, the **Museo Nazionale d'Arte Orientale** is a first-rate collection of oriental art. Italy's connection with the Far East goes back to Marco Polo in the thirteenth century, and the quality of this collection of Islamic, Chinese, Indian and Southeast Asian art reflects this long relationship. Highlights include finds dating back to 1500 BC from a necropolis in Pakistan; architectural fragments, art works and jewellery from

Tibet, Nepal and Pakistan; a solid collection from China, with predictable Buddhas and vases alongside curiosities such as a large Wei-dynasty Buddha with two boddhisatvas.

PIAZZA VITTORIO EMANUELE II

MAP P.92-93, POCKET MAP J5

Piazza Vittorio Emanuele II lies at the centre of a district that became known as the "quartiere piemontese" when the government located many of its major ministries here after Unification. The arcades of the square, certainly, recall central Turin, but it's more recently become the immigrant quarter of Rome, with a heavy concentration of African, Asian and Middle Eastern shops and restaurants. You'll hear a dozen different languages spoken as you pass through, although the morning **market** that used to take place here has moved a few blocks east to Via Giolitti, between Via Ricasoli and Via Lamarmora. Raucous and usually rammed with locals, this is a good place to shop for a picnic.

PIAZZA DELLA REPUBBLICA

MAP P.92-93, POCKET MAP H4

Typical of Rome's nineteenth-century regeneration, **Piazza della Repubblica** is a dignified semicircle of buildings that used to be rather dilapidated but is now – with the help of the very stylish *Hotel Exedra* – once again resurgent. The traffic roars ceaselessly around the centrepiece of the Fontana delle Naiadi, with its languishing nymphs and sea monsters. The piazza's shape follows the outline of the Baths of Diocletian, the remains of which lie across the piazza (see p.96).

PALAZZO DELLE ESPOSIZIONI

Via Nazionale 194 ☎ 06 3996 7500, ⟲ www .palazzoesposizioni.it. Tues–Thurs & Sun 10am–8pm, Fri & Sat 10am–10.30pm. Approx €12. MAP P.92-93, POCKET MAP G4

Via Nazionale connects Piazza Venezia and the centre of town with the area around Stazione Termini and the eastern districts beyond. A focus for development after Unification, its overbearing buildings are now occupied by hotels and bland, mid-range shops. It's worth strolling down as far as the imposing **Palazzo delle Esposizioni**, though, a cultural centre that hosts large-scale exhibitions and cultural events, and also houses a cinema, bookshop, café and restaurant (see p.100).

PALAZZO DELLE ESPOSIZIONI

SANTA MARIA DEGLI ANGELI

Piazza della Repubblica. Daily
7.30am–7.30pm. MAP P.92–93, POCKET MAP H4

The basilica of Santa Maria
degli Angeli was built on the
ruins of the Baths of Diocletian.
Designed by Michelangelo in
1563, a year before his death,
it gives a good impression of
the size and grandeur of the
baths complex: the crescent
shape of the facade remains
from the original caldarium,
the large transept was once
the tepidarium, and eight of
its huge pink-granite pillars
are originals from the baths.
Luigi Vanvitelli rearranged
the interior in 1749, by and
large imitating Michelangelo's
designs. The meridian that
strikes diagonally across the
floor in the south transept,
flanked by representations of
the twelve signs of the zodiac,
was until 1846 the regulator
of time for Romans (now a
cannon shot fires daily at noon
from the Janiculum Hill).

THE AULA OTTAGONA

Via Giuseppe Romita 8 ☎ 06 3996 7700.
Open rarely (for exhibitions only). MAP P.92–93,
POCKET MAP H4

The exit from the church
leaves you behind another
remnant of the baths, the **Aula
Ottagona**, which contains

marble statues taken from
the baths of Caracalla and
Diocletian, and two remarkable
statues of a boxer and athlete
from the Quirinale Hill. It also
holds underground furnaces
for heating water for the baths
and the foundations of another
building from the time of
Diocletian.

MUSEO DELLE TERME DI DIOCLEZIANO

Viale Enrico De Nicola 79 ☎ 06 3996 7700.
Tues–Sun 9am–7.45pm. €7 joint ticket
includes Palazzo Altemps, Palazzo Massimo
& Crypta Balbi, valid 3 days. MAP P.92–93,
POCKET MAP H3

Behind the church of Santa
Maria degli Angeli, the huge
halls and courtyards of the
Baths of Diocletian have
been renovated and they now
hold what is probably the least
interesting part of the Museo
Nazionale Romano – the **Museo
delle Terme di Diocleziano**,
the best bit of which is the large
cloister of the church whose
sides are crammed with statuary,
funerary monuments and
fragments from all over Rome.
The galleries that wrap around
the cloister hold a reasonable
collection of pre-Roman and
Roman finds: terracotta statues,
armour and weapons found in
Roman tombs.

PALAZZO MASSIMO ALLE TERME

Largo di Villa Peretti 1 ☏ 06 3996 7700.
Tues–Sun 9am–7.45pm. €7 joint ticket
includes Palazzo Altemps, Terme di Diocleziano
& Crypta Balbi, valid 3 days. MAP P.92–93,
POCKET MAP H4

The snazzily restored Palazzo
Massimo is home to one
of the two principal parts
of the **Museo Nazionale
Romano** (the other is in the
Palazzo Altemps) – a superb
collection of Greek and Roman
antiquities, second only to
the Vatican's. As one of the
great museums of Rome, there
are too many highlights to
do it justice here, and there
is something worth seeing
on every floor. Start at the
basement, which has displays
of exquisite gold jewellery
from the second century
AD, and – startlingly – the
mummified remains of an
8-year-old girl, along with a
coin collection. The **ground
floor** is devoted to statuary of
the early empire, including a
gallery with an unparalleled
selection of unidentified busts
found all over Rome – amazing
pieces of portraiture, and
as vivid a representation of
patrician Roman life as you'll
find. There are also identifiable
faces from the so-called
imperial family – a bronze
of Germanicus, a marvellous
small bust of Caligula, several
representations of Livia,
Antonia and Drusus and a
hooded statue of Augustus. On
the far side of the **courtyard**
is Greek sculpture, including
bronzes of a Hellenistic prince
holding a spear and a wounded
pugilist at rest.

The gallery on the **first
floor** has groupings of later
imperial dynasties in roughly
chronological order, starting
with the Flavian emperors and
ending with the Severans, with
the fierce-looking Caracalla
looking across past his father
Septimius Severus to his
brother Geta, whom he later
murdered.

The **second floor**, which you
can only visit on an organized
tour, takes in some of the finest
Roman frescoes and mosaics
ever found. There is a stunning
set of frescoes from the Casa
di Livia (see p.73), depicting
an orchard dense with fruit
and flowers and patrolled by
partridges and doves; wall
paintings rescued from what
was perhaps the riverside villa of
Julia and Agrippa; and mosaics
showing naturalistic scenes – sea
creatures, people boating – as
well as four finely crafted chariot
drivers and their horses.

SAN LORENZO FUORI LE MURA

Piazzale del Verano 3. Daily 7.30am–12.30pm & 4–8pm (winter 3.30–7pm). MAP P.92–93. POCKET MAP K4

The student neighbourhood of San Lorenzo, behind Termini, is home to **San Lorenzo fuori le Mura**, one of the seven great pilgrimage churches of Rome, and a typical Roman basilica, fronted by a columned portico and with a lovely twelfth-century cloister to its side. The original church was built by Constantine over the site of St Lawrence's martyrdom – the saint was reputedly burned to death on a gridiron, halfway through his ordeal apparently uttering the immortal words, "Turn me, I am done on this side." Because of its proximity to Rome's rail yards, the church was bombed heavily during World War II, but it has been rebuilt with sensitivity, and remains much as it was originally. Inside there are features from all periods, including a Cosmati mosaic floor and thirteenth-century pulpits. The mosaic on the inside of the triumphal arch is a sixth-century depiction of the founder offering his church to Christ. The catacombs below (rarely open) are where St Lawrence was apparently buried – a dank path leads to the pillars of Constantine's original structure. There's also a Romanesque cloister with a well-tended garden.

PIGNETO

Tram #5 or bus #105 from Termini.

Once a gritty inner-city district, **Pigneto** has been gentrified in recent years and is now firmly on the radar of Rome's cool set. The area has transformed itself into one of the city's best areas for a night out, with a selection of laid-back bars and intimate restaurants, particularly around Via del Pigneto, which is home to a lively morning **market** from Monday to Saturday.

Pigneto is a twenty-minute taxi ride from Termini, or a short hop on the tram, but well worth the trek.

SAN LORENZO FUORI LE MURA

Shops

BLUE GOOSE

Via del Boschetto 4. Mon–Sat 11am–8pm.
MAP P.92–93, POCKET MAP G5

This tiny store is crammed
full of rails of vintage designer
clothing, all in good condition
and at reasonable (if not
rock-bottom) prices. There's
a good selection of bags and
jewellery too.

BOSCHETTO TRE

Via del Boschetto 3. Daily 10.30am–8pm. MAP
P.92–93, POCKET MAP G5

Cool little homeware store,
with lots of northern European
design-led knick-knacks that
make great presents. You
can pick up anything from a
novelty lemon squeezer to a
pop art-influenced watch, at
affordable prices.

FELTRINELLI INTERNATIONAL

Via Emanuele Orlando 84. Mon–Sat
9am–8pm, Sun 10.30am–1.30pm & 4–8pm;
closed Sun in Aug. MAP P.92–93, POCKET MAP G4

This international branch
of the nationwide chain has
an excellent stock of books
in English, as well as in
French, German, Spanish and
Portuguese.

SUPER

Via Leonina 42. Mon–Sat 10.30am–2.30pm &
3.30–8pm. MAP P.92–93, POCKET MAP G5

Monti's original concept store
is still going strong. Though
space is tight, they manage
to pack in a well-curated
selection of cool womenswear,
menswear and quirky
homeware, with niche brands
you won't find anywhere else.

TRIMANI

Via Goito 20 ⓦ www.trimani.com. Mon–Sat
9am–8.30pm. MAP P.92–93, POCKET MAP H3

One of the city's best wine

BOSCHETTO TRE

shops, *Trimani* has been in
business since 1876 and is still
run by the same family. It's
close to Termini if you want
to stock up before heading off
to the airport; otherwise, they
can ship anywhere. There's also
a wine bar around the corner
serving decent food (see p.102).

Cafés and snacks

LA BOTTEGA DEL CAFFÈ

Piazza Madonna dei Monti 5. Daily 8am–2am.
MAP P.92–93, POCKET MAP G5

Right in the heart of Monti,
this is a good place for
breakfast, a lunchtime snack
or an early-evening drink,
with tables outside on a
picturesque square.

DAGNINO

Galleria Esedra, Via E. Orlando 75. Daily
7am–11pm. MAP P.92–93, POCKET MAP G4

Good for a coffee, snack
or light lunch, this
long-established Sicilian
bakery – ricotta-stuffed
cannoli are a speciality – is a
peaceful retreat in the
Termini area, with tables
outside in this small shopping
arcade.

PALAZZO DEL FREDDO DI GIOVANNI FASSI

Via Principe Eugenio 65. Tues–Sat noon–midnight, Sun 10am–midnight; closes 9pm Tues–Thurs & Sun in winter. MAP P.92–93, POCKET MAP J6

A wonderful, airy 1920s ice cream parlour. Brilliant fruit ice creams and great *frullati*, too.

Restaurants

AGATA E ROMEO

Via Carlo Alberto 45 ☎ 06 446 6115. Mon & Sat 7–10.30pm, Tues–Fri 12.30–2.30pm & 7–10.30pm; closed 3 weeks in Aug. MAP P.92–93, POCKET MAP H5

Much-lauded chef Agata Parisella takes classic Roman cuisine to refined heights, in dishes such as her *baccalà* (salt cod) cooked five ways. Pricey for this part of town, but a great place for a blow-the-budget feast. Booking essential.

L'ASINO D'ORO

Via del Boschetto 73 ☎ 06 4891 3832. Tues–Sat 12.30–2.30pm & 7.30–10.30pm. MAP P.92–93, POCKET MAP G5

The Rome location of legendary chef Lucio Sforza, who blends traditional Roman ingredients in both complex and simple combinations that you won't find anywhere else in the city. Great value at lunch (€13 for three courses). Credit cards not accepted at lunch.

ALLE CARRETTE

Via Madonna dei Monti 95 ☎ 06 679 2770. Mon & Wed–Sun noon–3pm & 7.30–11.30pm; in winter open dinner only and also open Tues. MAP P.92–93, POCKET MAP G5

Inexpensive large pizzeria just up Via Cavour that normally has long queues for the exceptional pizza and phenomenal desserts they serve here.

DOOZO

Via Palermo 51/53 ☎ 06 481 5655, ⓦ www.doozo.it. Tues–Sat 12.30–3pm & 7.30–11pm, Sun 7.30–10.30pm; tearoom Tues–Sat 4–7pm. MAP P.92–93, POCKET MAP G4

Arguably the best Japanese restaurant in Monti. Part restaurant and tearoom, part art gallery and bookshop, *Doozo* serves affordable lunch menus (around €15); dinner is pricier (€35 and up). Outdoor seating is in a leafy courtyard with an ancient wall.

HANG ZHOU

Via di San Martino ai Monti 33 ☎ 06 487 2732. Daily noon–3pm & 7–11.30pm. MAP P.92–93, POCKET MAP H5

Rome isn't great for Chinese food, but this old Monti favourite is a cut above the rest. Plastered with photos of the sociable owner, it's cheap too.

MONTI DOC

Via G. Lanza 93 ☎ 06 4893 0427. Tues–Sun 11.30am–3pm & 6pm–1am. MAP P.92–93, POCKET MAP H5

Comfortable Santa Maria Maggiore-neighbourhood wine bar, with a comprehensive wine list and nice food: cold cuts and cheese, soups and a few pastas and *secondi*. There's a good *aperitivo* buffet too (6–8pm).

TRAM TRAM

LA MUCCA BISCHERA

Via degli Equi 56 ☎ 06 446 9349. Mon–Fri 7.30pm–1am, Sat & Sun noon–3.30pm & 7.30pm–1am. MAP P.92–93, POCKET MAP K5

This cheap-and-cheerful place is packed with locals every night. The decor is kitsch – plastic vines, twinkling fairy lights and stuffed cows – but the food is hearty: Tuscan steaks and grilled meats from about €12.

NECCI DAL 1924

Via Fanfulla da Lodi 68 ☎ 06 9760 1552. Daily 8am–1am. Bus #105 or tram #5 or #14 from Termini.

Pasolini shot some of his films in Pigneto, and this bar-restaurant was apparently one of his favourite haunts. Now a trendy, buzzing spot throughout the day, it has a lovely shady garden where you can have a drink, snack or a full meal, with its creative dishes chalked afresh on the blackboard each day.

OPEN COLONNA

Palazzo delle Esposizioni, Via Milano 9a ☎ 06 4782 2641. Tues–Sat 12.30–3.30pm & 8–10.30pm, Mon & Sun 12.30–3.30pm. MAP P.92–93, POCKET MAP G4

The top floor of the Palazzo delle Esposizioni (see p.95) is the domain of big-shot Italian chef Antonello Colonna. The €16 weekday lunch buffet is a hit with local office workers, while the €30 weekend brunch attracts more of a mixed crowd.

PIGNETO QUARANTUNO

Via del Pigneto 41–43 ☎ 06 7039 9483. Tues–Sun 11.30am–midnight. Bus #105 or tram #5 or #14 from Termini.

In the heart of the action, on Via del Pigneto's pedestrianized strip, this excellent-value trattoria with outdoor tables has a short but ever-changing menu, though their fantastic carbonara (€8) is always on the menu.

POMMIDORO

Piazza dei Sanniti 46 ☎ 06 445 2692. Mon–Sat 1–3pm & 8–11pm. MAP P.92–93, POCKET MAP K4

This family-run Roman trattoria has a breezy open veranda in summer and a fireplace in winter, and a great menu: try the tasty *pappardelle* with a wild boar sauce, and *abbacchio allo scottadito*, perfectly grilled lamb.

PRIMO AL PIGNETO

Via del Pigneto 46 ☎ 06 701 3827. Tues–Sat 7pm–1am, Sun 12.30–2.30pm & 7pm–1am. Bus #105 or tram #5 or #14 from Termini

The top Pigneto restaurant, distinguished by its clean, contemporary interior and short menu of unfussy, seasonal dishes made using the freshest of ingredients – the mezze maniche pasta with amatriciana sauce is a favourite. Primi €10–14, secondi €18–20. It's a good idea to book.

TRAM TRAM

Via dei Reti 44 ☎ 06 490 416. Tues–Sun 12.30–3pm & 7.30–11.30pm; July & Aug closed Sun & open Mon. MAP P.92–93, POCKET MAP K5

Despite the grungy location, this trendy San Lorenzo restaurant is a cosy spot, and serves good pasta dishes, seafood and unusual salads. Reserve ahead. There's a bar if you want to carry on drinking after dinner.

TRATTORIA MONTI

Via di San Vito 13a ☎ 06 446 6573. Tues–Sat 1–2.45pm & 8–11pm, Sun 1–2.45pm. MAP P.92–93, POCKET MAP H5

A small family-run restaurant specializing in the cuisine of the Marche region, meaning hearty food from a short menu. As homely and friendly a restaurant as you could want.

VALENTINO

Via del Boschetto 37 ☎ 06 488 0643.
Mon–Sat 1–3pm & 7.45–11.15pm. MAP P.92–93,
POCKET MAP G5

With only a faded Peroni sign
above the door, this trattoria on
an atmospheric street is easy
to miss. Inside, it's buzzing,
with waiters zipping between
the closely packed tables. You'll
find grilled meat options, and
a *scamorza* (grilled cheese)
menu.

Bars

2PERIODICO CAFÉ

Via Leonina 77 ☎ 06 4890 6600
ⓦ www.2periodicocafe.it. Mon–Fri 4pm–2am,
Sat & Sun 9am–2am; opens earlier in winter.
MAP P.92–93, POCKET MAP G5

This new bar, all mismatched
furniture and chilled-out tunes,
has a good *aperitivo* buffet
(from 6.30pm), and there's a
clubby feel in the back room
later on. The Sunday brunch
with DJ is worth dropping
by for (from 12.30pm; €20
including drinks).

AL VINO AL VINO

Via dei Serpenti 19. Daily 6pm–midnight;
closed Aug. MAP P.92–93, POCKET MAP G5

Seriously good wine bar with
a choice of over 500 labels,
many by the glass. Snacks
are generally Sicilian
specialities.

LA BARRIQUE

Via del Boschetto 41b ☎ 06 4782 5953.
Mon–Fri 1–4pm & 6.30pm–midnight,
Sat 6.30pm–midnight. MAP P.92–93, POCKET
MAP G5

This labyrinthine wine bar is
a great spot for an *aperitivo*.
French and Italian wines
are the main attraction –
champagne is a speciality – and
there are platters of meats and
cheeses.

CAVOUR 313

Via Cavour 313. Daily 12.30–2.45pm &
7.30pm–12.30am; closed Sun in summer.
MAP P.92–93, POCKET MAP G5

A lovely old wine bar that
makes a handy retreat after
seeing the ancient sites.
The interior is cosy and
wood-panelled, and delicious
(though not cheap) snacks are
served – cheese platters, salads
and the like.

FINNEGAN

Via Leonina 66 ☎ 06 474 7026. Mon–Fri
1pm–12.30am, Sat & Sun noon–1am. MAP
P.92–93, POCKET MAP G5

Decent Irish pub with live
football on TV, pool, and a
friendly expat crowd. There's
seating outside, too, on this
bustling Monti street.

RIVE GAUCHE

Via dei Sabelli 43. Daily 7pm–2am.
MAP P.92–93, POCKET MAP K5

This large San Lorenzo pub
is noisy, cavernous and
beery – one of the best and
longest-established night haunts
in an area that is full of them.
Aperitivi with buffet till 9pm.

IL TIASO

Via Ascoli Piceno 20 ☎ 333 284 5283. Daily
6pm–2am. Bus #105 or tram #5 or #14
from Termini

This relaxed wine bar with

free wi-fi has book-lined shelves and a large selection of wines to try by the glass, accompanied by cheese and salami platters, as well as some more substantial meals. There are often live acoustic sets, too – a great place to kick off an evening out.

AI TRE SCALINI

Via Panisperna 251 ☎ 06 4890 7495. Daily 12.30pm–1.30am. MAP P.92–93, POCKET MAP G5

Easy-to-miss Monti bar, cosy and comfortable, with a great wine list but beer too if you want it, and decent food – cheese and salami plates, porchetta and a few hot dishes.

TRIMANI

Via Cernaia 37b. Mon–Sat 11.30am–3pm & 5.30pm–12.30am. MAP P.92–93, POCKET MAP H3

Classy wine bar that's good for a lunchtime tipple. You'll spend around €18 to sample a range of cheeses and cured pork, or soup and salad, with a glass of wine.

IL TIASO

Clubs and venues

CIRCOLO DEGLI ARTISTI

Via Casilina Vecchia 42 ☎ 06 7030 5684, Ⓦ www.circoloartisti.it. Open most days 9pm–2am. Admission from €5. Bus #105 from Termini. MAP P.92–93, POCKET MAP K7

Alternative live music venue, with emerging talent and established indie bands, both Italian and international. Sundays see events such as vintage markets or swing classes. The garden in the shade of an ancient Roman aqueduct is an atmospheric spot in summer. They serve great pizzas too.

TEATRO DELL'OPERA DI ROMA

Piazza Beniamino Gigli 1 ☎ 06 4816 0255, Ⓦ www.operaroma.it. Box office Tues–Sat 9am–5pm, Sun 9am–1.30pm. MAP P.92–93, POCKET MAP H4

Nobody compares it to La Scala, but cheap tickets are a lot easier to come by at Rome's opera and ballet venue – they start at around €20 for opera, less for ballet. If you buy the very cheapest tickets, bring some high-powered binoculars: you'll need them in order to see anything at all.

VICIOUS CLUB

Via Achille Grandi 7/a ☎ 06 7061 4349, Ⓦ www.viciousclub.com. Tues–Thurs 10pm–4am, Fri & Sat 11pm–6am. MAP P.92–93, POCKET MAP K6

Its interior lined with mirrors and black walls, *Vicious Club*'s underground feel marks it out from many Roman clubs. It's a cocktail bar on Tuesday and Wednesday, and the rest of the week it hosts djs. Friday's Rock'n Yolk night (indie, nu-wave, electronica, rap) is popular, and there's a monthly gay night.

The Celian Hill and San Giovanni

Just behind the Colosseum, the Celian Hill is the most southerly of Rome's seven hills, and one of its most peaceful, home to a handful of churches and a quiet park. Just to the south and east are some of Rome's most interesting churches: triple-layered San Clemente and nearby Quattro Coronati, and the complex of San Giovanni in Laterano – which gives its name to the surrounding San Giovanni district – all well worth the walk from the Colosseum. Nearby also is the wartime headquarters of the Nazi SS, now the home of an affecting commemorative museum.

VILLA CELIMONTANA

Via della Navicella 12 ⓦ www
.villacelimontanajazzfestival.com. MAP P.106–107,
POCKET MAP G7

Much of the Celian Hill is taken up by the park of **Villa Celimontana**, whose gardens make a nice spot for a picnic, with lots of leafy walkways and grassy slopes. There are pony rides and a playground, and outdoor jazz concerts are performed on summer evenings.

THE PARK OF VILLA CELIMONTANA

SANTA MARIA IN DOMINICA

Via della Navicella 10. Daily 9am–noon & 3–6pm. MAP P.106–107, POCKET MAP H7

Also known as Santa Maria in Navicella after the ancient Roman stone boat that sits outside, this sixth-century church is just outside the entrance to the Villa Celimontana, and is worth visiting for the ninth-century mosaic above the apse, which shows Paschal I, who restored the church, kneeling at the feet of the Virgin.

SANTO STEFANO ROTONDO

Via di Santo Stefano Rotondo 7. Tues–Sat 9.30am–12.30pm & 3–6pm (2–5pm in winter). Sun 9.30am–12.30pm. MAP P.106–107, POCKET MAP H7

This church is an ancient structure, illuminated by 22 windows – a magnificent and wonderfully moody circular space, though the feature that really sticks in the mind is the series of stomach-churning frescoes that grace the walls, showing various saints being martyred in different ways, all in graphic and vividly restored detail.

SANTI GIOVANNI E PAOLO

Piazza dei Santi Giovanni e Paolo 13. Daily
8.30am–noon & 3.30–6pm. MAP P.106-107,
POCKET MAP G7

Recognized by its colourful
campanile, this church is
dedicated to two dignitaries in
the court of Constantine who
were beheaded here in 361 AD
after refusing military service.
A railed-off tablet in mid-nave
marks the shrine where the
saints were martyred and buried.
The church is best known today
as a wedding venue.

CASE ROMANE

Clivo di Scauro ☎ 06 7045 4544. Daily except
Tues & Wed 10am–1pm & 3–6pm. €6. MAP
P.106-107, POCKET MAP G7

The relics of what is believed to
be the residence of the martyrs
Giovanni and Paolo (see above)
– around twenty rooms, patchily
frescoed with pagan and
Christian subjects. Standouts
include the **Casa dei Genii,**
frescoed with winged youths
and cupids, and the courtyard
or nymphaeum, which has a
marvellous fresco of a goddess
preparing for her marriage to
Pluto, sandwiched between
cupids in boats, fishing and
loading supplies. There's also an
interesting antiquarium, with a
good haul of finds from the site.

SAN GREGORIO MAGNO

Piazza di San Gregorio 1. Daily 9am–1pm &
3.30–7.30pm; ring the bell marked "portinare"
to gain admission. MAP P.106-107, POCKET MAP G7

St Gregory the Great founded
a monastery that still exists,
and was a monk here before
becoming pope in 590 AD.
The church's interior is fairly
ordinary, but the lovely
Cosmati floor remains intact,
and the chapel of the saint
at the end of the south aisle
has a beautifully carved
altar showing scenes from St
Gregory's life, along with his
marble throne, that actually
pre-dates the saint by 500 years.

SANTI QUATTRO CORONATI

Via dei Querceti. Daily 9.30am–noon &
4.30–6pm. €1. MAP P.106-107, POCKET MAP H6-H7

Originally built in 1110, the
interior feels a world away from
the crowds around the nearby
Colosseum – an atmosphere
that is intensified by the pretty
cloister (ring the bell for access),
where the community of nuns
sings beautifully at mass. But
its real treasure is the chapel of
San Silvestro, whose frescoes,
painted in 1248, relate the story
of how the fourth-century pope
cured the emperor Constantine
of leprosy and then went on to
baptize him.

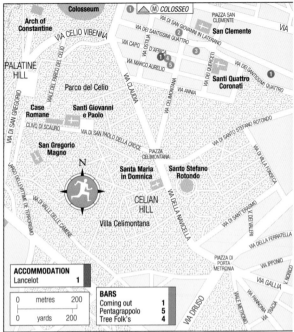

ACCOMMODATION
Lancelot   **1**

| 0 | metres | 200 |
| 0 | yards | 200 |

BARS
Coming out   **1**
Pentagrappolo   **5**
Tree Folk's   **4**

SAN CLEMENTE

Via Labicana 95. Mon–Sat 9am–12.30pm &
3–6pm, Sun noon–6pm. €5. MAP P.106–107,
POCKET MAP H6

This church perhaps
encapsulates better than any
other the continuity of history
in Rome – a conglomeration
of three places of worship
from three very different eras.
The ground-floor church
is a superb example of a
medieval basilica, with some
fine mosaics in the apse and
some beautiful and vivid
fifteenth-century frescoes.
Downstairs there's the nave of
an earlier church, dating back
to 392 AD, and the **tomb of
Pope Clement I**, the saint to
whom the church is dedicated.
At the eastern end of the
fourth-century church, steps
lead down to a third level, the

remains of a Roman house –
a labyrinthine set of rooms
that includes a dank Mithraic
temple of the late second
century.

SAN GIOVANNI IN LATERANO

Piazza di San Giovanni in Laterano. Daily
7am–6.30pm. Cloisters daily 9am–6pm. MAP
P.106–107, POCKET MAP J7

The area immediately south
and east of the Esquiline
Hill is known as **San
Giovanni**, after the great
basilica that lies at its heart
– the city's cathedral, and the
headquarters of the Catholic
Church before the creation
of the Vatican state. There
has been a church on this site
since the fourth century, and
the present building evokes
Rome's staggering wealth of
history, with features from

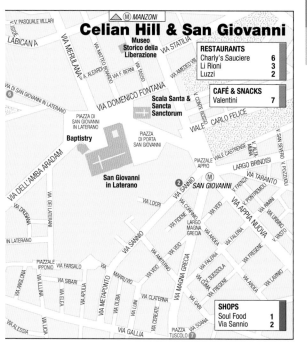

different periods. The doors to the church were taken from the Roman Curia or Senate House, while the obelisk outside dates from the fifteenth century BC. Inside, the first pillar on the left of the right-hand aisle shows a fragment of Giotto's fresco of Boniface VIII proclaiming the first Holy Year in 1300. On the next pillar, a more recent monument commemorates Sylvester I, and incorporates part of his original tomb, said to sweat and rattle its bones when a pope is about to die. The nave itself is lined with eighteenth-century statues of the apostles: St Matthew, the tax collector, is shown with coins falling out of a sack; St Bartholomew holds a knife

and his own skin (he was flayed alive). The heads of St Peter and St Paul are kept secure behind the altar, while the baldacchino just in front is a splash of Gothic grandeur made by the Tuscan sculptor Giovanni di Stefano in the fourteenth century: it shelters the glassed-over bronze tomb of Martin V, the Colonna pope who was responsible for returning the papacy to Rome from Avignon in 1419. Outside the church, the cloisters are decorated with early thirteenth-century Cosmati work, while next door the Lateran Palace, home of the popes in the Middle Ages, has a small historical museum.

THE BAPTISTRY

San Giovanni in Laterano. Daily 7am–12.30pm & 4–6.30pm. Free. MAP P.106–107, POCKET MAP J7

San Giovanni's **baptistry** is the oldest surviving in the Christian world – the octagonal structure was built during the fifth century and has been the model for many such buildings since. Even though it doesn't feel this old, the mosaics in the side chapels and the bronze doors to the chapel on the right, brought here from the Baths of Caracalla, quickly remind you that you're in an ancient church.

THE SCALA SANTA AND SANCTA SANCTORUM

Piazza di San Giovanni in Laterano 14. Daily 6am–12.30pm & 3–6.30pm. MAP P.106–107, POCKET MAP J7

The **Scala Santa** is claimed to be the staircase from Pontius Pilate's house down which Christ walked after his trial. The 28 steps are protected by boards, and the only way you're allowed to climb them is on your knees, which pilgrims do regularly – although there are other staircases either side for the less penitent. At the top, the Sancta Sanctorum holds an ancient (sixth- or seventh-century) painting of Christ said to be the work of an angel, hence its name – *acheiropoeton*, Greek for "not done by human hands". You can't enter the chapel, and, fittingly perhaps, you can only really get a view of it by kneeling and peering through the grilles.

MUSEO STORICO DELLA LIBERAZIONE

Via Tasso 145. Tues–Sun 9.30am–12.30pm, Tues, Thurs, Fri also 3.30–7.30pm. Free. MAP P.106–107, POCKET MAP J6

Occupying two floors of the building the Nazis used as a prison during World War II, this museum (signage in Italian only) incorporates the prison cells, left deliberately untouched. It's extremely well done, and perhaps the most seriously affecting free attraction in town.

Shops

SOUL FOOD

Via San Giovanni in Laterano 192. Tues–Sat 10.30am–1.30pm & 3.30–8pm. MAP P.106–107, POCKET MAP H7

Great, mainly vinyl, music store, with lots of rare as well as mainstream rock and punk discs. Flyers and information on gigs and venues too.

VIA SANNIO

Mon–Sat 7.30am–2pm, Sat sometimes till 5pm. MAP P.106–107, POCKET MAP J7

Long-standing market that creeps down the Aurelian Wall just beyond San Giovanni. Cheap clothes, luggage and shoes.

Café

VALENTINI

Piazza Tuscolo 2. Mon–Sat 6am–11pm, Sun 7am–11pm. MAP P.106–107, POCKET MAP J8

Café, pastry shop and *tavola calda*, just five minutes' from San Giovanni and a great spot for lunch, with outside seating too.

Restaurants

CHARLY'S SAUCIERE

Via San Giovanni in Laterano 270 ☎ 06 7049 5666. Mon & Sat 8–11.30pm, Tues–Fri 1–3pm & 8–11.30pm. MAP P.106–107, POCKET MAP H7

Lots of French classics – including fondues (the owner is Swiss), onion soup and excellent steaks, not to mention a good selection of real French cheeses. Moderate to high prices, but the food, service and overall atmosphere are worth every cent. Best to book.

LI RIONI

Via SS. Quattro 24 ☎ 06 7045 0605. Mon & Wed–Sun 7pm–midnight. MAP P.106–107, POCKET MAP H6

With its street lamps and tiled roofs, *Li Rioni's* interior resembles an Italian piazza, especially after trying the robust house wine. At dinner it's packed with locals enjoying crispy Roman-style pizza; a meal with wine costs less than €20.

LUZZI

Via San Giovanni in Laterano 88 ☎ 06 709 6332. Mon, Tues & Thurs–Sun noon–midnight. MAP P.106–107, POCKET MAP H6

Between San Giovanni in Laterano and the Colosseum, *Luzzi* sits amid the tourist joints of the neighbourhood. There's hearty food and outside seating. It's very cheap – *secondi* are €6–9 and they do pizzas too.

Bars

COMING OUT

Via San Giovanni in Laterano 8 ☎ 06 700 9871 ⓦ www.comingout.it. Daily 7.30am–2am. MAP P.106–107, POCKET MAP G6

Laid-back gay bar that serves food and hosts karaoke and live music nights.

PENTAGRAPPOLO

Via Celimontana 21b ☎ 06 709 6301. Tues–Sun noon–3pm & 6pm–1am. MAP P.106–107, POCKET MAP G7

Celian Hill wine bar with good wines by the glass, cheese plates and cold cuts. Live music plus a lively *aperitivo* with tapas Thursday to Sunday.

TREE FOLK'S

Via Capo d'Africa. Daily 6pm–2am. MAP P.106–107, POCKET MAP G6

Lots of Belgian and German brews, along with whisky – their selection of single malts must be the city's best. Food served, too.

The Aventine Hill and south

The leafy Aventine Hill – once the heart of plebeian Rome – is now an upscale residential area and one of the city's most pleasant corners. South and west from the hill are two distinct neighbourhoods: Testaccio, a working-class enclave that's become increasingly hip and gentrified (and home to much of the city's nightlife), and the more up-and-coming Ostiense, beyond the ancient city wall, worth a visit for the Centrale Montemartini branch of the Capitoline Museums. Between these districts is Rome's Protestant Cemetery, where the poets Keats and Shelley are buried. Further south lie the magnificent basilica of San Paolo fuori le Mura and the Via Appia Antica with its atmospheric catacombs, and beyond, EUR: Rome's futuristic 1930s experiment in town planning.

CIRCUS MAXIMUS

MAP P.112-113, POCKET MAP F7

The southern side of the Palatine Hill drops down to **Circus Maximus**, a long green expanse that was the ancient city's main venue for chariot races. At one time this arena had a capacity of up to 400,000 spectators, and it still retains something of its original purpose as an occasional venue for festivals and concerts.

THE BATHS OF CARACALLA

Viale Terme di Caracalla 52 ☎ 06 3996 7700. Mon 8.30am–2pm, Tues–Sun 9am–1 hr before sunset. €6 joint ticket includes Tomb of Cecilia Metella & Villa dei Quintili (valid for 7 days) Tours (Sun 3pm; Italian only) free. MAP P.112-113, POCKET MAP H8

The remains of this ancient Roman leisure centre give a far better sense of the monumental scale of Roman architecture than most of the extant ruins in the city – so much so that Shelley was moved to write *Prometheus Unbound* here in 1819. The walls still rise to very nearly their original height and there are many fragments of mosaics – none spectacular, but quite a few bright and well preserved. The complex included gymnasiums, gardens and an open-air swimming pool as well as the hot, tepid and cold series of baths. As for Caracalla, he was one of Rome's worst and shortest-lived rulers, so it's no wonder there's nothing else in the city built by him. The baths make an

LATIN PLAQUE ON SANTA SABINA

the saint. Wherever the truth lies, the views from the park are splendid – across the Tiber to the centre of Rome and St Peter's.

PIAZZA DEI CAVALIERI DI MALTA

MAP P.112–113, POCKET MAP E7

As if to reward those who venture this far up the Aventine Hill, the minuscule **Piazza dei Cavalieri di Malta** holds an intriguing attraction: the imposing doorway to the **Priory of the Knights of Malta** is kept firmly closed to the public, but you can peek through the keyhole for a perfectly framed, dead-ahead view of St Peter's: the work of Giovanni Battista Piranesi.

TESTACCIO

MAP P.112–113, POCKET MAP E9

The working-class neighbourhood of **Testaccio** was for many years synonymous with its slaughterhouse, or *mattatoio*. In recent years the area has become fashionable, and is best known for its clubs. For a taste of old Testaccio, head for one of the district's many **restaurants**; this is the best place in town to sample traditional *cucina povera* – offal-heavy "poor cuisine", best sampled at *Checchino dal 1887* (see p.120). Testaccio's historic **market** (Mon–Sat 7am–3pm) recently moved to bright new premises between Via Galvani and Via Alessandro Volta, and is a great place to pick up a picnic lunch. Near the old slaughterhouse at Piazza Giustiniani 4 is a branch of the **Museum of Contemporary Art of Rome** (MACRO Testaccio; Tues–Sun 4–10pm; €6; ⓦwww.museomacro.org), home to innovative temporary exhibitions.

atmospheric setting for opera performances during the summer (one of Mussolini's better ideas); for tickets and programme information, see ⓦwww.operaroma.it.

SANTA SABINA

Piazza Pietro d'Illiria. Daily 8.15am–12.30pm & 3.30–6pm. MAP P.112–113, POCKET MAP E7

Crowning the Aventine Hill, **Santa Sabina** is a strong contender for Rome's most beautiful basilica. Look at the main doors, which are contemporary with the church and boast eighteen panels carved with Christian scenes (including one of the oldest representations of the Crucifixion). Santa Sabina is also the principal church of the Dominicans, and inside, just near the doors, a smooth piece of black marble, pitted with holes, was apparently thrown by the devil at St Dominic himself while at prayer, shattering the marble pavement but miraculously not harming the saint. It's also claimed that the orange trees behind, which you can glimpse on your way to a room once occupied by St Dominic himself, are descendants of those planted by

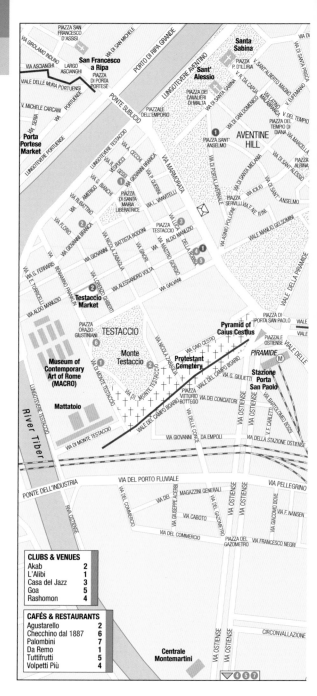

CLUBS & VENUES

Akab	2
L'Alibi	1
Casa del Jazz	3
Goa	5
Rashomon	4

CAFÉS & RESTAURANTS

Agustarello	2
Checchino dal 1887	6
Palombini	7
Da Remo	1
Tuttifrutti	5
Volpetti Più	4

Aventine Hill & south

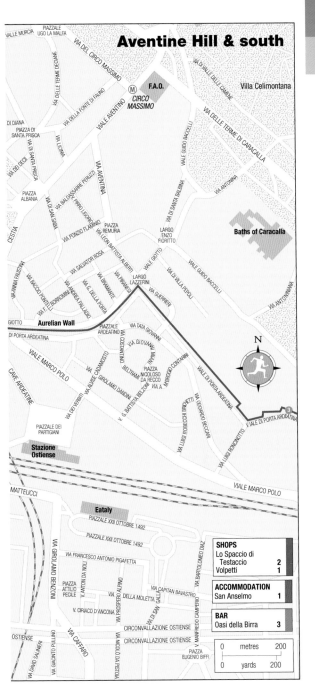

Villa Celimontana

F.A.O.

M CIRCO MASSIMO

Baths of Caracalla

Aurelian Wall

N

Stazione Ostiense

VIALE MARCO POLO

Eataly

PIAZZALE XXII OTTOBRE 1492

PIAZZALE XXII OTTOBRE 1492

PIAZZA EUGENIO BIFFI

SHOPS	
Lo Spaccio di Testaccio	2
Volpetti	1

ACCOMMODATION	
San Anselmo	1

BAR	
Oasi della Birra	3

0	metres	200
0	yards	200

MONTE TESTACCIO

MAP P.112–113, POCKET MAP E9

Monte Testaccio, which gives the area its name, is a 35-metre-high mound created out of the shards of Roman amphorae that were dumped here over several centuries. It's an odd sight, the ceramic curls clearly visible through the tufts of grass that crown its higher reaches, the bottom layers hollowed out by the workshops of car and bike mechanics – and, now, clubs and bars.

THE PROTESTANT CEMETERY

Entrance on Via Caio Cestio 6 ☎ 06 574 1900, ⓦ www.cemeteryrome.it. Mon–Sat 9am–5pm, Sun 9am–1pm; last entrance 30min before closing. €3 donation expected. Bus 23 to Piazzale Ostiense. MAP P.112–113, POCKET MAP E9

The **Protestant Cemetery** isn't in fact a Protestant cemetery at all, but is reserved for non-Roman Catholics of all nationalities. It is nonetheless one of the shrines to the English in Rome, and a fitting conclusion to a visit to the Keats-Shelley Memorial House on Piazza di Spagna (see p.74) since it is here that both poets are buried, along with a handful of other well-known names. Most visitors come to see the grave of Keats, who lies next to his friend, the painter Joseph Severn, in a corner of the old part of the cemetery, his stone inscribed, according to his wishes, with the words "Here lies one whose name was writ in water". Shelley's ashes were brought here at his wife's request and interred, after much obstruction by the papal authorities, in the newer part of the cemetery at the top – the Shelleys had visited several years earlier, the poet praising it as "the most beautiful and solemn cemetery I ever beheld".

THE PYRAMID OF CAIUS CESTIUS

Piazzale Ostiense ☎ 06 3996 7700. Guided tours in Italian only: 2nd and 4th Sat of the month at 11am; 1hr. €5.50. Book in advance. MAP P.112–113, POCKET MAP E9

The most distinctive landmark in this part of town is the **pyramidal tomb** of Caius Cestius, who died in 12 BC. Cestius had spent some time in Egypt, and part of his will decreed that all his slaves should be freed – the white pyramid here today was thrown up by them in only 330 days of what must have been joyful building.

EATALY

Piazzale XII Ottobre 1492. ☎ 06 9027 9201. ⓦ www.roma.eataly.it. Daily 8am–midnight. Metro B Piramide. MAP P.112–113. POCKET MAP F10

High-end supermarket chain **Eataly** now has a hangar-like branch in Rome, with four storeys full of Italian produce, from microbrewed beers to fresh fish. As an experience, it's more American mall than authentic Italian food shop, and prices are higher than elsewhere, but its air-conditioned spaces are a relief on a hot day.

CENTRALE MONTEMARTINI

Via Ostiense 106 ☎ 06 0608. ⓦ www.centralemontemartini.org. Tues–Sun 9am–7pm. €6.50, or €11.50 for joint ticket with Capitoline Museums, valid 7 days. Metro B Garbatella. MAP P.112–113. POCKET MAP E11

This former power station is a permanent outpost of the Capitoline Museums, attracting visitors to formerly industrial Ostiense. The huge rooms are suited to showcasing ancient sculpture, although the massive turbines and furnaces have a fascination of their own. Among many compelling objects are the head, feet and an arm from a colossal statue, once 8m high, found in Largo Torre Argentina, a large Roman copy of Athena, a fragmented mosaic of hunting scenes, and a lovely naturalistic statue of a girl seated on a stool with her legs crossed, from the third century BC. There's also a figure of Hercules and next to it a soft Muse Polymnia, the former braced for activity, the latter leaning on a rock and staring into the distance.

SAN PAOLO FUORI LE MURA

Via Ostiense 190. Basilica daily 7am–6.30pm, cloister daily 8am–6.15pm. €4. Metro B San Paolo. MAP P.112–113. POCKET MAP E12

The basilica of **San Paolo fuori le Mura** (St Paul's Outside the Walls) is one of Rome's five patriarchal basilicas, occupying the site of St Paul's tomb. Victim of a devastating fire in 1823, today its largely nineteenth-century reconstruction. The huge structure has a powerful and authentic sense of occasion: evidenced by the medallions of the popes fringing the nave and transepts above, starting with St Peter to the right of the apse and ending with Benedict XVI at the top of the south aisle. The cloister holds probably Rome's finest piece of Cosmatesque work, its spiralling, mosaic-encrusted columns enclosing a peaceful rose garden.

THE AURELIAN WALL

MAP P.112–113, POCKET MAP E10–H9

Built by the Emperor Aurelian in 275 AD to enclose Rome's hills and protect the city from invasion, the Aurelian Wall still surrounds much of the city, but its best-preserved stretch runs 2km between Porta San Paolo and Porta San Sebastiano (which lies a few hundred metres of Largo Terme di Caracalla). Here, the **Museo delle Mura** at Via di Porta San Sebastiano 18 (☎ 06 0608, ⍵ www.museodelle muraroma.it; Tues–Sun 9am–2pm; €5) occupies two floors of the city gate and has displays showing Aurelian's original plans and lots of photos of the walls past and present. You can climb up to the top of the gate for great views over the Roman countryside beyond, and walk a few hundred metres along the wall itself. From here it's only a short walk up Via di Porta San Sebastiano to the Baths of Caracalla.

VIA APPIA ANTICA

POCKET MAP H10–K12

The **Via Appia Antica**, which starts at the Porta San Sebastiano, is the most famous of the consular roads that used to strike out in each direction from ancient Rome. It was built by one Appio Claudio in 312 BC, and is the only Roman landmark mentioned in the Bible. During classical times the "Appian Way" was the most important of all the Roman trade routes, carrying supplies right down through Campania to the port of Brindisi. It's no longer the main route south out of the city – that's Via Appia Nuova from nearby Porta San Giovanni – but it remains an important part of early Christian Rome, its verges lined with numerous pagan and Christian sites, including, most famously, the underground burial cemeteries, or catacombs, of the first Christians.

Visiting Via Appia Antica and the catacombs

Buses run south along Via Appia Antica and conveniently stop at, or near to, most of the main attractions, starting with Porta San Sebastiano. You can walk it, but bear in mind that much of the Via Appia Antica isn't particularly picturesque, at least until you get down to the Catacombs of San Sebastiano, and the best thing to do is take a bus to San Sebastiano and double back or walk on further for the attractions you want to see. Bus #118 runs from Piazzale Ostiense almost as far as the San Sebastiano catacombs; you can also take bus #218 from Piazza San Giovanni, which goes down Via Ardeatina, or bus #660 from Colli Albani metro station (line A), which goes beyond the Tomb of Cecilia Metella. Another option is to take the **Archeobus** (wwww.trambusopen.com), which runs from Termini and Piazza Venezia, among other city-centre locations, every 30min (April–Oct 9am–12.30pm & 1.30–4.30pm); tickets cost €12 for a 48-hour ticket and you can hop on and off as you wish. Or you could walk from Porta San Sebastiano and take everything in on foot, which allows you to stop off at the Parco Regionale dell'Appia Antica **information office** for the area – it's actually classified as a national park – at Via Appia Antica 58, on the right just before you get to Domine Quo Vadis (Mon–Sat 9.30am– 1.30pm & 2–5/5.30pm, Sun 9.30am–5/6.30pm; 06 513 6314; wwww. parcoappiaantica.it). You can pick up a good map and other information on the various Appia Antica sights here, as well as hire **bikes** (€3/hour or €15/day). You can take a tour of the catacombs and nearby sights with Enjoy Rome (see p.183; Mon, Tues, Thurs, Fri & Sat at 10am; 3hr; €50). Finally, there are a couple of decent **restaurants** down by San Sebastiano: **L'Archeologia** (06 788 0494; closed Tues), just past the church, and the **Cecilia Metella** (06 5136 743; closed Mon) right opposite.

DOMINE QUO VADIS

Via Appia Antica 51. Daily 8am–7pm, 6pm in winter. POCKET MAP J11

About 500m from Porta San Sebastiano, where the road forks, the church of Domine Quo Vadis is the first sight on Via Appia. Legend has this as the place where St Peter saw Christ while fleeing from certain death in Rome and asked "Where goest thou, Lord?", to which Christ replied that he was going to be crucified once more, leading Peter to turn around and accept his fate. The small church is ordinary enough inside, except for its replica of a piece of marble that's said to be marked with the footprints of Christ –

the original is in the church of San Sebastiano (see p.119).

CATACOMBS OF SAN CALLISTO

Via Appia Antica 110/126 ☎ 06 513 0151, Ⓦ www.catacombe.roma.it. Thurs–Tues 9am–noon & 2–5pm. €8. POCKET MAP J12

The largest of Rome's catacombs, the Catacombs of San Callisto were founded in the second century AD and many of the early popes are buried here. There are regular free tours (40min) in English, and the site also features some seventh- and eighth-century frescoes, and the crypt of Santa Cecilia, who was buried here after her martyrdom, before being moved to the church dedicated to her in Trastevere – a copy of Carlo Maderno's famous statue marks the spot.

MAUSOLEO DELLE FOSSE ARDEATINE

Via Ardeatina 174 ☎ 06 513 6742. Mon–Fri 8.15am–3.15pm, Sat & Sun 8.15am–4.45pm. Free. POCKET MAP K12

A ten-minute walk from San Callisto, close by the #218 bus stop, is a site that remembers the **massacre** of over 300 civilians during the Nazi occupation of Rome, after the Resistance had ambushed and killed 32 soldiers in the centre of the city. The Nazis exacted a harsh vengeance, killing ten civilians for every dead

German, burying the bodies here and then exploding mines to cover up their crime. The bodies were dug up after the war and reinterred in the mausoleum here.

CATACOMBS OF SAN SEBASTIANO

Via Appia Antica 136 ☎ 06 785 0350, Ⓦ www.catacombe.org. Mon–Sat 10am–4.30pm; closed mid-Nov to mid-Dec. €8. POCKET MAP K12

These **catacombs** sit under a much-renovated basilica that was originally built by Constantine on the spot where the bodies of the apostles Peter and Paul are said to have lain for a time. Half-hour tours take in paintings of doves and fish, a contemporary carved oil lamp and inscriptions dating the tombs themselves. The most striking features are three pagan tombs (one painted, two stuccoed) discovered when archeologists were investigating the floor of the basilica upstairs. Just above here, Constantine reputedly raised his chapel, and although St Peter was later removed to the Vatican and St Paul to San Paolo fuori le Mura, the graffiti records the fact that this was indeed where the two Apostles' remains rested.

TOMB OF CECILIA METELLA

VILLA AND CIRCUS OF MAXENTIUS

Via Appia Antica 153 ☎ 06 0608, ⓦ www
.villadimassenzio.it. Tues–Sun 10am–4pm.
€5. POCKET MAP K12

A few hundred metres further on from the San Sebastiano catacombs, the group of brick ruins trailing off into the fields to the left are the remains of the **Villa and Circus of Maxentius**, a complex built by the emperor in the early fourth century AD before his defeat by Constantine. It's a clear, long oval of grass, similar to the Circus Maximus (see p.110), but slightly better preserved.

THE TOMB OF CECILIA METELLA

Via Appia Antica 161 ☎ 06 780 0093. Tues–
Sun 9am–1hr before sunset. €6 joint ticket
including Baths of Caracalla and Villa dei
Quintili. POCKET MAP K12

Further along the Via Appia, this circular tomb dates from the Augustan period, and was converted into a castle in the fourteenth century. Known as "Capo di Bove" for the bulls on the frieze around it, the tomb itself, a huge brick-built drum, is little more than a large pigeon coop these days; various fragments and finds are littered around the

adjacent, later courtyards, and down below you can see what's left of an ancient lava flow from thousands of years earlier.

EUR

Main piazzas at south end of Via Cristoforo
Colombo. Bus #714 from Termini or metro
line B to Laurentina. POCKET MAP E12

The **EUR** district was planned by Mussolini for the 1942 Esposizione Universale Roma, but not finished until after the war. Its monumental fascist architecture and grand processional boulevards recall Imperial Rome (especially the Palazzo della Civiltà or "Square Colosseum"). Overall it's a pretty strange and soulless place, something of a white elephant despite the busy offices. Apart from the **shops** – the city's biggest mall, Euroma2, is on Via Cristoforo Colombo (Metro EUR Fermi, then bus 70, 700 or 709) – EUR's main attraction is its museums. The **Museo della Civiltà Romana**, Piazza Agnelli 10 (closed for renovation at the time of writing; ⓦ www.museocivilta romana.it) has a large model of the fourth-century city and also incorporates the Planetario e Museo Astronomico.

Shops

LO SPACCIO DI TESTACCIO

Stall no. 39, Testaccio market, between Via Galvani and Via Alessandro Volta. Mon–Sat 9am–2pm. MAP P.112–113, POCKET MAP E9

Amid the hustle and bustle of Testaccio market is this little kitchenware stall with a vintage feel, selling enamel saucepans, glassware and all manner of wooden utensils that you soon won't be able to do without.

VOLPETTI

VOLPETTI

Via Marmorata 47. Mon–Sat 8am–2pm & 5–8.15pm. MAP P.112–113, POCKET MAP E8

It's worth seeking out this Testaccio deli, truly one of Rome's very best, with a fantastic selection of cold meats and cheeses.

Cafés and restaurants

AGUSTARELLO

Via Giovanni Branca 98–100 ☎ 06 574 6585. Mon–Sat 12.30–3pm & 7.30pm–midnight. MAP P.112–113, POCKET MAP E8

Just off busy Piazza di Santa Maria Liberatrice, this small and simple trattoria is strong

on the *quinto quarto* (offal) dishes that Testaccio is known for, and also serves all the classics of Roman cuisine (roast lamb with potatoes €18).

CHECCHINO DAL 1887

Via di Monte Testaccio 30 ☎ 06 574 6318. Tues–Sat 12.30–3pm & 8–midnight. MAP P.112–113, POCKET MAP E9

A historic symbol of Testaccio cookery, with an excellent wine cellar, too. Expensive, but worth it for its rustic atmosphere and excellent menu of authentic Roman meat and offal dishes.

PALOMBINI

Piazzale Adenauer 12. Mon–Thurs 7am–10pm, Fri & Sat 7am–1am, Sun 8am–10pm. MAP P.112–113, POCKET MAP H12

Great EUR café whose outside terrace and large interior are a haven amidst EUR's brutal boulevards. Appropriately housed on the ground floor of EUR's official "restaurant building", it's a café, *tabacchi* and wine shop all rolled into one, and serves excellent cakes and sandwiches.

DA REMO

Piazza Santa Maria Liberatrice 44 ☎ 06 574 6270. Mon–Sat 7pm–1am; closed three weeks in Aug. MAP P.112–113, POCKET MAP E8

Remo is the best kind of pizzeria: usually crowded with locals, very basic, and serving the thinnest, crispiest Roman pizza you'll find. It's also worth trying the heavenly *bruschette* and other snacks like *supplì* and *fiori di zucca*. Perfect pre-clubbing food – and very cheap (pizzas from €6).

TUTTIFRUTTI

Via Luca della Robbia 3a ☎ 06 575 7902. Mon–Fri 7.30–11.30pm, Sat & Sun noon–3.30pm & 7.30–11.30pm. MAP P.112–113, POCKET MAP E8

This Testaccio favourite is pretty much the perfect

restaurant – family-run, with good food and fair prices. The menu changes daily, and offers interesting variations on traditional Roman dishes.

VOLPETTI PIÙ

Via A. Volta 8. Mon-Sat 10.30am-3.30pm & 5.30–9.30pm; closed afternoons in Aug. MAP P.112-113, POCKET MAP E8

Tavola calda that's attached to the famous deli a few doors down. Great pizza, *supplì*, chicken, deep-fried veg and much more.

Bar

OASI DELLA BIRRA

Piazza Testaccio 41. Mon-Sat 8am-2.30pm, & 4.30pm-1am, Sun 7.30pm-1am. MAP P.112-113, POCKET MAP E8

Unassumingly situated under a Piazza Testaccio wine bar, the cosy basement rooms here house an international selection of beers that arguably rivals anywhere in the world – 500 in all, and with plenty of wines to choose from as well. You can eat generously assembled plates of cheese and salami, as well as a great selection of *bruschette* and polenta dishes.

Clubs

AKAB

Via di Monte Testaccio 69 ☎ 06 5725 0585, Ⓦ www.akabclub.com. Metro B Piramide or bus #23. Wed-Sat 10pm-4am. €10–20, including 1 drink. MAP P.112-113, POCKET MAP E9

This club is built into an old carpenter's shop on two floors, one on ground level, the other a cavelike room below. Head down for Thursday's popular "Milkshake" (r'n'b, hip-hop) night.

L'ALIBI

Via di Monte Testaccio 44 ☎ 06 574 3448, Ⓦ www.lalibi.it. Metro B Piramide or bus #23. Thurs-Sun midnight-5am. Admission €10–€15, including 1 drink. MAP P.112-113, POCKET MAP E9

Predominantly – but by no means exclusively – male venue that's one of Rome's oldest and best gay clubs. Thursday night's Gloss is ever-popular. Downstairs there's a multi-room cellar disco and upstairs an open-air bar. The big terrace is perfect during the warm months.

CASA DEL JAZZ

Viale di Porta Ardeatina 55 ☎ 06 704 731, Ⓦ www.casajazz.it. Metro #B to Piramide or bus #714. Closed Tues & Sun evenings. Admission €5-15. MAP P.112-113, POCKET MAP G9

Sponsored by the city, this converted villa in leafy surroundings is the ultimate jazz-lovers' complex, with a book and CD store and restaurant, recording studios and a 150-seat auditorium that hosts gigs on most nights.

GOA

Via Libetta 13 ☎ 06 574 8277 Ⓦ www .goaclub.com. Metro B Garbatella or Bus #29, 769, 770. Thurs-Sat 11pm-4am. Admission €10–25, including 1 drink. MAP P.112-113, POCKET MAP E11

Long-running Ostiense club near the Basilica San Paolo, playing techno, house and drum'n'bass, with a top-of-the-range sound system.

RASHOMON

Via degli Argonauti 16 Ⓦ www.rashomonclub .com. Metro B Garbatella. Wed & Thurs 8pm-2am, Fri & Sat 11pm-4am. Admission around €10. MAP P.112-113, POCKET MAP F11

A two-room live music space with good music and dj sets at weekends. On Thursdays it's a loungey cocktail bar (drink and buffet €10).

Trastevere and the Janiculum Hill

Across the river from the centre of town, Trastevere (the name means literally "across the Tiber") was the artisan area of the city in classical times, neatly placed for the trade that came upriver from Ostia. Nowadays the area is a long way from its working-class roots, and its many bars and restaurants can be thronged with tourists. But its narrow streets and closeted squares are charming, peaceful in the morning, lively come the evening, with dozens of trattorias setting tables out along the cobbled streets – and still buzzing late at night, when its bars and clubs host one of Rome's most dynamic after-dark scenes.

SAN FRANCESCO A RIPA

Piazza San Francesco d'Assisi 88. Daily 7am–1pm & 2–7.30pm. MAP P.124–125, POCKET MAP D7–E7

The church of **San Francesco a Ripa** is best known for two things: the fact that St Francis himself once stayed here – you can see the actual room he stayed in if you're lucky enough to find it open – and the writhing, orgasmic statue of a minor saint, the Blessed Ludovica Albertoni, sculpted by Bernini towards the end of his career. As a work of Baroque

emotiveness, it's perhaps even more frank in its depiction of an earthly realized divine ecstasy than his more famous *Ecstasy of St Theresa* in the church of Santa Maria della Vittoria (see p.84).

SANTA CECILIA IN TRASTEVERE

Piazza Santa Cecilia 22. Basilica and excavations Mon–Sat 9.30am–1pm & 4–6.30pm, Sun 11.30am–12.30pm & 4–6.30pm; singing gallery Mon–Sat 10.15am–12.15am, Sun 11.30am–12.30pm. Basilica €2.50, singing gallery €2.50, excavations €3. MAP P.124–125, POCKET MAP E18

In its own quiet piazza off Via

Anicia, the basilica of **Santa Cecilia in Trastevere** was originally built over the site of the second-century home of St Cecilia, who was – along with her husband – persecuted for her Christian beliefs. The story has it that Cecilia was locked in the caldarium of her own baths for several days but refused to die, singing her way through the ordeal (Cecilia is patron saint of music). Her head was finally half hacked off with an axe, though it took several blows before she died. Below the high altar, under a Gothic baldacchino, Stefano Maderno's statue of the limp saint shows her incorruptible body as it was found when exhumed in 1599, with three deep cuts in her neck. Downstairs, excavations of the baths and the rest of the Roman house are on view in the crypt. But more alluring by far is the singing gallery above the nave of the church (ring the bell to the left of the church door), where Pietro Cavallini's late thirteenth-century fresco of the *Last Judgement* – all that remains of the decoration that once covered the entire church – is a powerful, amazingly naturalistic piece of work for its time, centring on Christ in quiet majesty, flanked by angels.

SANTA MARIA IN TRASTEVERE

Piazza Santa Maria in Trastevere. Daily 7am–9pm. MAP P.124–125, POCKET MAP C16

In the heart of old Trastevere, Piazza **Santa Maria in Trastevere** is named after the church in its northwest corner. Held to be the first Christian place of worship in Rome, it was built on a site where a fountain of oil is said to have sprung on the day of Christ's birth. The church's mosaics are among the city's most impressive: mostly Byzantine-inspired works depicting a solemn yet sensitive parade of saints thronged around Christ and Mary – the *Coronation of the Virgin* – beneath which are scenes from her life by the Santa Cecilia artist, Pietro Cavallini. Under the high altar on the right, an inscription – "FONS OLEI" – marks the spot where the oil is supposed to have sprung up.

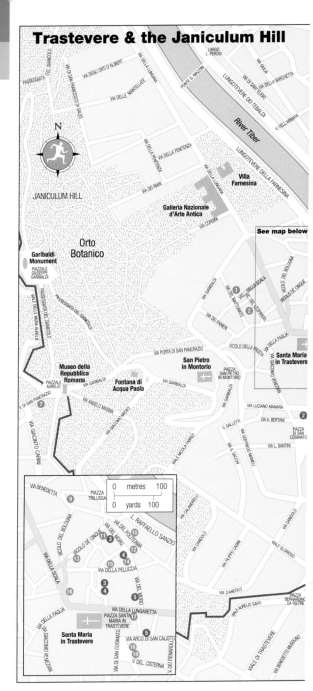

Trastevere & the Janiculum Hill

Villa Farnesina

Galleria Nazionale d'Arte Antica

Orto Botanico

Garibaldi Monument

Museo della Repubblica Romana

Fontana di Acqua Paola

San Pietro in Montorio

Santa Maria in Trastevere

JANICULUM HILL

River Tiber

Santa Maria in Trastevere

| 0 | metres | 100 |
| 0 | yards | 100 |

See map below

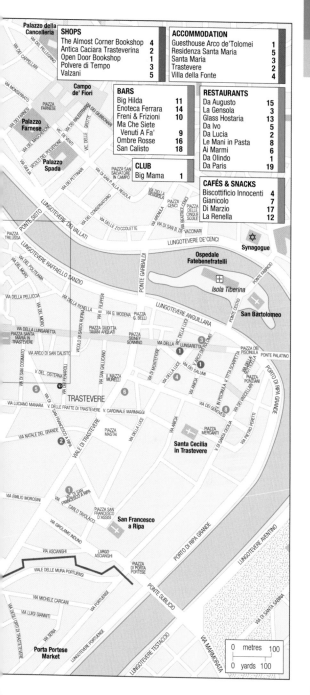

SHOPS
The Almost Corner Bookshop	4
Antica Caciara Trasteverina	2
Open Door Bookshop	1
Polvere di Tempo	3
Valzani	5

ACCOMMODATION
Guesthouse Arco de'Tolomei	1
Residenza Santa Maria	5
Santa Maria	3
Trastevere	2
Villa della Fonte	4

BARS
Big Hilda	11
Enoteca Ferrara	14
Freni & Frizioni	10
Ma Che Siete Venuti A Fa'	9
Ombre Rosse	16
San Calisto	18

RESTAURANTS
Da Augusto	15
La Gensola	3
Glass Hostaria	13
Da Ivo	5
Da Lucia	2
Le Mani in Pasta	8
Ai Marmi	6
Da Olindo	1
Da Paris	19

CLUB
| Big Mama | 1 |

CAFÉS & SNACKS
Biscottificio Innocenti	4
Gianicolo	7
Di Marzio	17
La Renella	12

VILLA FARNESINA

Via della Lungara 230 ☎ 06 6802 7268.
Mon–Sat 9am–2pm, second Sun of the month
9am–5pm. €6. MAP P.124–125, POCKET MAP C16

The early sixteenth-century
Villa Farnesina was built by
Baldassare Peruzzi for the
Sienese banker Agostino Chigi.
Its opulent rooms are decorated
with marvellous frescoes and
most people come to view the
Raphael-designed painting of
Cupid and Psyche in the now
glassed-in loggia, completed in
1517 by the artist's assistants.
The painter and art historian
Vasari claims Raphael didn't
complete the work because his
infatuation with his mistress –
"La Fornarina", whose father's
bakery was situated nearby
– was making it difficult to
concentrate. Nonetheless it's
very impressive: a flowing,
animated work bursting
with muscular men and
bare-bosomed women, although
the only part Raphael is said
to have actually completed is
the female figure with her back
turned on the lunette (to the
right of the door leading out
to the east). He did, however,
apparently manage to finish
the Galatea in the room next
door. The ceiling illustrates
Chigi's horoscope constellations,
frescoed by the architect of the
building, Peruzzi, who also
decorated the upstairs Salone
delle Prospettive, where trompe
l'oeil balconies give views onto
contemporary Rome.

PALAZZO CORSINI

Via della Lungara 10 ☎ 06 6880 2323, ⓦ www
.galleriaborghese.it. Tues–Sun 8.30am–7.30pm.
€5. MAP P.124–125, POCKET MAP C16–17

Housed in the **Palazzo Corsini**,
the **Galleria Nazionale d'Arte
Antica** is a relatively small
collection that takes up a few
rooms of the giant palace.
There's a grouping of Flemish
paintings, including works by
Rubens and Van Dyck; a room
full of landscapes, including lush
scenes by Dughet and a fanciful
depiction of the Pantheon by
Charles Clérisseau. Look out
for the famous portrayal of
*Salome with the Head of St
John the Baptist* by Guido Reni
and a painting of *Prometheus*
by Salvatore Rosa that is one
of the most vivid and detailed
expositions of human internal
anatomy you'll see. You can also
visit the bedchamber of Queen
Christina, who renounced
Protestantism and, with it, the
Swedish throne in 1655, and
brought her library and fortune
to Rome – she died, here in the
palace, in 1689, and is one of
only three women to be buried

PALAZZO CORSINI

in St Peter's. Also worth a look is the curious Aldobrandini Throne, thought to be a Roman copy of an Etruscan throne of the second or first century.

THE ORTO BOTANICO

Largo Cristina di Svezia 24 📞 06 4991 7107. Mon–Sat: April to mid-Oct 9.30am–6.30pm, mid-Oct to March 9.30am–5.30pm. €8. MAP P.124–125, POCKET MAP B17

The **Orto Botanico** occupies the eastern side of the Janiculum Hill. It's a pleasantly neglected expanse these days where you can clamber up to high stands of bamboo and ferns cut by rivulets of water, stroll through a wood of century-old oaks, cedars and conifers, and relax in a grove of acclimatized palm trees. There's also a herbal garden with medicinal plants, a collection of orchids that bloom in springtime and early summer, and a garden of aromatic herbs put together for the blind. The garden also has the distinction of being home to one of the oldest plane trees in Rome, between 350 and 400 years old.

THE JANICULUM HILL

MAP P.124–125, POCKET MAP A17–B17

It's about a fifteen-minute walk up Via Garibaldi from lively Piazza di Sant'Egidio to the summit of the **Janiculum**

Hill – not one of the original seven hills of Rome, but the one with the best and most accessible views of the centre. Follow Vicolo del Cedro from Via della Scala and take the steps up from the end, cross the main road, and continue on the steps that lead up to **San Pietro in Montorio**, best known – and worth stopping off for – the Renaissance architect Bramante's little **Tempietto** in its courtyard. Head up from here past the gigantic **Fontana di Acqua Paola** – which starred in the opening scene of Paolo Sorrentino's 2013 film *The Great Beauty* – up to the Porta San Pancrazio, home to the new **Museo della Repubblica Romana e della Memoria Garibaldina** (Tues– Fri 10am–2pm, Sat & Sun 10am–6pm; €5.50). Dedicated to Garibaldi's unsuccessful defence of the Roman republic of 1849, it holds multimedia displays, photographs and artefacts. From here, it's a short stroll uphill to the statues of the 1849 martyrs – as well as spectacular views across the city. Below the equestrian **monument to Garibaldi**, a **cannon** fires a single shot at exactly noon each day that can be heard as far away as the Colosseum.

Shops

THE ALMOST CORNER BOOKSHOP

Via del Moro 45. Mon–Sat 10am–1.30pm &
3.30–8pm, Sun 11am–1.30pm & 3.30–8pm.
MAP P.124–125, POCKET MAP D17

Of all Rome's English
bookshops, this is the best bet
for finding the very latest titles,
and staff are helpful too.

ANTICA CACIARA TRASTEVERINA

Via San Francesco a Ripa 140a/b. Mon–Sat
7am–2pm & 4–8pm. MAP P.124–125, POCKET
MAP D18

This wonderful cheese shop
is piled high with ricotta,
pecorino romano and creamy
burrata from Puglia, as
well as cold meats, porcini
mushrooms and juicy Sicilian
olives.

OPEN DOOR BOOKSHOP

Via della Lungaretta 23. Mon–Sat
10am–8pm, Aug closed Sat pm. MAP P.124–125,
POCKET MAP E18

Although they do have some
new titles, especially on Rome
and Roman history, used
books in English dominate

the shelves at this friendly
bookshop, where you never
know what treasures you
might happen upon. They also
have a selection of books in
Italian, German, French and
Spanish.

POLVERE DI TEMPO

Via del Moro 59. Mon–Sat 10am–1.30pm
& 3–8pm, Sun 4–8pm. MAP P.124–125, POCKET
MAP D17

This treasure trove of a
shop selling antique lamps,
hourglasses and globes is a
great place to pick up unusual
gifts.

PORTA PORTESE MARKET

Via Portuense. Sun 7am–2pm. MAP
P.124–125, POCKET MAP D8.

On a Sunday it's worth
approaching Trastevere from
the south, walking over
the Ponte Sublicio to Porta
Portese; from here the Porta
Portese flea market stretches
down Via Portuense to
Trastevere train station in a
congested medley of antiques,
old motor spares, cheap and
trendy clothing items, and
assorted junk. Haggling is
the rule here, and remember
to keep a good hold of your
wallet or purse. Plan to come
early if you want to buy –
most of the bargains have gone
by 10am, by which time the
crush of people can be rather
intense.

VALZANI

Via del Moro 37a/b. Daily 9am–7.30pm.
MAP P.124–125, POCKET MAP D18

Specializing in the art of
confectionary since 1925,
this small shop is stuffed full
of calorific treats. *Valzani* is
most famous for its sublime
chocolate, but the traditional
Roman treats such as *bigne*
and *frappe* are just as hard
to resist.

PORTA PORTESE MARKET

Cafés and snacks

BISCOTTIFICIO INNOCENTI

Via della Luce 21. Mon–Sat 8am–8pm, Sun 9.30am–2pm. MAP P.124–125, POCKET MAP E18

Tucked away on a Trastevere backstreet is this wonderfully old-fashioned bakery, run by three generations of the same family. Pride of place is given to the enormous 1950s-vintage oven, which wafts out the delicious aroma of freshly baked biscuits.

GIANICOLO

Piazzale Aurelia 5. Tues–Sat 6am–1am, Sun 6am–11pm. MAP P.124–125, POCKET MAP A18

Quite an ordinary bar, but in a picturesque location and a bit of a hangout for Italian media stars, writers and academics from the nearby Spanish and American academies. Tasty sandwiches, too, and a couple of tables inside as well as out.

DI MARZIO

Piazza di Santa Maria in Trastevere 15. Mon & Wed–Sun 8am–2am, Tues 10am–10pm. MAP P.124–125, POCKET MAP D18

This bar isn't much on the inside, but it's a friendly place that does decent sandwiches and whose terrace right on Piazza Santa Maria makes it the best people-watching spot in Trastevere.

LA RENELLA

Via del Moro 15. Daily 7am–10pm. MAP P.124–125, POCKET MAP D17

Arguably the best bakery in Rome, with great foccaccia and superb *pizza al taglio*. Take a number and be prepared to wait at busy times. You can take away or eat on the premises at the long counter.

Restaurants

DA AUGUSTO

Piazza de Renzi 15 ☎ 06 580 3798. Daily 12.30–3pm & 8–11pm. MAP P.124–125, POCKET MAP D17

A Trastevere old-timer serving Roman basics outside on the cobbles in the summer months. You can get a good meal for about €14 here, including a glass of robust house wine. Expect offerings such as pasta and soup starters, and daily meat and fish specials – not haute cuisine, but decent, hearty Roman cooking. No bookings taken.

LA GENSOLA

Piazza della Gensola 15 ☎ 06 5833 2758 & 06 581 6312. Daily 12.45–3pm & 7.45–11.30pm; closed Sun in Aug. MAP P.124–125, POCKET MAP E18

This place, with charming and simple decor, is a lovely place for a special meal: the Sicilian cuisine is faultless and the atmosphere warm and convivial. The predominantly fishy specialities include tagliolini with tuna and asparagus, and the desserts are excellent too: you can't go wrong with the crumbly apple pie served with deliciously creamy cinnamon ice cream.

DA AUGUSTO

GLASS HOSTARIA

Vicolo dè Cinque 58 ☎ 06 5833 3920. Tues–Sun 7.30–11pm. MAP P.124–125, POCKET MAP C17

Trastevere's smartest dining option is this Michelin-starred restaurant, with brick walls, glass floor and polished service. On the menu you might find tagliatelle with wild asparagus, black garlic and lemon, or crab with truffle sauce. The five-course tasting menu is €75.

DA IVO

Via di San Francesco a Ripa 158 ☎ 06 581 7082. Wed–Mon 7.30pm–1am. MAP P.124–125, POCKET MAP D18

The Trastevere pizzeria, almost in danger of becoming a caricature, but still good and very reasonable. A nice assortment of desserts, too – try the *monte bianco* for the ultimate chestnut cream and meringue confection. Arrive early to avoid a chaotic queue.

DA LUCIA

Vicolo del Mattonato 2 ☎ 06 580 3601. Tues–Sun 12.30–3pm & 7.30–11pm. MAP P.124–125, POCKET MAP C17

Reliable, moderately priced old Roman trattoria that is the best place for summer outdoor dining in Trastevere. *Spaghetti cacio e pepe* is the speciality here – arrive early for one of the in-demand tables on the attractive alleyway outside.

LE MANI IN PASTA

Via dei Genovesi 37 ☎ 06 581 6017. Tues–Sun 12.30–3pm & 7.30–11.30pm. MAP P.124–125, POCKET MAP E18

Tucked down an alley, this small and unassuming place has a tiny kitchen in view and specializes in pasta and fish. A full – and excellent – meal with wine will set you back around €40–50 per person. It's deservedly busy, so be sure to book.

AI MARMI

Viale di Trastevere 53 ☎ 06 580 0919. Thurs–Tues 6.30pm–2.30am. MAP P.124–125, POCKET MAP D18

Very reasonably priced place, nicknamed "the mortuary" because of its stark interior and marble tables, and serving superior *supplì al telefono* (so named because of the string of mozzarella it forms when you take a bite), fresh *baccalà* and some of Rome's best pizza.

DA OLINDO

Vicolo della Scala 8 ☎ 06 581 8835. Mon–Sat 7.30–11pm. MAP P.124–125, POCKET MAP C17

With no sign outside, it's easy to miss this great, family-run Trastevere trattoria with just a few tables. There's a small menu of staples – traditional Roman fare – and prices are cheap and easy to remember: *primi* cost €8, *secondi* €10.

DA PARIS

Piazza San Calisto 7a ☎ 06 581 5378. Mon 7.30–11.30pm, Tues–Sun 12.30–3pm & 7.30–11.30pm. MAP P.124–125, POCKET MAP D18

The menu at this moderately priced Trastevere favourite is a roll-call of traditional Roman-Jewish dishes such as *abbacchio* (lamb) and *carciofi* (artichokes). You can either eat outside, on one of Trastevere's most atmospheric piazzas, or in an elegant dining room.

GLASS HOSTARIA

FREN: E FRIZIONI

Bars

BIG HILDA

Vicolo dè Cinque 33. Mon–Fri 9am–2am, Sat & Sun 10am–2am. MAP P.124–125, POCKET MAP D17

This cosy, English-style pub is always buzzing with an Italian and international crowd. There are plenty of tables, inside and out, so you can settle in and enjoy the ultra-long happy hour (11am until around 10pm).

ENOTECA FERRARA

Piazza Trilussa 41 ☎ 06 5833 5903. Daily 6pm–2am. MAP P.124–125, POCKET MAP D17

This cavernous place incorporates a pricey restaurant, a cheaper *osteria* and, best of the lot, a cosy wine-bar, *La Mescita*. Drop by in the evening for a superior *aperitivo*: there's a huge selection of wines by the glass, accompanied by free nibbles.

FRENI & FRIZIONI

Via del Politeama 4/6. Daily 6.30pm–2am. MAP P.124–125, POCKET MAP D17

Just off Piazza Trilussa, this former mechanic's workshop (the name means "Brakes and clutches") is now home to one of the city's best bars. The *aperitivo* buffet (7–10pm) is worth dropping by for, too.

MA CHE SIETE VENUTI A FA'

Via Benedetta 25. Daily 11am–2am. MAP P.124–125, POCKET MAP D6

There's an amazing choice of artisanal beers from all over the world in this tiny bar. Some of them can't be found anywhere else in the city, or even Italy, and this is a cosy place to work your way through them.

OMBRE ROSSE

Piazza di Sant'Egidio 12 ☎ 06 588 4155. Daily 7.30am–1.45am. MAP P.124–125, POCKET MAP C18

A great place for a morning cappuccino, with seating on one of Trastevere's most charming piazzas. Light meals are served, and there's live jazz and blues on Tuesday and Thursday nights.

SAN CALISTO

Piazza San Calisto 4. Mon–Sat 6am–2am. MAP P.124–125, POCKET MAP D18

This old-guard Trastevere bar attracts a huge, mixed crowd on late summer nights; the booze is cheap, and you can sit at outside tables for no extra cost. Things are slightly less *demimonde*-ish during the day, when it's simply a great spot to sip a cappuccino, read and enjoy the sun.

Club

BIG MAMA

Vicolo San Francesco a Ripa 18 ☎ 06 581 2551. ⓦ www.bigmama.it. Tues–Sat (and occasionally on Mon) 9pm–1.30am; concerts start at 10.30pm. MAP P.124–125, POCKET MAP D7

Trastevere-based jazz/blues club of long standing, hosting nightly acts. Book ahead for star attractions. Food is served too.

Villa Borghese and north

During the Renaissance, the market gardens and olive groves north of the city walls were appropriated as summer estates by Rome's wealthy elite, particularly those affiliated to the papal court. One of the most notable of these, the Villa Borghese, was the summer playground of the Borghese family and is now a public park and home to two of Rome's best museums: the unmissable art collection of the Galleria Borghese, and the Villa Giulia, built by Pope Julius II and now the National Etruscan Museum. North of Villa Borghese stretch Rome's nineteenth- and early twentieth-century residential districts – not of much interest in themselves except perhaps for the Mussolini-era Foro Italico and the Auditorium music complex.

VILLA BORGHESE

Bus #116 (city-centre stops include the Pantheon) does a circuit of the park. MAP P.134–135, POCKET MAP G2

The vast green expanse of the **Villa Borghese** – accessible by way of the Pincio Gardens, or from entrances at the top of Via Veneto or Via Porta Pinciana – is about as near as you can get to peace in the city centre. The beautiful landscaped grounds and palace were designed for Cardinal Scipione Borghese in 1605 and bought by the city at the turn of the nineteenth century; they now form the city's most central park. There are plenty of attractions for those who want to do more than just stroll or sunbathe, not least a zoo and some of the city's finest museums (see below), but it's full of pockets of interest if you just want to wander. You can rent bikes outside the Galleria Nazionale d'Arte Moderna and other places in the Pincio Gardens (from €4/hr, €15/day), but most people take a two- or four-person chariot known as a *risciò*, operated by a mixture of pedal and electrical power, which make for a very relaxed way to see the park (€15–25/hr).

LAKE IN THE GROUNDS OF VILLA BORGHESE

GALLERIA BORGHESE

Piazzale Scipione Borghese ☎ 06 32 810.
ⓦ www.galleriaborghese.it. Tues–Sun
8.30am–7.30pm. €13 (including booking
fee). Pre-book at least a day in advance;
pre-booked visits are obligatory. MAP P.134–135,
POCKET MAP G2

The collection of Cardinal
Scipione Borghese in the
Galleria Borghese is one of
the city's most compelling.
The first room has as its
centrepiece Canova's infamous
statue of the half-naked
Pauline Borghese posed as
Venus, but otherwise the focus
is on **Bernini**. The face of his
marvellous statue of David
is a self-portrait, said to have
been carved with the help
of a mirror held by Scipione
Borghese himself. Other
highlights include his dramatic,
poised *Apollo and Daphne*;
The Rape of Proserpine from
1622; and a larger-than-life
statue of Aeneas, carrying
his father, Anchises, out of
the burning city of Troy,
sculpted by both Bernini and
his then 15-year-old son in
1613. There are paintings,
too, including notable works
such as Caravaggio's *David
Holding the Head of Goliath*,
and a self-portrait as *Bacchus*,
among others, and the upstairs
Pinacoteca comprises one
of the richest collections of
paintings in the world, with
canvases by Raphael, his
teacher Perugino and other
masters of the Umbrian school
from the late fifteenth and
sixteenth centuries. Look for
the *Deposition*, *Lady with a
Unicorn*, and *Portrait of a Man*,
by Raphael, and a copy of the
artist's portrait of a tired-out
Julius II, painted in 1513.
There's also *Venus and Cupid
with a Honeycomb* by Cranach,
Lorenzo Lotto's touching
Portrait of a Man and works
by the Venetians of the early
1500s, including Titian's *Sacred
and Profane Love*, painted
in 1514. Check out also the
gallery on the first floor,
where there are a series of
self-portraits done by Bernini
at various stages of his life
and a bust of Cardinal
Scipione executed in 1632,
portraying him as the worldly
connoisseur of fine art and
living that he was.

10

VILLA BORGHESE AND NORTH

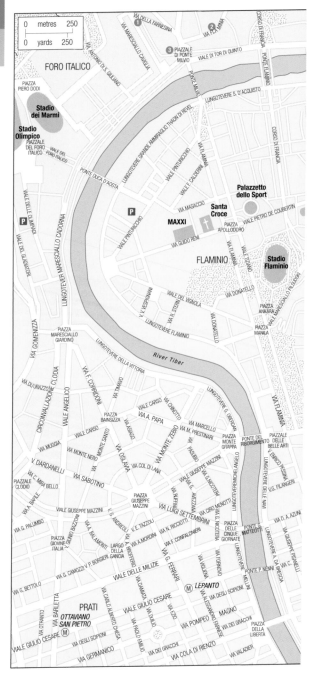

| 0 | metres | 250 |
| 0 | yards | 250 |

FORO ITALICO

VIA DELLA FARNESINA

VIA FLAMINIA

PIAZZALE DI PONTE MILVIO

VIALE DI TOR DI QUINTO

CORSO DI FRANCIA

PONTE FLAMINIO

PIAZZA PIERO DODI

VIA ANTONIO DI S. GIULIANO

VIA MARESCIALLO CADUNA

LUNGOTEVERE S. D'ACQUISTO

Stadio dei Marmi

Stadio Olimpico

PIAZZALE DEL FORO ITALICO

VIALE DEL FORO ITALICO

VIALE DEI GLADIATORI

VIALE DELLE OLIMPIADI

PONTE DUCA D'AOSTA

LUNGOTEVERE GRANDE AMMIRAGLIO THAON DI REVEL

VIA PINTURICCHIO

VIA F. CALDERINI

VIA FLAMINIA

CORSO DI FRANCIA

Palazzetto dello Sport

VIA MASACCIO

VIA PIETRO DE COUBERTIN

MAXXI

Santa Croce

PIAZZA APOLLODORO

Stadio Flaminio

P

P

VIA PINTURICCHIO

VIA GUIDO RENI

FLAMINIO

VIA FLAMINIA

VIA TIZIANO

LUNGOTEVERE MARESCIALLO CADORNA

VIALE DEL VIGNOLA

VIA DONATELLO

PIAZZA ANKARA

VIALE MARESCIALLO PILSUDSKI

V. V. VESPIGNANI

VIA R.R. STERN

LUNGOTEVERE FLAMINIO

VIA DONATELLO

PIAZZA MANILA

PIAZZA MARESCIALLO GIARDINO

LUNGOTEVERE DELLA VITTORIA

River Tiber

VIA GOMENIZZA

CIRCONVALLAZIONE CLODIA

VIALE ANGELICO

VIA F. CORRIDONI

VIA TIMAVO

PIAZZA BAINSIZZA

VIALE CARSO

VIA CIMINITO

LUNGOTEVERE G. OREFDAN

VIA FLAMINIA

VIALE CARSO

VIA A. PAPA

VIA MARCELLO

VIA M. PRESTINARI

PIAZZA MONTE GRAPPA

PONTE DEL RISORGIMENTO

PIAZZALE DELLE BELLE ARTI

VIA MUGGIA

VIA ASIAGO

VIA MONTE NERO

VIA MONTE SANTO

VIA MONTE ZEBIO

VIA PASUBIO

LUNGOTEVERE DELLE NAVI

V. G. FILANGERI

V. DARDANELLI

VIA OSLAVIA

VIA COL DI LANA

VIALE GIUSEPPE MAZZINI

VIALE MICHELANGELO

VIA C. MIRA BELLO

VIA SABOTINO

VIA G. AVEZZANA

VIA CIRO MENOTTI

PIAZZALE CLODIO

PIAZZA GIUSEPPE MAZZINI

VIA RUFFINI

VIA LUIGI SETTEMBRINI

VIA G. NICOTERA

VIA D.A. AZUNI

VIA A. BAFILE

VIA G. PALUMBO

V. G. ANDREOLI

V.E. TAZZOLI

VIA N. RICCIOTTI

PIAZZA DELLE CINQUE GIORNATE

PONTE G. MATTEOTTI

LUNGOTEVERE A. DA PRESCIA

VIA GIUSEPPE PISANELLI

PIAZZA GIOVINE ITALIA

VIA G. BALAMONTI

GIINO BAZZONI

LARGO DELLA GANCIA

VIA A. MORDINI

VIA F. CONFALONIERI

VIA VIGLENA

LUNGOTEVERE MELLINI

PONTE P. NENNI

VIA A BRUFFERIO

VIA G. FERRARI

VIA FORNOVO

VIA G. BETTOLO

VIA G. CAMOZZI

V. P. BORSIERI

VIALE DELLE MILIZIE

VIA DAMIATA

M **LEPANTO**

VIA DEGLI SCIPIONI

VIA BARLETTA

VIA OTRANTO

VIA CARLO ALBERTO DI CHIESA

VIA DAMIATA

VIALE GIULIO CESARE

VIA IZDO

VIA POMPEO MAGNO

VIA ALESSANDRO FARNESE

VIA DEI GRACCHI

PIAZZA DELLA LIBERTA

PRATI

OTTAVIANO SAN PIETRO M

VIA PAOLO EMILIO

VIALE GIULIO CESARE

VIA DEGLI SCIPIONI

VIA GERMANICO

VIA DEI GRACCHI

VIA COLA DI RIENZO

VIA VALADIER

Villa Borghese & north

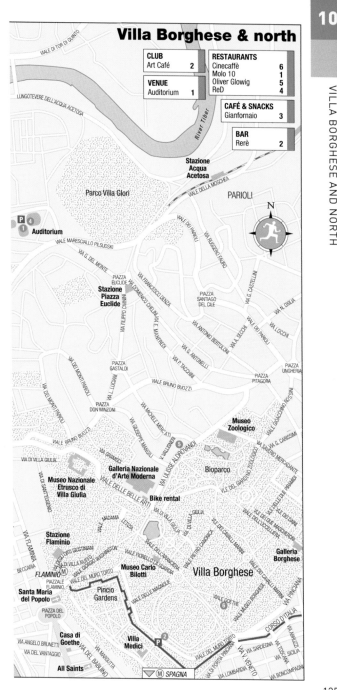

CLUB	
Art Café	2

VENUE	
Auditorium	1

RESTAURANTS	
Cinecaffè	6
Molo 10	1
Oliver Glowig	5
ReD	4

CAFÉ & SNACKS	
Gianfornaio	3

BAR	
Rerè	2

MUSEO CARLO BILOTTI

Viale Fiorello La Guardia ☎ 06 0608, ⓦ www
.museocarlobilotti.it. June–Sept Tues–Fri
1–7pm, Sat & Sun 10am–7pm; Oct–May
Tues–Fri 10am–4pm, Sat & Sun 10am–7pm.
€8. MAP P.134–135, POCKET MAP F2

Housed in the orangery of the
Villa Borghese, this museum
is, like the Galleria Borghese,
made up of a family bequest,
this time of **Carlo Bilotti** – a
perfume and cosmetics baron
who, until his death in 2006,
collected art and hobnobbed
with the brightest and best in
the international art world.
Good portraits of him by Larry
Rivers, and of his wife and
daughter by Andy Warhol,
open the exhibition and add to
the slightly self-congratulatory
air of the place, but the real
reason for coming is to
enjoy the small collection of
high-quality works by the
great modern Greek-Italian
painter, Giorgio De Chirico,
who lived in Rome for many
years (see p.75).

BIOPARCO

Via del Giardino Zoologico, Villa Borghese
☎ 06 360 8211, ⓦ www.bioparco.it. Daily:
Jan–March & Nov–Dec 9.30am–5pm; April–
Oct 9.30am–6pm, open till 7pm Sat & Sun
April–Sept. €15 adults, €12 children over 1m
tall. MAP P.134–135, POCKET MAP F1

Large, typical city-centre zoo,
much improved and reinvented
as the **"Bioparco"**, focusing on
conservation and education
yet still providing the usual
animals kids are after – tigers,
apes, giraffes, elephants, hippos
and much more. The zoological
museum next door – accessible
from the main road (left out of
the zoo and then left again) is
less engaging but worth a visit –
recently revamped, with displays
on different animal habitats as
well as lots of more traditional
stuffed mammals and birds.

GALLERIA NAZIONALE D'ARTE
MODERNA

Via delle Belle Arti 131 ☎ 06 322 981,
ⓦ www.gnam.beniculturali.it. Tues–Sun
8.30am–7.30pm. €8. MAP P.134–135, POCKET
MAP F1

Rome's **museum of
modern art** is a lumbering,
Neoclassical building housing
a collection of nineteenth-
and twentieth-century Italian
(and a few foreign) names.
It can make a refreshing
change after several days of
having the senses bombarded
with Etruscan, Roman

and Renaissance art. The nineteenth-century collection contains a splendid range of paintings by the Tuscan Impressionists (the Macchiaioli school), as well as works by Monet, Van Gogh and Cézanne, not to mention a giant statue of Hercules by the nineteenth-century Italian sculptor Canova and some mighty battle scenes celebrating Italian Unification. The twentieth-century collection features work by Giacomo Balla (a view of the Villa Borghese divided into 15 panels), his student Boccioni and other Futurists, along with work by Modigliani and De Chirico, whose paintings dominate one room. There are also some postwar canvases by the likes of Rothko, Pollock and Cy Twombly, Rome's own American artist, who lived in the city for most of his life.

The sun-trap terrace of the museum's smart **café** is a good spot for a coffee; they serve full meals too.

MUSEO NAZIONALE ETRUSCO DI VILLA GIULIA

Piazzale Villa Giulia 9 ⓦ www.villagiulia .beniculturali.it. Tues–Sun 8.30am–7.30pm. €8. MAP P.134–135, POCKET MAP E1

The Villa Giulia is a lovely collection of courtyards, loggias, gardens and temples put together in a playful Mannerist style for Pope Julius III in the mid-sixteenth century. It now houses the **Museo Nazionale Etrusco di Villa Giulia**, the world's primary collection of Etruscan treasures, along with the Etruscan collection in the Vatican (see p.147). Not much is known about the Etruscans, but the Roman's predecessors were a creative and civilized people, evidenced here by a wealth of sensual sculpture, jewellery

and art. They were also deeply religious and much of the collection focuses on preparing for the afterlife. The most famous exhibit is the remarkable *Sarcophagus of the Married Couple* (in the octagonal room in the east wing) – a touchingly lifelike portrayal of a husband and wife lying on a couch. It dates from the sixth century BC and was discovered in the tombs at Cerveteri. Look also at the delicate and beautiful cistae – drum-like objects, engraved and adorned with figures, that were supposed to hold all the things needed for the care of the body after death – and, in the same room, marvellously intricate pieces of gold jewellery, delicately worked into tiny horses, birds, camels and other animals, as well as mirrors, candelabra and religious statues – votive offerings designed to appease the gods. Further on you'll find a drinking horn in the shape of a dog's head that is so lifelike you almost expect it to bark; a *holmos*, or small table, to which the maker attached 24 little pendants around the edge; and a bronze disc breastplate from the seventh century BC decorated with a weird, almost modern abstract pattern of galloping creatures.

EXHIBIT IN THE MUSEO NAZIONALE ETRUSCO

FORO ITALICO

Bus #32 (Ple. M. Giardino), 271 (Ple. M. Diaz), 280 (P. Mancini), Tram #2 (P. Mancini). MAP P.134-135

The **Foro Italico** sports complex is one of the few parts of Rome to survive intact pretty much the way Mussolini planned it. The centrepiece is the Ponte Duca d'Aosta, which connects Foro Italico to the town side of the river, and is headed by a white marble obelisk capped with a gold pyramid, engraved MUSSOLINI DUX in beautiful 1930s calligraphy. Beyond the bridge, an avenue patched with mosaics revering the Duce leads up to a fountain surrounded by more mosaics of muscle-bound figures revelling in healthful sporting activities. Either side of the fountain are the two main stadiums: the larger of the two, the Stadio Olimpico on the left, was used for the Olympic Games in 1960 and is still the venue for Rome's two soccer teams; the smaller, the **Stadio dei Marmi** ("stadium of marbles"), is ringed by sixty great male statues, groins modestly hidden by fig leafs, in a variety of elegantly macho poses.

MAXXI

Via Guido Reni 4a ⓦ www.maxxi.beniculturali .it. Tues, Wed, Thurs, Fri & Sun 11am–7pm, Sat 11am–10pm; €11. Tram #2 from Piazzale Fiaminio (Metro A). MAP P.134-135, POCKET MAP D1

This new museum of twenty-first-century art and architecture is housed in a landmark building by the Anglo-Iraqi architect Zaha Hadid. It's mainly a venue for temporary exhibitions, but there are small permanent collections, and the building – a jagged, concrete spaceship that looks like it's just landed in this otherwise rather ordinary part of the city – is worth a visit just for itself.

PONTE MILVIO

MAP P.134-135

This footbridge across the Tiber was the site of the battle in which Constantine defeated Maxentius in 312 AD, a victory that brought about the end of Roman paganism. More recently, it became the home to numerous padlocks, placed here by lovers who then throw the keys into the river – a romantic ritual that the authorities recently put a stop to, for fear that the weight of the locks would cause permanent damage.

FORO ITALICO

Café and snacks

GIANFORNAIO

Largo Maresciallo Piaz 16. Mon–Sat
7.30am–9pm, Sun 9am–3pm. MAP P.134–135

Great bakery selling tasty pizza
and other goodies.

Restaurants

CINECAFFÈ

Casina delle Rose, Largo Marcello
Mastroianni 1 ☎ 06 4201 6224. Café daily
9am–7pm, restaurant daily 12.30–3.30pm.
MAP P.134–135, POCKET MAP F2

A great option for lunch in
Villa Borghese, this restaurant
puts on a huge buffet at
lunchtime (€25 at weekends,
including a drink; €15 on
weekdays), with salads, cold
meats and cheeses, pastas and
desserts. There's a large, sunny
terrace too.

MOLO 10

Via Prati della Farnesina 10 ☎ 06 333 6166.
Mon–Sat12.30–3pm & 7.30–11.30pm.
MAP P.134–135, POCKET MAP D1

An excellent fish restaurant
with an informal but elegant
atmosphere. Standout dishes
include the *tonnarelli* with
scampi, courgette flowers and
pecorino, and the crispy tuna
with wild chicory. The desserts
are delicious too.

OLIVER GLOWIG

Aldrovandi Palace Hotel, Via Ulisse
Aldrovandi 15 ☎ 06 321 6126, ⓦ www.oliver
glowig.com. Tues–Sat 12.30–2.30pm &
7.30–10.30pm. MAP P.134–135, POCKET MAP F1

Creative cuisine and
impeccable service distinguish
this two-Michelin-starred
restaurant. The emphasis is on
the two tasting menus (€140
and €160), but there are plenty
of a la carte options. The simple,
crisply modern dining room,
looking out onto lovely gardens,

makes a pleasant backdrop to a
special-occasion meal.

RED

Via Pietro de Coubertin 30 ☎ 06 8069 1630.
Daily 9am–2am. MAP P.134–135, POCKET MAP D1

Part of the Auditorium
complex, this sleek designer
bar-restaurant is good for a
drink or a meal before or after
a performance.

Club

ART CAFÉ

Via del Galoppatoio 33 ☎ 06 322 0994.
ⓦ www.art-cafe.it. Tues–Sat 9pm–6am.
MAP P.134–135, POCKET MAP F2

In the underground car park
in Villa Borghese, this is one
of Rome's trendiest clubs. Next
door is *The Place*, with live
music Thursday–Saturday.
Expect to queue, and dress up.

Venue

AUDITORIUM

Via Pietro de Coubertin 15. Bus #53, 280, 910
or Tram #2, 19. Box office daily 11am–8pm.
Concert tickets €15–30. Buy tickets online,
or in Italy on ☎ 892982 or from abroad on
☎ 06 4411 7799. Tours Sat & Sun every hour
11.30am–4.30pm, weekdays groups only;
book in advance on ☎ 06 8024 1281.
ⓦ www.auditorium.com; €9. MAP P.134–135,
POCKET MAP D1

Designed by Renzo Piano, this is
one of Rome's most prestigious
serious music venues, home
to its premier orchestra, the
Accademia Nazionale di Santa
Cecilia. Two smaller venues
host chamber, choral, recital
and experimental works. The
complex also hosts major rock
and jazz names when they come
to town. And there's a great
book and CD shop and a decent
café too if you just want to hang
out and admire the building –
of which there are regular tours.

The Vatican

Situated on the west bank of the Tiber, just across from the city centre, the Vatican City has been a sovereign state since 1929, and its 1000 inhabitants have their own radio station, daily newspaper, postal service, and security service, in the colourfully dressed Swiss Guards. It's believed that St Peter was buried in a pagan cemetery on the Vatican hill, giving rise to the building of a basilica to venerate his name and the siting of the headquarters of the Catholic Church here. Stretching north from St Peter's, the Renaissance papal palaces are now home to the Vatican Museums – quite simply, the largest, richest, most compelling and perhaps most exhausting museum complex in the world. The other main Vatican sight worth visiting is the Castel Sant'Angelo on the riverside, a huge fortress which once harboured the popes in times of danger. Apart from visiting the main attractions, you wouldn't know at any point that you had left Rome and entered the Vatican; indeed the area around it, known as the Borgo, is one of the most cosmopolitan districts – full of mid-range hotels, restaurants and scurrying tourists and pilgrims, while the district just beyond, Prati, is a comfortable middle-class neighbourhood that's home to some of the city's best and often least touristy restaurants.

CASTEL SANT'ANGELO

CASTEL SANT'ANGELO

Lungotevere Castello 50 ⓦ www.castel
santangelo.com. Tues–Sun 9am–7.30pm
€10.50. MAP P.142–143, POCKET MAP C13

The great circular hulk of the
Castel Sant'Angelo marks the
edge of the Vatican, designed
and built by Hadrian as his
own mausoleum. It was
renamed in the sixth century,
when Pope Gregory the Great
witnessed a vision of St Michael
here that ended a terrible
plague. The papal authorities
converted the building for
use as a fortress and built a
passageway to link it with the
Vatican as a refuge in times
of siege or invasion. Inside, a
spiral ramp leads up into the
centre of the mausoleum, over
a drawbridge, to the main
level at the top, where a small
palace was built to house the
papal residents in appropriate
splendour. Pope Paul III had
some especially fine renovations
made, including the beautiful
Paolina rooms, where the
gilded ceilings display the
Farnese family arms, and
you'll also notice the pope's
personal motto, *Festina Lenta*
("Make haste slowly"), scattered
throughout the ceilings and
in various corners of all his
rooms. Elsewhere, rooms hold
swords, armour, guns and the
like, while below are dungeons
and storerooms which can be
glimpsed from the spiralling
ramp, testament to the castle's
grisly past as the city's most
notorious Renaissance prison.
Off the Paolina rooms, a
terrace runs around the whole
building and holds a shady
bar for pick-me-up drinks
and sandwiches – and some
great views of Rome, best from
the terrace on the top of the
whole structure – from which
Tosca famously flung herself in
Puccini's eponymous opera.

ST PETER'S SQUARE

ST PETER'S SQUARE

MAP P.142–143, POCKET MAP A14

Perhaps the most famous of
Rome's many piazzas, Bernini's
St Peter's Square doesn't
disappoint, although its size
isn't really apparent until you're
right on top of it, its colonnade
arms symbolically welcoming
the world into the lap of the
Catholic Church. The obelisk
in the centre was brought to
Rome by Caligula in 36 AD,
and was moved here in 1586,
when Sixtus V ordered that
it be erected in front of the
basilica, a task that took four
months and was apparently
done in silence, on pain of
death. The matching fountains
on either side are the work of
Carlo Maderno (on the right)
and Bernini (on the left). In
between the obelisk and each
fountain, a circular stone
set into the pavement marks
the focal points of an ellipse,
from which the four rows of
columns on the perimeter of
the piazza line up perfectly,
making the colonnade appear
to be supported by a single line
of columns.

The Vatican

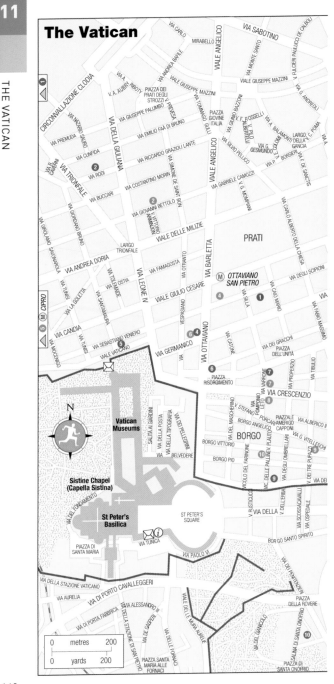

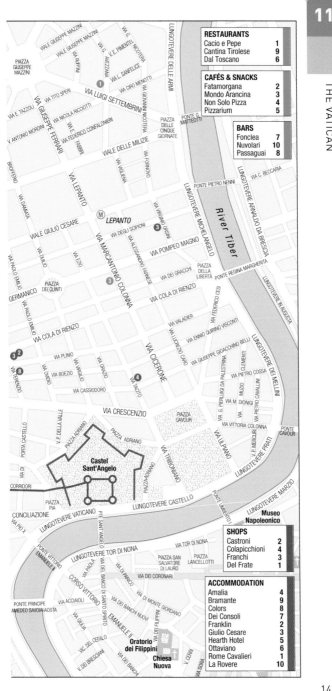

RESTAURANTS

Cacio e Pepe	1
Cantina Tirolese	9
Dal Toscano	6

CAFÉS & SNACKS

Fatamorgana	2
Mondo Arancina	3
Non Solo Pizza	4
Pizzarium	5

BARS

Fonclea	7
Nuvolari	10
Passaguai	8

SHOPS

Castroni	2
Colapicchioni	4
Franchi	3
Del Frate	1

ACCOMMODATION

Amalia	4
Bramante	9
Colors	8
Dei Consoli	7
Franklin	2
Giulio Cesare	3
Hearth Hotel	5
Ottaviano	6
Rome Cavalieri	1
La Rovere	10

ST PETER'S

Daily: April–Sept 7am–7pm; Oct–March 7am–6.30pm. Strict dress code – knees and shoulders must be covered. MAP P.142–143, POCKET MAP B4

The Basilica di San Pietro, better known to many as **St Peter's**, is the principal shrine of the Catholic Church, built on the site of St Peter's tomb, and worked on by the greatest Italian architects of the sixteenth and seventeenth centuries. Not so long ago you could freely stroll around the piazza and wander into the basilica when you felt like it. Now much of the square is fenced off, and you can only enter St Peter's from the right-hand side (exiting to the left); you also have to go through security first, and the queues can be horrendous unless you get here before 9am or after 5pm. Once you get close to the basilica, you're channelled through various entrances depending on what you want to see first – all of which is strictly enforced by the unsmiling besuited functionaries that appear at every turn. A carefree experience it is not.

Inside the **basilica**, on the right, is Michelangelo's graceful *Pietà*, completed when he was just 24. Following an attack by a vandal, it sits behind glass, strangely remote from the rest of the building. Further into the church, the dome is breathtakingly imposing, rising high above the supposed site of St Peter's tomb. With a diameter of 41.5m it is Rome's largest dome, supported by four enormous piers, decorated with reliefs depicting the basilica's so-called "major relics": St Veronica's handkerchief, which was used to wipe the face of Christ; the lance of St Longinus, which pierced Christ's side; and a piece of the True Cross. On the right side of the nave is the bronze statue of St Peter, its right foot polished smooth by the attentions of pilgrims. Bronze was also the material used in Bernini's 26-metre high baldacchino, cast out of 927 tonnes of metal removed from the Pantheon roof in 1633. To modern eyes, it's an almost grotesque piece of work, its wild spiralling columns copied from those in the Constantine basilica. Bernini's feverish sculpting decorates the apse too, his bronze *Cattedra* enclosing the supposed chair of St Peter, though his monument to Alexander VII in the south transept is more interesting, its winged skeleton struggling underneath the heavy marble drapes, upon which the Chigi pope is kneeling in prayer.

MICHELANGELO'S PIETA

An entrance off the aisle leads to the steeply priced **Treasury** (daily: April–Sept 8am–7pm; Oct–March 8am–6.15pm; €6), while back outside steps lead down to the **Grottoes** (daily: April–Sept 8am–6pm; Oct–March 8am–5.30pm), where the majority of the popes are buried. Directly beneath St Peter's baldacchino, the **necropolis** contains a row of Roman tombs with inscriptions confirming that the Vatican Hill was a burial ground in classical times.

Whether the tomb claimed as that of St Peter really is the saint's resting place is unclear, although it does tally with some historical descriptions. To be sure of getting a place on the English-language **tour**, book two or three months in advance via the Scavi office, through the arch to the left of St Peter's (Mon–Sat 9am–3.30pm; €13; no under-15s; ☎06 6988 5318; ✉scavi@fsp.va).

The worthwhile ascent to the **roof and dome** (daily: April–Sept 8am–6pm; Oct–March 8am–5pm; €7 via lift, €5 using the stairs) – is also outside by the entrance to the church. The views from the gallery around the interior of the dome give you a sense of the vastness of the church, and from there the roof grants views from behind the huge statues onto the piazza below, before the (challenging) climb to the lantern at the top of the dome – the views over the city are as glorious as you'd expect.

THE VATICAN MUSEUMS

Viale Vaticano 13 Ⓦ mv.vatican.va. Mon–Sat 9am–6pm, last entrance at 4pm, last Sun of each month 9am–2pm, last entrance at 12.30pm; Fridays May–July, Sept & Oct open 7–11pm, online booking obligatory; closed public and religious holidays. €16, under-18s and under-26s with student ID €8; audio guides €6; €4 extra for online booking; last Sun of the month free. MAP P.142–143, POCKET MAP B3

If you have found any of Rome's other museums disappointing, the Vatican is probably the reason why: so much booty from the city's history has ended up here, and so many of the Renaissance's finest artists were in the employ of the pope, that the result is a set of museums which put most other European collections to shame. As its name suggests, the complex actually holds a number of museums on very diverse subjects – displays of classical statuary, Renaissance painting, Etruscan relics and Egyptian artefacts, not to mention the furnishings and decoration of the building itself. There's no point in trying to see everything, at least not on one visit, and the only features you really shouldn't miss are the Raphael Rooms and the Sistine Chapel, and perhaps the Museo Pio-Clementino and Pinacoteca. Above all, decide how long you want to spend here, and what you want to see, before you start; it's easy to collapse from museum fatigue before you've even got to your main target of interest. In high season there may be a queue to get in, but getting to the museums late morning or after lunch can mean a shorter wait. Try to avoid Mondays, Saturdays and the days before and after Catholic holidays. Or buy your ticket in advance online and go to the front of the queue.

MUSEO PIO-CLEMENTINO

Vatican Museums. MAP P.142–143, POCKET MAP B3

To the left of the entrance, the **Museo Pio-Clementino** is home to some of the Vatican's best classical statuary, including two pieces that influenced Renaissance artists more than any others – the serene *Apollo Belvedere*, a Roman copy of a fourth-century BC original, and the first-century BC *Laocoön*. The former is generally thought to be a near-perfect example of male anatomy and was studied by Michelangelo; the latter depicts the prophetic Trojan priest being crushed by a serpent as he warned of the danger of the Trojan horse, and is perhaps the most famous classical statue of all time. Beyond here there are busts of Roman emperors, the statue of *Venus of Cnidos*, the first known representation of the goddess, the so-called *Belvedere Torso*, found in the Campo de' Fiori during the reign of Julius II, and much, much more sublime classical statuary.

MUSEO GREGORIANO EGIZIO

Vatican Museums. MAP P.142–143, POCKET MAP B3
It may not be one of the Vatican's highlights, but the **Museo Gregoriano Egizio** holds a distinguished collection of ancient Egyptian artefacts, including some vividly painted mummy cases (and two mummies), along with canopic jars, the alabaster vessels into which the entrails of the deceased were placed.

GALLERIA DELLE CARTE GEOGRAFICHE

MUSEO GREGORIANO ETRUSCO

Vatican Museums. MAP P.142–143, POCKET MAP B3
The **Museo Gregoriano Etrusco** holds Etruscan sculpture, funerary art and applied art. Especially worth seeing are the finds from the Regolini-Galassi tomb, from the seventh century BC, discovered near Cerveteri, which contained the remains of three Etruscan nobles. There's gold armour, a bronze bedstead, a funeral chariot and a wagon, as well as a great number of enormous storage jars, in which food, oil and wine were contained for use in the afterlife.

GALLERIA DEI CANDELABRI, DEGLI ARAZZI, AND DELLE CARTE GEOGRAFICHE

Vatican Museums. MAP P.142–143, POCKET MAP B3
Outside the Etruscan Museum, a large monumental staircase leads back down to the **Galleria dei Candelabri**, the niches of which are adorned with huge candelabra taken from imperial Roman villas. This gallery is also stuffed with ancient sculpture, its most memorable piece being a copy of the famous statue of *Diana of Ephesus*, whose multiple breasts are according to the Vatican official line in fact bees' eggs. Beyond here the **Galleria degli Arazzi** has Belgian tapestries to designs by the school of Raphael and tapestries made in Rome during the 1600s. The **Galleria delle Carte Geografiche** was decorated in the late sixteenth century with maps of all Italy, the major islands in the Mediterranean, the papal possessions in France, as well as large-scale maps of the maritime republics of Venice and Genoa.

RAPHAEL ROOMS

Vatican Museums. MAP P.142–143, POCKET MAP B3

At the end of the various galleries, the **Raphael Rooms** formed the private apartments of Pope Julius II, and when he moved in here he commissioned Raphael to redecorate them in a style more in tune with the times. Raphael died in 1520 before the scheme was complete, but the two rooms that were painted by him, as well as others completed by pupils, stand as one of the highlights of the Renaissance. The Stanza di Eliodoro, the first room you come to, was painted by three of Raphael's students five years after his death, and is best known for its painting of the *Mass of Bolsena* which relates a miracle that occurred in the town in northern Lazio in the 1260s, and, on the window wall opposite, the *Deliverance of St Peter*. The other main room, the Stanza della Segnatura, or pope's study, was painted between 1508 and 1511, when Raphael first came to Rome, and comes close to the peak of the painter's art. *The School of Athens*, on the near wall as you come in, steals the show, a representation of the triumph of scientific truth in which all

the great minds from antiquity are represented. It pairs with the *Disputation of the Sacrament* opposite, which is a reassertion of religious dogma – an allegorical mass of popes, cardinals, bishops, doctors and even the poet Dante.

APPARTAMENTO BORGIA

Vatican Museums. MAP P.142–143, POCKET MAP B3

Outside the Raphael Rooms, the **Appartamento Borgia** was inhabited by Julius II's hated predecessor, Alexander VI, and is host to a large collection of modern religious art, although its ceiling frescoes, the work of Pinturicchio between 1492 and 1495, are really the main reason to visit, especially those of the Sala dei Santi, where the figure of St Catherine is said to be a portrait of Lucrezia Borgia.

SISTINE CHAPEL

Vatican Museums. MAP P.142–143, POCKET MAP B4

Steps lead from the Raphael Rooms to the **Sistine Chapel**, a huge barn-like structure that is the pope's official private chapel and the scene of the conclaves of cardinals for the election of each new pontiff. The walls of the chapel were decorated by several prominent painters of the Renaissance – Pinturicchio, Perugino, Botticelli and

Ghirlandaio. However they are entirely overshadowed by Michelangelo's more famous **ceiling frescoes**, commissioned by Pope Julius II in 1508, and perhaps the most viewed set of paintings in the world. The frescoes were done by **Michelangelo** single-handed over a four year period and depict scenes from the Old Testament, from the *Creation of Light* at the altar end to *The Drunkenness of Noah* over the door. Look also at the pagan sibyls and biblical prophets which Michelangelo incorporated in his scheme – some of the most dramatic figures in the entire work, and all clearly labelled by the painter, from the sensitive figure of the Delphic Sybil to the hag-like Cumaean Sybil and the prophet Jeremiah – a brooding self-portrait of an exhausted-looking Michelangelo. Julius II lived only a few months after the Sistine Chapel ceiling was finished, but the fame of the work he had commissioned spread. It's staggeringly impressive, all the more so for its restoration, which lifted centuries of accumulated soot and candle grime off the paintings to reveal a much brighter painting. Michaelangelo's other great work here, *The Last Judgement*, is on the altar wall of the chapel, and was painted by the artist more than twenty years later. Michelangelo wasn't especially keen to work on this, but Pope Paul III, an old acquaintance of the artist, was keen to complete the decoration of the chapel. The painting took five years, again single-handed, and is probably the most inspired and most homogeneous large-scale painting you're ever likely to see. The centre is occupied by Christ, turning angrily as he gestures the condemned to the underworld. St Peter, carrying his keys, looks on in astonishment, while Mary averts her eyes from the scene. Below Christ a group of angels blasts their trumpets to summon the dead from their sleep. On the left, the dead awaken from their graves, tombs and sarcophagi, and are levitating into the heavens or being pulled by ropes and the napes of their necks by angels who take them before Christ. At the bottom right, Charon, keeper of the underworld, swings his oar at the damned souls as they fall off the boat into the waiting gates of hell.

MUSEUM OF CHRISTIAN ART AND THE VATICAN LIBRARY

Vatican Museums. MAP P.142-143, POCKET MAP B4

After the Sistine Chapel, you're channelled to the exit by way of the **Museum of Christian Art**, which is not of great interest in itself, but does give access to a small room off to the left that contains a number of ancient Roman frescoes and mosaics, among them the *Aldobrandini Wedding*, a first-century BC Roman fresco that shows the preparations for a wedding in touching detail. Back down the main corridor, the **Vatican Library** is decorated with scenes of Rome and the Vatican, and beyond, the corridor opens out into the dramatic **Library of Sixtus V**, a vast hall built across the courtyard in the late sixteenth century to glorify literature – and of course Sixtus V himself.

BRACCIO NUOVO AND MUSEO CHIARAMONTI

Vatican Museums. MAP P.142-143, POCKET MAP B4

The **Braccio Nuovo** and **Museo Chiaramonti** both hold classical sculpture, although they are the Vatican at its most overwhelming – close on a thousand statues crammed into two long galleries. The Braccio Nuovo was built in the early 1800s and it contains, among other things, probably the most famous extant image of Augustus, and a bizarre-looking statue depicting the Nile. The 300-metre-long Chiaramonti gallery is lined with the chill marble busts of hundreds of nameless ancient Romans, along with the odd deity. It pays to have a leisurely wander, for there are some real characters here: sour, thin-lipped matrons with their hair tortured into pleats, curls and spirals; kids, caught in a sulk or mid-chortle; and ancient old men, their flesh sagging and wrinkling to reveal the skull beneath.

THE PINACOTECA

Vatican Museums. MAP P.142-143, POCKET MAP B4

The **Pinacoteca** is housed in a separate building on the far side of the Vatican Museums' main spine, and is among Rome's picture galleries, with works from the early to high Renaissance and right up to the nineteenth century. Among early works, there is an amazing *Last Judgement* by Nicolò and Giovanni from the twelfth century, the stunning *Simoneschi* triptych by Giotto, painted in the early 1300s for the old St Peter's, and fragments of Melozzo de Forli's *Musical Angels*, painted for the church of Santi Apostoli. Further on are the rich backdrops and elegantly clad figures of the Umbrian School painters, Perugino and Pinturicchio. Raphael has a room to himself, where you'll find his *Transfiguration*, which he had nearly completed when he died in 1520, *The Coronation of the Virgin*,

THE TRANSFIGURATION

painted when he was only 19 years old, and, on the left, the *Madonna of Foligno*, showing Sts John the Baptist, Francis of Assisi and Jerome. Leonardo's *St Jerome*, in the next room, is a remarkable piece of work with Jerome a rake-like ascetic torn between suffering and a good meal, while Caravaggio's *Descent from the Cross*, two rooms on, is a warts-and-all canvas that unusually shows the Virgin Mary as a middle-aged mother grieving over her dead son. Take a look too at the most gruesome painting in the collection, Poussin's *Martyrdom of St Erasmus,* which shows the saint stretched out on a table with his hands bound above his head in the process of having his small intestine wound onto a drum – basically being "drawn" prior to "quartering".

MUSEI GREGORIANO PROFANO, PIO CRISTIANO AND MISSIONARIO ETNOLOGICO

Vatican Museums. MAP P.142–143. POCKET MAP B4
Next door to the Pinacoteca, the **Museo Gregoriano Profano** holds more classical sculpture, mounted on scaffolds for all-round viewing, including mosaics of athletes from the Baths of Caracalla and Roman funerary work, notably the Haterii tomb friezes, which show backdrops of ancient Rome and realistic portrayals of contemporary life. The adjacent **Museo Pio Cristiano** has intricate early Christian sarcophagi and, most famously, an expressive third-century AD statue of the Good Shepherd. The **Museo Missionario Etnologico** displays art and artefacts from all over the world, collected by Catholic missionaries.

VATICAN GARDENS

Daily except Wed & Sun; €32, includes access to the Vatican Museums; visits last about two hours and tickets must be booked in advance on ☎ 06 6988 4676, ⓦ mv.vatican.va, ⓦ www .vatican.va. MAP P.142–143. POCKET MAP A4
It's possible to visit the lovely **Vatican Gardens** on one guided tour a day – well worth doing for the great views of St Peter's. But you have to be organized and book in advance. The dress code is as for St Peter's – so no bare knees or shoulders.

Shops

CASTRONI

Via Cola di Rienzo 196. Mon–Sat
7.45am–8pm. MAP P.142–143, POCKET MAP C3

Huge, labyrinthine food store
with a large selection of Italian
treats as well as hard-to-find
international favourites – plus
a café with coffee, cakes and
sandwiches. There's another
branch at Via Frattina 79, near
the Spanish Steps.

COLAPICCHIONI

Via Tacito 76/78. Mon–Fri 7am–2.30pm
& 5–7.30pm, Sat 7am–4pm. MAP P.142–143,
POCKET MAP D3

Long-running food store,
mainly a bakery, selling the
family's excellent *pangiallo* and
other foodie goodies.

FRANCHI

Via Cola di Rienzo 200. Mon–Sat
8.30am–8.30pm. MAP P.142–143, POCKET MAP C3

One of the best delis in Rome
– a triumph of cheeses and
sausages with an ample choice
of cold or hot food to go,
including delicious *torta rustica*
and roast chicken. They'll make
up customized lunches for you,
and they have the wines to go
with it.

FRANCHI

DEL FRATE

Via degli Scipioni 118/124 ☎ 06 323 6437.
Mon–Sat 9am–1.30pm & 3.30–8pm. MAP
P.142–143, POCKET MAP C3

This large wine and spirits shop
is located on a quiet street near
the Vatican, and has all the
Barolos and Chiantis you could
want, alongside shelves full of
grappa in all shapes and sizes.
There's a wine bar/restaurant
attached, too.

Cafés and snacks

FATAMORGANA

Via Giovanni Bettolo ☎ 06 8639 1589. Daily
noon–10pm. MAP P.142–143, POCKET MAP B2

This is undoubtedly one of
the top three *gelaterie* in
Rome. *Fatamorgana* serves up
perfectly spherical scoops of
creative and seasonal flavours,
and is just a short walk from
the Vatican Museums.

MONDO ARANCINA

Via Marcantonio Colonna 38 ☎ 06 9761
9213. Daily 10.30am–12.30am. MAP P.142–143,
POCKET MAP D2

Great *pizza al taglio* at this
Prati Sicilian takeaway, but the
real treats are the *arancini* –
any number of varieties, from
tomato and mozzarella to
Bolognese, and cheap too, at
€2.50 each. Just the thing for
post-Vatican recovery.

NON SOLO PIZZA

Via degli Scipioni 95/97. Tues–Sun
8.30am–9.30pm. MAP P.142–143, POCKET MAP B3

Enjoy pizza by the slice, as
well as *supplì*, *olive ascolane*,
fiori di zucca, *crocchette*, etc,
and a complete selection of
good hot dishes. At lunch a
made-to-order round pizza,
plus a drink costs €7. There's no
extra charge to sit, inside or out.

PIZZARIUM

Via della Meloria 43 ☎ 06 3974 5416. Mon–
Sat 11am–10pm, Sun noon–4pm & 6–10pm.
MAP P.142–143, POCKET MAP A3

Celebrity *pizzaiolo* Gabriele
Bonci lures foodies to this
hole-in-the-wall spot near
Cipro metro. Join the hordes
for top-notch pizza by the slice,
made with slow-leavened dough
and with gourmet toppings.
There's very little seating, but it's
perfect for lunch on the run.

DAL TOSCANO

Restaurants

CACIO E PEPE

Via Avezzana 11 ☎ 06 321 7268. Mon–Fri
12.30pm–3pm & 7.30–11.30pm, Sat
12.30pm–3pm. MAP P.142–143, POCKET MAP D1

Rough-and-ready Prati cheapie
with a menu taped to the wall
but the food can't be beat.
You can't book, and should
expect to wait for a table, but
it's well worth it: great *cacio
e pepe* (naturally), *alla gricia*,
carbonara and other pasta
staples, and good *secondi* too.

CANTINA TIROLESE

Via Vitelleschi 23 ☎ 06 6813 5297. Tues–Fri
& Sun noon–3pm & 7pm–midnight, Sat 7pm–
midnight. MAP P.142–143, POCKET MAP B13

The hearty and wholesome
Austrian and German fare
served at this long-established
Prati standby is excellent, and
there's lots of it. A nice option
if you're craving a change from
Rome's usual offerings.

DAL TOSCANO

Via Germanico 58/60 ☎ 06 3972 5717. Tues–
Sun 12.30–3pm & 8–11.15pm. MAP P.142–143,
POCKET MAP B3

Tuscan food, and very popular,
with great steaks and other
meat dishes, perfectly grilled on
charcoal, delicious *pici* (thick
home-made spaghetti) and
ribollita (veg & bread soup)

– all at moderate prices. A treat,
and very handy for the Vatican.

Bars

FONCLEA

Via Crescenzio 82a ☎ 06 689 6302. Daily
7pm–2am; concerts start at 9.30pm. MAP
P.142–143, POCKET MAP C3

This historic basement joint
is loaded both with devoted
regulars and visitors who
have happily discovered that
there is life in the Vatican's
sometimes somnolent Borgo
and Prati area. Free live music
every evening, and happy hour
7–8.30pm.

NUVOLARI

Via degli Ombrellari 10 ☎ 06 6880 3018.
Mon–Sat 6.30pm–2am. MAP 142–143, POCKET
MAP A13

Welcoming Borgo wine bar
that has a good choice of wines
by the glass and does a free
buffet (6.30–8.30pm). A local
vibe, quite unexpected in this
part of town.

PASSAGUAI

Via Pomponio Leto 1 ☎ 06 8745 1358.
Mon–Fri 10am–2am, Sat & Sun 6pm–2am..
MAP P.142–143, POCKET MAP C3

Busy basement wine bar that
serves great platters of cheese,
meats and salads to go with its
excellent wine. Unusually there's
no cover or bread charge.

Day-trips

You may find there's quite enough in Rome to keep you occupied during your stay. But it can be a hot, oppressive city, and its churches, museums and ruins are sometimes wearing – so if you're around long enough it's worth getting out to see something of the countryside or going to the beach. Two of the main attractions close to Rome are among the most compelling attractions in the country, let alone the Rome area: Tivoli, about an hour by bus northeast of Rome, is a small provincial town famous not only for the travertine quarries nearby, but also for its villas, complete with landscaped gardens and parks; southwest of Rome, Ostia is the city's busiest seaside resort, but more importantly was the site of the port of Rome in classical times, the ruins of which – Ostia Antica – are well preserved and worth seeing.

Tivoli

Cotral buses leave Rome for Tivoli every 10min from Ponte Mammolo metro station (line B); journey time 30–45min, or 35min by train from Tiburtina station.

Perched high on a hill, with fresh mountain air and a pleasant position on the Aniene River, **Tivoli** has always been a retreat from the city. In classical days it was a retirement town for wealthy Romans; during the Renaissance it again became the playground of the moneyed classes, attracting some of the city's most well-to-do families and their new-built villas. Nowadays the leisured classes have mostly gone, but Tivoli does very nicely on the fruits of its still-thriving travertine business and the relics from its ritzier days. To do justice to the gardens and villas – especially if Villa Adriana is on your list – you'll need the whole day.

VILLA D'ESTE

VILLA D'ESTE

Piazza Trento 5 ☎ 0774 332 920, ⓦ www
.villadestetivoli.info. Tues–Sun 8.30am–1hr
before sunset. €8..

Tivoli's major sight is the **Villa
d'Este**, across the main square
of Largo Garibaldi. This was
the country villa of Cardinal
Ippolito d'Este, and has since
been restored to its original
state. Beautiful Mannerist
frescoes in its rooms show
scenes from the history of the
d'Este family in Tivoli, but it's
the gardens that most people
come to see, peeling away
down the hill in a succession
of terraces, their carefully
tended lawns, shrubs and
hedges interrupted by one
fountain after another. Among
the highlights, the central,
almost Gaudí-like Fontana del
Bicchierone, by Bernini, is one
of the most elegant; to the left
of this, the Rometta, or "Little
Rome", has reproductions of
the city's major buildings and
a boat holding an obelisk;
while perhaps the best is the
Fontana dell'Ovato on the
opposite side, fringed with
statues, underneath which is a
rather dank arcade, in which
you can walk.

VILLA GREGORIANA

☎ 0774 332 650, ⓦ www.villagregoriana.it.
Tues–Sun: April–Oct 10am–6.30pm; March,
Nov & Dec 10am–4pm. €6.

Tivoli's other main attraction,
the **Villa Gregoriana** was
created when Pope Gregory
XVI diverted the flow of the
river here to ease the periodic
flooding of the town in 1831.
As interesting and beautiful as
the d'Este estate, it remains less
well known and less visited, and
has none of the latter's conceits
– its vegetation is lush and
overgrown, descending into a
gorge over 60m deep. There are
two main waterfalls – the larger
Grande Cascata on the far side,
and a smaller one at the neck of
the gorge. Cross the bridge and
go in the back entrance, from
where the path winds down
to the bottom of the canyon,
passing a ruined Roman villa.
Climb up the other side through
hollowed-out rock to where you
can get right up to the roaring
falls; beyond here the path leads
up to the far side to the main
entrance and the substantial
remains of a **Temple of Vesta**,
clinging to the side of the hill.
The paths can be steep and
slippery, so wear sturdy shoes.

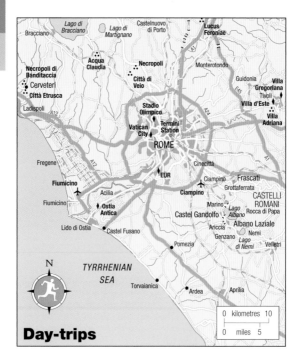

Day-trips

VILLA ADRIANA

Largo Yourcenarz ☎ 0774 382 733. Ask the Rome–Tivoli bus to drop you off or take the local CAT #4 bus from Largo Garibaldi in Tivoli. It's a 10min walk from the main road. Daily 9am–1hr before sunset; €8.

Probably the largest and most sumptuous villa in the Roman Empire, **Villa Adriana**, just outside Tivoli, was the retirement home of the Emperor Hadrian for a short while between 135 AD and his death three years later. Hadrian was a great traveller and a keen architect, and parts of the enormous site were inspired by buildings he had seen around the world. The massive Pecile, for instance, through which you enter, is a reproduction of a building in Athens; the Canopus, on the opposite side of the site, is a copy of the sanctuary of Serapis near Alexandria, its long, elegant channel of water fringed by sporadic columns and statues leading up to a temple of Serapis at the far end. Near the Canopus, a museum displays the latest finds from the ongoing excavations here, though most of the discoveries have found their way to museums in Rome. Back towards the entrance there are the remains of two bath complexes, a fishpond with a cryptoporticus (underground passageway) underneath, marked with the names of the seventeenth- and eighteenth-century artists who visited here, and finally the Teatro Marittimo, with its island in the middle of a circular pond – the place to which it's believed Hadrian would retire for a siesta.

Hitting the beach

OSTIA

Lido di Ostia has for years been the number one, or at any rate the closest and most accessible seaside resort for Romans. The beaches are ok, and much cleaner than they used to be, but you have to pay to use them and the town doesn't have a great deal to recommend it apart from its thumping nightlife in summer, and with a little more time you could do better. Ostia is, however, easy to get to, just half an hour by train from Porta San Paolo station, next door to Piramide mero on line #B; get off at Lido Centro or the last stop, Cristoforo Colombo, where the crowds might be thinner.

TORVAIANICA

South of Ostia, the water is cleaner here and the crowds not so thick, plus there are gay and nudist sections of the beach if these are your fancy, and not a lot of development. Buses run from Cristoforo Colombo station in Ostia; take #061.

FREGENE

Like Ostia, **Fregene,** a little way north, is one of the busier resorts of the Rome area but posher and more family-orientated than Ostia – its beaches are equally crowded and expensive though. Take a train to Maccarese from Rome Trastevere or Ostiense – a roughly 20min journey – and it's a short local bus ride from there to Fregene.

ANZIO

SPERLONGA

SANTA SEVERA

There's not much to sleepy **Santa Severa** but it's easy to get to and has everything you need for a day at the beach, with long stretches of sandy beach – some free, the rest given over to the usual *letti* and *ombrelloni* – and a *tavola calda* right on the seafront; there's also a castle at the southern end of the beach, home to a small municipal museum, if you get bored. The only drawback is the fact that the train station is a 20min walk from town, with erratic connecting buses and no real alternative transport. But trains are regular and quick: hourly from Termini, and the journey takes about an hour.

SANTA MARINELLA

The next stop on the train after Santa Severa, **Santa Marinella**, is one of the most popular spots north of the capital. It has a lovely crescent beach, 5min walk from the train station, and although most of it is pay-only the sand is fine and clean and the water shallow – perfect for kids. Trains are hourly from Termini, and take about an hour.

CAPALBIO

Just over the border in Tuscany, about 100km northwest of Rome, **Capalbio** is just about possible on a day-trip, and its beaches are worth the journey. The station is a shortish walk from the beach and the village, a little way inland, is an upscale, artsy sort of place, and only a bus-ride from the late Niki St-Phalle's sculpture garden, the **Giardino dei Tarocchi** (April to mid-Oct 2.30–7.30pm; €12), which the French artist created over twenty years with her husband, Jean Tinguely.

ANZIO

About 40km south of Rome, and fairly free of the pull of the capital, **Anzio** is worth visiting both for its beaches and its history – much of the town was damaged during a difficult Allied landing here on January 22, 1944, to which two military cemeteries (one British, another, at nearby Nettuno, American), as well as a small museum, bear testimony. It was also a favoured spot of the Roman emperor, the ruins of whose villa spread along the cliffs above and even down onto the beach. Anzio is a good place to eat: it hosts a thriving fishing fleet and some great restaurants down on the harbour. The resort is easy to get to, with trains every hour from Termini; the journey is an hour and from the station it's just a ten-minute walk down to the main square and harbour, with the beaches stretching out north of the centre.

TERRACINA AND SPERLONGA

Both of these are a bit of a schlep compared to the other nearby resorts, and as such you might want to consider staying overnight. But they are do-able for a day-trip and **Terracina** has great sandy beaches and a welcoming small-town feel, as well as a couple of good restaurants. A little further south from Terracina, little **Sperlonga** is a more chi-chi resort, with equally good beaches and an attractive old quarter piled up on the headland just beyond; the remains of the Emperor Tiberius' villa, conserved as part of the Museo Archeologico (Tues–Sun 8.30am–7.30pm; E5; ☎0771 768 3850), are a 10-minute walk along the beach from the town. There are direct trains from Termini to Terracina (1hr 30min) and buses from Terracina station to Sperlonga.

TERRACINA

Ostia Antica

Viale dei Romagnoli 717 ☎ 06 5635 0215,
🌐 www.ostiaantica.beniculturali.it.
Tues–Sun: April-Aug 8.30am–6.15pm, Sept
8.30am–6pm, Oct 8.30am–5.30pm, Nov
to mid-Feb 8.30am–3.30pm, mid-Feb to
mid-March 8.30am–4pm, mid-to end March
8.30am–4.30pm; museum opens at 9.30am.
€8. Regular trains from Roma–Porta San
Paolo (next door to Piramide metro station, on
line B); journey time 30min.

The excavations of the port of
Ostia – **Ostia Antica** – are one
of the finest ancient Roman
sites you'll see anywhere. Until
its harbour silted up and the
town was abandoned in the
fourth century, Ostia was Rome's
principal port and a commercial
hub. Over the centuries the
Tiber's mud preserved its
buildings incredibly well and the
place is now an evocative sight:
it's easier to visualize a Roman
town here than at the Forum
– and it compares pretty well
with better-known sights like
Pompeii.

From the entrance, the
Decumanus Maximus, Ostia's
main street, leads west, past the
Baths of Neptune on the right
(with its interesting mosaic) to
the town's commercial centre,
the Piazzale delle Corporazioni.
On the way, detour down
Via della Fontana, a street
which gives a good idea of
the typical Roman urban
layout: ground-floor shops and
upper-floor apartments. There
are more shops on Piazzale
delle Corporazioni, which
specialized in enterprises from
all over the ancient world, and
the mosaics just in front denote
their trade – grain merchants,
ship-fitters, ropemakers and
the like. On one side of the
square, Ostia's theatre has
been much restored and

sometimes hosts performances of classical drama during summer. Left of the square, the **House of Apulius** preserves mosaic floors and, beyond, a dark-aisled Mithraeum with more mosaics illustrating the cult's practices. Behind here, the **House of Diana** is probably the best-preserved private house in Ostia, with a dark, mysterious set of rooms around a central courtyard, and another Mithraeum at the back (tours can be pre-booked for Sun 10.30am). Head to the roof for a fine view of the rest of the site, then cross the road to the Thermopolium – an ancient Roman café, complete with seats outside, a high counter, display shelves and wall paintings of parts of the menu. North of the House of Diana, the **museum** holds a variety of articles from the site, including wall paintings

depicting domestic life in Ostia and some fine sarcophagi and statuary, notably *Mithras Slaying the Bull* from one of Ostia's Mithraeums. Left from here, the Forum centres on the Capitol building, reached by a wide flight of steps, and fringed by the remains of baths and a basilica. Further on, the Porta Occidentale, or western gate, and the Via delle Foce beyond lead to the **Terme dei Sette Sapienti baths** complex, with a wonderfully intact floor mosaic and atmospheric arcaded passageways that lead to the large **Casa degli Aurighi**. From the roof you can enjoy great views over the whole site.

Near the entrance, the Castle of Julius II was commissioned by the future pope; enjoy the lovely views from the third-floor walkway (entrance Thurs at 11am, Sun at 11am & noon).

OSTIA ANTICA

Hotels and B&Bs

There's no shortage of places to stay in Rome – but accommodation here tends to be pricier than in other European cities. Location is important: many of the cheaper options are clustered around Termini district, which, despite having improved dramatically in recent years, is not the city's most picturesque. Via Veneto is traditionally home to Rome's fanciest five-stars, and is somewhere to consider if you're looking for some old-world luxury, though much trendier these days are the cobbled lanes of the Monti district, a stone's throw from the Colosseum. You'll feel more in the thick of things in the Tridente area near the Spanish Steps or in the centro storico and around Campo de' Fiori, from where you can walk just about every-where. Across the river, Prati is a pleasant, well-heeled neighbourhood handy for the Vatican. Trastevere is close to the main sights, and comes into its own after dark.

Accommodation prices

All accommodation prices in this chapter are for the cheapest double room in high season but remember that rates are very much driven by demand – never be afraid to ask for a better rate; they can only say no. Most hotels now offer **discounted online rates** – anything from ten to forty percent off the official price – when you book make a non-refundable booking in advance; the prices quoted below are the standard rates, without discounts. Note that rates do not include Rome's **accommodation tax** (€2–3 per person, per night, for up to ten consecutive nights), which will be added to your bill. **Breakfast** is included in all but the five-stars, where you can expect to be charged an extra €28–38. Book in advance if you want to snag a bargain, especially when the city is at its busiest (March–July, Sept, Oct and Christmas).

If you arrive without a reservation, Enjoy Rome is your best bet (see p.183), while the free Hotel Reservation Service, by platform 24 in Termini train station, can check vacancies for you (daily 7am–10pm, or call ☎06 699 1000).

The centro storico

ALBERGO DEL SENATO > Piazza della Rotonda 73, Bus #116 ☎ 06 678 4343, Ⓦ www.albergodelsenato.it. MAP P.36–37, POCKET MAP E15. A classy choice next door to the Pantheon, with friendly service and knockout views of the city from the roof and the Pantheon from some of the rooms. €340

CESÀRI > Via di Pietra 89a, Bus #116 ☎ 06 674 9701, Ⓦ www.albergocesari.it. MAP P.36–37, POCKET MAP F14 In a perfect position close to the Pantheon, this has been a hotel since 1787 – as they will be sure to tell you. The, comfortable rooms are elegantly and traditionally furnished and you can enjoy the roof terrace at breakfast and for drinks on summer evenings. €336

DUE TORRI > Vicolo del Leonetto 23, Bus #116 ☎ 06 6880 6956, Ⓦ www.hotelduetorriroma.com. MAP P.36–37, POCKET MAP E14. Cosy hotel with a personal touch tucked away in a warren of streets a couple of minutes from Piazza Navona. Once a residence for cardinals, then a brothel, some rooms are on the small side but have been well renovated, and there's a comfy reception area. Family rooms available too. €180

NAVONA > Via dei Sediari 8, Bus #492 ☎ 06 6821 1392, Ⓦ www.hotelnavona.com. MAP P.36–37, POCKET MAP E15. Constructed on the site of the ancient Baths of Agrippa, this is a moderately priced hotel located between the Pantheon and Piazza Navona – really you couldn't ask for a better location if you want to be in the centre of Rome. Rooms are decently furnished, with their own bathrooms, and the welcome is warm. They also rent apartments nearby and have a sister hotel, the *Zanardelli* (see p.166). €152

PORTOGHESI > Via dei Portoghesi 1, Bus #116 ☎ 06 686 4231, Ⓦ www.hotelportoghesiroma.it. MAP P.36–37, POCKET MAP E14. Decent and well-equipped modern rooms 5min from most centro storico attractions. Breakfast is served on the roof terrace upstairs. It's worth paying a little extra for one of the roomier junior suites (€230). €200

RAPHAËL > Largo Febo 2, Bus #64 ☎ 06 682 831, Ⓦ www.raphaelhotel.com. MAP P.36–37, POCKET MAP D14. Set on a quiet, picturesque piazza just off Piazza Navona, the *Raphaël* is a mix of plush traditional style – antiques and rich colours – and sleek contemporary rooms designed by American architect Richard Meier (of Ara Pacis fame). There's also a rooftop terrace – one of Rome's loveliest – where you can try to identify the city's domes over a cocktail. €520

RESIDENZA CANALI > Via dei Tre Archi 13, Bus #492 ☎ 06 6830 9541, Ⓦ www.residenzacanali.com. MAP P.36–37, POCKET MAP D14. Tucked away on a side street just a 3min walk from Piazza Navona, this family-run hotel is hard to beat for location and service. The bright rooms, with wood-beamed ceilings and modern en-suite bathrooms, are great value too, especially the junior suites, each with their own terrace. Note that there are several flights of stairs – and no lift. €215

Apartments and B&Bs

A few hotels rent out apartments, and a number of agencies specialize in short lets. One of the best options is Rome Apartments (UK ☎ 0203 608 0580, US ☎ 202 618 9600, Ⓦ www.romeapartments.com). Cross-Pollinate (Ⓦ www.cross-pollinate.com), run by the owners of *The Beehive* (see p.170), is a good source of budget apartments; Ⓦ www.romeloft.com, Ⓦ www.romecityapartments.com and Ⓦ www.aplaceinrome.com are also worth a browse. See Ⓦ www.b-b.rm.it for a good range of B&Bs all over the city. Prices start relatively low – around €70 for a double – with the more upscale options going for up to €160.

SANTA CHIARA > Via Santa Chiara 21, Bus #116 ☎ 06 687 2979, Ⓦ www .albergosantachiara.com. MAP P.36–37, POCKET MAP E15. The *Santa Chiara*'s location is superb: on a quiet piazza right behind the Pantheon. Some of the rooms overlook the church of Santa Maria sopra Minerva; ask for one of the recently renovated rooms, which are bright, modern and comfortable. €260

TEATRO PACE 33 > Via del Teatro Pace 33, Bus #64 ☎ 06 687 9075, Ⓦ www.hotelteatropace.com. MAP P.36–37, POCKET MAP D15. This beautifully restored *palazzo*, a few paces from Piazza Navona, was once home to one of the Vatican's most prominent cardinals. Leading off an impressive Baroque spiral staircase (no lift) are four floors of elegant, spacious rooms with original wood beams, floor-sweeping drapes and luxurious bathrooms. €200

ZANARDELLI > Via G. Zanardelli 7, Bus #492 ☎ 06 6821 1392, Ⓦ www .residenzazanardelli.com. MAP P.36–37, POCKET MAP D14. Run by the same family as the *Navona* (see p.165). Located just north of Piazza Navona, the building used to be a papal residence and has many original fixtures and furnishings. The rooms are elegant, but still decently priced, especially considering the location. €140

Campo de' Fiori and the Ghetto

ARGENTINA RESIDENZA > Via di Torre Argentina 47, Bus #64 ☎ 06 6819 3267, Ⓦ www.argentinaresidenza.com. MAP P.52–53, POCKET MAP E16. This former noble carriage house has been converted to a six-room hotel and it's an elegant affair, with antique ceilings combining with well-chosen modern furnishings and amenitites. It's in a perfect location, too, close to the major transport hub of Largo Argentina. €185

CAMPO DE' FIORI > Via del Biscione 6, Bus #64 ☎ 06 6880 6865, Ⓦ www .hotelcampodefiori.com. MAP P.52–53, POCKET MAP D16. A friendly place in a

good location just off Campo de' Fiori with 23 individually designed rooms, each a different colour. The sixth-floor roof terrace has great views and the hotel owns a number of recently restored apartments nearby if you're keen to self-cater (from €250 for two, €330 for four). €300

FORTYSEVEN > Via Petroselli 47, Bus #170 ☎ 06 678 7816, Ⓦ www .fortysevenhotel.com. MAP P.52–53, POCKET MAP F17. Tasteful, elegant rooms above the ancient cattle market just outside the Ghetto. Within striking distance of the Forum, Trastevere and the Ghetto, it has a rooftop bar and restaurant too. €290

RESIDENZA FARNESE > Via del Mascherone 59, Bus #64 ☎ 06 6821 0980, Ⓦ www.residenzafarneseroma .it. MAP P.52–53, POCKET MAP D16. Situated on a quiet side street right by the Palazzo Farnese, this hotel has tastefully appointed rooms – though some are showing signs of wear and tear – and helpful staff. The location is excellent too – it's great for both the centro storico and Trastevere, just across the water by way of the Ponte Sisto footbridge. Do ask, though, to see several rooms – they vary a lot and some can be on the small side. €220

TEATRO DI POMPEO > Largo del Pallaro 8, Bus #64 ☎ 06 687 2812, Ⓦ www.hotelteatrodipompeo.it. MAP P.52–53, POCKET MAP D16. Built above the remains of Pompey's ancient Roman theatre, this moderately priced hotel has a great location just off the Campo, and comfortable rooms, with high-beamed wooden ceilings, marble-topped furniture and – in some – great views. €220

The Tridente, Trevi and Quirinale

BABUINO 181 > Via del Babuino 181 Ⓜ Spagna ☎ 06 3229 5295, Ⓦ www .romeluxurysuites.com. MAP P.76–77, POCKET MAP E13. *Rome Luxury Suites* operates this and two other locations at

Via Margutta 54 and Via Mario de'Fiori 37. Decorated with contemporary Italian flair, the accommodation is stylishly comfortable and includes breakfast and concierge service. €320

DEI BORGOGNONI > Via del Bufalo 126, Bus #175 📞 06 6994 1505, 🌐 www.hotelborgognoni.it. MAP P.76–77, POCKET MAP F13. Nicely situated four-star that has pleasant, well-renovated rooms. A surprisingly large hotel, considering its location down a side street not far from Piazza di Spagna, and handy for this part of town and for the centro storico. €290

CASA HOWARD > Via Capo le Case 18; Via Sistina 149 Ⓜ Spagna 📞 06 6992 4555, 🌐 www.casahoward. com. MAP P.76–77, POCKET MAP G13. This small boutique hotel offers a series of themed rooms, varying considerably in price, in two locations, one close to Piazza di Spagna, the other just off Piazza Barberini. Rooms are on the small side, but elegantly and stylishly furnished; service is very personal and welcoming and there's free wi-fi in each room. Breakfast is served to you in your room. €175

CASA MONTANI > Piazzale Flaminio 9 Ⓜ Flaminio 📞 06 3260 0421, 🌐 www .casamontani.com. MAP P.76–77, POCKET MAP E2. This self-styled "luxury town house" is a boutique hotel with a personal feel. The rooms – all designed by the owners, a friendly French-Italian couple – are decked out in a chic palette of neutrals, with touches of luxury: designer bathrooms, wide-screen TVs and breakfast served on fine porcelain. The five rooms are rightly popular – book well ahead. €210

CONDOTTI > Via Mario de' Fiori 37 Ⓜ Spagna 📞 06 679 4661, 🌐 www.hotelcondotti.com. MAP P.76–77, POCKET MAP E3. This cosy and inviting three-star, with comfortable rooms and cheery, welcoming staff, now has two other locations nearby (reception for all is at the *Condotti*). The most appealing of these is the *Condotti Palace* at Via della Croce 15, whose luxury suites have a refined, elegant feel. €270

DAPHNE > Via di San Basilio 55; Via degli Avignonesi 20 Ⓜ Spagna, 📞 06 8745 0086, 🌐 www.daphne-rome .com. MAP P.76–77, POCKET, MAP F4. Welcoming place in two locations either side of Piazza Barberini, run by an American woman and her Roman husband. Most of the rooms are bright, modern and spacious, and you can choose between shared bathrooms and en-suite. €160

DEKO ROME > Via Toscana 1, Ⓜ Barberini 📞 06 4202 0032, 🌐 www .dekorome.com. MAP P.76–77, POCKET MAP G3. This little hotel, run by the ever-helpful Marco and Serena, gets everything right, from the glass of prosecco on arrival to the complimentary iPad and free minibar. The rooms are modern and spotless, and it's in a great location too. It's understandably popular, so book ahead. €170

HASSLER > Piazza Trinità dei Monti 6 Ⓜ Spagna 📞 06 699 340, 🌐 www .hotelhasslerroma.com. MAP P.76–77, POCKET MAP F3. You can't get much closer to the heart of Rome than this – and you certainly can't get a much better view. Situated right at the top of the Spanish Steps, this luxury hotel has elegant rooms and every convenience a guest could possibly require. €500

HOTEL ART > Via Margutta 56 Ⓜ Spagna 📞 06 328 711, 🌐 www .hotelartrome.com. MAP P.76–77, POCKET MAP E3. Tucked away on Via Margutta, this has an impressive bar and lobby fashioned out of a vaulted chapel. Rooms are excellent, too, with plenty of luxurious touches – Frette linens, Etro toiletries – and breakfast is a feast. €325

HOTEL BAROCCO > Via della Purificazione 4, Ⓜ Barberini 📞 06 487 2001, 🌐 www.hotelbarocco.com. MAP P.76–77, POCKET MAP F3. Overlooking Bernini's Fontana del Tritone in Piazza Barberini, this smart four-star is within walking distance of all the main sights. Extremely comfortable, if a little old-fashioned, the rooms are all thick carpets, swagged curtains and gilt-framed art. Great breakfasts, too. €299

Our Picks

Budget choice: *The Beehive* p.170
Central hotel: *Navona* p.165
Boutique: *Casa Montani* p.167
Room with a view: *Hassler* p.167
Romance: *Casa Howard* p.167
Celebs: *De Russie* p.169
Luxury: *Portrait Roma* p.169

HOTEL D'INGHILTERRA > Via Bocca di Leone 14 Ⓜ Spagna ☎ 06 699 811, Ⓦ www.royaldemeure.com. MAP P.76–77, POCKET MAP F13. This old favourite, formerly the apartments of the princes of Torlonia, has had a striking makeover, incorporating chic design touches while retaining an old-world elegance. Rooms are furnished with antiques and have Murano glass chandeliers and marble bathrooms. **€570**

HOTEL PANDA > Via della Croce 35, Ⓜ Spagna ☎ 06 678 0179, Ⓦ www .hotelpanda.it. MAP P.76–77, POCKET MAP E3. If you don't mind lugging your cases up two floors (there's no lift), this no-frills little hotel, just steps from Piazza di Spagna, is a bargain. Rooms – both en-suite and with shared bathroom – are on the small side but are clean and comfortable. Breakfast is not included but there are plenty of cafés nearby. **€85**

JK PLACE ROMA > Via di Monte d'Oro 30, Ⓜ Spagna ☎ 06 982 634, Ⓦ www .jkroma.com. MAP P.76–77, POCKET MAP E13. The ultra-exclusive JK chain, with two other Italian locations, has recently opened this chic bolthole in the centre of Rome. It oozes sophisticated style, from the tasteful rooms – whose marble-clad bathrooms are bigger than most hotel bedrooms – to the airy lounge, dotted with art and sculpture, and the mirror-lined dining room, which sparkles like a jewellery box. Expensive, but a Roman one-off. **€800**

LOCARNO > Via della Penna 22 Ⓜ Flaminio ☎ 06 361 0841, Ⓦ www .hotellocarno.com. MAP P.76–77, POCKET MAP E2. Arguably the most characterful and inviting hotel in central Rome, a quirky and engaging place whose courtyard bar draws a crowd every evening. The rooms aren't the most luxurious or facility-laden but they're comfy and individually furnished. Considering the location, it's well-priced, too and there is a fleet of bikes for guest's use. **€198**

MODIGLIANI > Via della Purificazione 42 Ⓜ Barberini ☎ 06 4281 5226, Ⓦ www.hotelmodigliani.com. MAP P.76–77, POCKET MAP F3. A friendly, modern hotel on a quiet street just off Piazza Barberini. Rooms are comfortable, and have a/c. Splash out on a superior room – they have views of St Peter's. There's a small garden courtyard. **€182**

IL PALAZZETTO > Vicolo del Bottino 8 Ⓜ Spagna ☎ 06 6993 41000, Ⓦ www .ilpalazzettoroma.com. MAP P.76–77, POCKET MAP F3. Located at the top of the Spanish Steps, this is an elegant hotel with just four rooms, all differently designed in chic monochrome. It also has a panoramic rooftop bar and guests can use the facilities of the *Hassler* (see p.167). **€360**

PIAZZA DI SPAGNA > Via Mario de' Fiori 61 Ⓜ Spagna ☎ 06 679 3061, Ⓦ www.hotelpiazzadispagna.it. MAP P.76–77, POCKET MAP F3. This small hotel, just a few minutes' walk from the Spanish Steps, is a good alternative to the opulent palaces that dominate the area. Rooms are comfortable, and all have a/c. Friendly staff too. **€235**

PORTRAIT ROMA > Via Bocca di Leone 23 Ⓜ Spagna ☎ 06 6938 0742, Ⓦ www.lungarnocollection.com. MAP P.76–77, POCKET MAP E3. This converted town house with fourteen rooms, owned and designed by fashion designer Salvatore Ferragamo, is a bastion of luxury and comfort. Prices are high – but the suites are superbly appointed, and there's a lovely rooftop bar. **€880**

LA RESIDENZA > Via Emilia 22 Ⓜ Barberini ☎ 06 488 0789, Ⓦ www .hotel-la-residenza.com. MAP P.76–77, POCKET MAP G3. A great option in the expensive Via Veneto area, this place combines the luxuries and atmosphere of a grand hotel with the easy-going comforts and intimacy of a private home. It's set off the busy main drag and is very tranquil. **€190**

RESIDENZA DI RIPETTA > Via di Ripetta 231, Ⓜ Spagna ☎ 06 323 1144, Ⓦ www.residenzadiripetta.com. MAP P.76–77, POCKET MAP E3. Set in a seventeenth-century cloister, the *Hotel d'Inghilterra*'s sister hotel has very comfortably furnished rooms; it's worth paying a little extra for the superior and deluxe rooms, which come with hidden kitchenettes and marble bathrooms. The hotel's biggest draw, though, is its large plant-filled terrace – a rarity in the centre of Rome. It also has an intimate restaurant. **€300**

DE RUSSIE > Via del Babuino 9 Ⓜ Flaminio ☎ 06 328 881, Ⓦ www .roccofortehotels.com. MAP P.76–77, POCKET MAP E2. Coolly elegant and gorgeously understated, this hotel's emphasis on comfort and quality, not to mention its stellar location just off Piazza del Popolo, make it first choice for the hip traveller spending someone else's money – it's popular among visiting movie stars. **€728**

VILLA SPALLETTI TRIVELLI > Via Piacenza 4, Bus #64 ☎ 06 4890 7934, Ⓦ www.villaspalletti.it. MAP P.76–77, POCKET MAP G4. In a fantastic location – a five-minute walk from Piazza Venezia – this aristocratic villa is one of Rome's most luxurious accommodation

options. The twelve rooms are impeccably furnished with antiques, and the common areas – including a lovely garden – exude an aura of exclusivity. **€705**

The Esquiline, Monti and Termini

ALPI > Via Castelfidardo 84 Ⓜ Termini ☎ 06 444 1257, Ⓦ www.hotelalpi.com. MAP P.92–93, POCKET MAP J3. One of the more peaceful hotels close to Termini, with pleasant (if somewhat small) rooms, a terrace and a great buffet breakfast – better than you would normally expect from a hotel in this bracket. **€242**

ARTEMIDE > Via Nazionale 22, Ⓜ Repubblica ☎ 06 489 911, Ⓦ www .hotelartemide.it. MAP P.92–93, POCKET MAP G4. If you're after a grand hotel without the five-star price tag, head to the handsome *Artemide*, which combines an imposing, old-world feel with a warm welcome. The comfortable rooms come with a free minibar, and the rooftop bar is a lovely spot on a sunny day. **€303**

DES ARTISTES > Via Villafranca 20 Ⓜ Castro Pretorio ☎ 06 445 4365, Ⓦ www.hoteldesartistes.com. MAP P.92–93, POCKET MAP J3. Exceptionally good value, spotlessly clean and with a wide range of rooms, including dorm beds for €19–23. Doubles are available with and without en-suite facilities. You can eat breakfast or recover from a long day of sightseeing on the lovely roof terrace. **€139**

ARTORIUS > Via del Boschetto 13, Bus #64 ☎ 06 482 1196, Ⓦ www.hotel artoriusrome.com. MAP P.92–93, POCKET MAP G5. On a cobbled Monti street and with just ten rooms, the family-run *Artorius* is an appealing mid-range option. The attractive courtyard makes a pleasant spot for breakfast in fine weather, and for drinks after dark. **€183**

THE BEEHIVE > Via Marghera 8 Ⓜ Termini ☎ 06 4470 4553, Ⓦ www .the-beehive.com. MAP P.92–93, POCKET MAP J4. This ecological – and economical – hotel run by an American couple is one of Rome's most popular budget options. The doubles – all of which share bathrooms – are basic but stylishly decorated; a few en-suites (€10 extra) are available in a separate part of the building, more spartan dorms go for €35 a head, and you can also stay in one of three nearby guestrooms with communal ktchen (€80 for a double room). There is free internet access, and a restaurant that serves breakfast, as well as vegetarian dinner on some evenings. **€80**

DUCA D'ALBA > Via Leonina 14, Bus #84 ☎ 06 484 471, Ⓦ www.hotelduca dalba.com. MAP P.92–93, POCKET MAP G5. A stylish four-star in the heart of Monti, just steps from the district's best restaurants and nightlife. All of the attractively furnished rooms have en-suite bathrooms and a/c, and some have balconies. Rooms are heavily discounted in low season. **€197**

LEON'S PLACE > Via XX Settembre 90/94 Ⓜ Termini ☎ 06 890 871, Ⓦ www.leonsplacehotel.it. MAP P.92–93, POCKET MAP H3. Walking distance from Termini but on the edge of an upscale residential area. The rooms are on the small side but sleekly modern, all black and white with splashes of colour and trendy design touches. **€257**

NICOLAS INN > Via Cavour 295 Ⓜ Cavour ☎ 06 9761 8483, Ⓦ www .nicolasinn.com. MAP P.92–93, POCKET MAP G5. A brief stroll from the Colosseum, this B&B is run by a friendly American-Italian couple, who are keen to make guests feel at home. The rooms are a good size, spotless and elegant. Breakfast is served in a nearby bar. **€180**

RESIDENZA CELLINI > Via Modena 5, Ⓜ Repubblica ☎ 06 4782 5204, Ⓦ www .residenzacellini.it. MAP P.92–93, POCKET MAP G4. The rooms here are large with a slightly old-fashioned feel; it's worth paying the extra for a spacious junior suite (€280), which comes with a hydromassage bath. Staff are extremely friendly. **€240**

ROMAE > Via Palestro 49 Ⓜ Termini ☎ 06 446 3554, Ⓦ www.hotelromae .com. MAP P.92–93, POCKET MAP J3. Rome's self-styled "groovy hotel" is a thoroughly welcoming and extremely comfortable place, with thirty contemporary rooms that offer some of the best value in the Termini area. They also run the *Yellow* hostel (see p.173) across the road. No breakfast but still great value. **€110**

SUITE DREAMS > Via Modena 5 Ⓜ Repubblica ☎ 06 4891 3907, Ⓦ www.suitedreams.it. MAP P.92–93, POCKET MAP G4. The rooms at this mid-range hotel are simple but stylish, with generous bathrooms, but it's the attention to detail and friendly customer care that really stand out. Services such as free a bottle water and a DVD library for guests' use are an unexpected bonus for a place in this price bracket. **€184**

VILLA DELLE ROSE > Via Vicenza 5 Ⓜ Termini ☎ 06 445 1788, Ⓦ www .villadellerose.it. MAP P.92–93, POCKET MAP J4. This centuries-old villa sits amidst its own tranquil rose gardens, belying the fact that it's only a block from Termini train station. The decor is a little tired, but it has bags of old-world charm, and staff are friendly. Ask for one of the rooms with a terrace. **€130**

YES HOTEL > Via Magenta 15 Ⓜ Termini ☎ 06 4436 3836, Ⓦ www .yeshotelrome.com. MAP P.92–93, POCKET MAP H4. The location – just down the road from Termini – might not be brilliant, but *Yes* is a huge step up from the grotty options that litter the area, and you'll pay considerably less here than for a similar room in the centre. Tailored to the needs of Termini's business travellers – rooms are comfortable but bland. **€170**

The Celian and Aventine Hills

LANCELOT > Via Capo d'Africa 47 Ⓜ Colosseo ☎ 06 7045 0615, Ⓦ www.lancelothotel.com. MAP P.92–93, POCKET MAP H6. Just two minutes from the Colosseum, this friendly family-run hotel has rooms with views of the Colosseum and staff that are well-informed and helpful. They have limited parking for €10. **€196**

SAN ANSELMO > Piazza Sant'Anselmo 2 Ⓜ Piramide ☎ 06 570 057, Ⓦ www.aventinohotels.com. MAP P.92–93, POCKET MAP E8. One of the most peaceful places you could stay, and arguably in Central Rome's most upscale residential neighbourhood, the *San Anselmo*, has beautifully furnished rooms (each with a different theme). Breakfast is good, there's a nice lounge and garden, and parking is free. Deals available outside high season. **€255**

Trastevere

GUESTHOUSE ARCO DE' TOLOMEI > Via Arco de' Tolomei 27, Bus #H ☎ 06 5832 0819, Ⓦ www.bbarcodeitolomei .com. MAP P.124–125, POCKET MAP E18. In an attractively crumbling *palazzo* on Trastevere's quieter, eastern side, this old-world B&B is full of antiques passed down from generation to generation of the Italian owners' family, but the atmosphere is anything but stuffy. The generous breakfast is served in the conservatory. Ten percent discount for cash payment. **€205**

RESIDENZA SANTA MARIA > Via dell'Arco di San Calisto 20, Bus #H ☎ 06 5833 5103, Ⓦ www .residenzasantamaria.com. MAP P.124–125, POCKET MAP D18. In an eighteenth-century building – which once housed crafts workshops – this intimate hotel has been attractively restored, with features such as brick arches, wood-beamed ceilings and an internal courtyard giving it a welcoming feel. It's especially recommended for families: four of the six rooms are triples or quads. **€195**

SANTA MARIA > Vicolo del Piede 2, Bus #H ☎ 06 589 4626, Ⓦ www .hotelsantamariatrastevere.it. MAP P.124–125, POCKET MAP D18. Just off Piazza Santa Maria in the heart of Trastevere, the rooms of this friendly three-star surround a garden filled with lovely orange trees. There's free internet access, and bikes are provided for guests' use. **€230**

TRASTEVERE > Via Luciano Manara 24a/25, Bus #H ☎ 06 581 4713, Ⓦ www.hoteltrastevere.net. MAP P.124–125, POCKET MAP C18. A good choice if you want to be in the heart of Trastevere, with nicely decorated – though small – doubles, and apartments to rent for up to five people. Request a room overlooking the little piazza, rather than the interior courtyard. **€103**

VILLA DELLA FONTE > Via della Fonte d'Olio 8, Bus #H ☎ 06 580 3797, Ⓦ www.villafonte.com. MAP P.124–125, POCKET MAP C18. This attractive hidden-away place feels almost secret, yet it is just a few steps from Piazza Santa Maria in Trastevere. The rooms are cosy and comfortable and there's a lovely sun-trap terrace. **€169**

Vatican

AMALIA > Via Germanico 66 Ⓜ Ottaviano ☎ 06 3972 3356, Ⓦ www.hotelamalia.com. MAP P.142–143, POCKET MAP B3. Located not far from the Vatican, this place has bright, nicely renovated double rooms with generous en-suite bathrooms. Rates can go as low as €99 in low season. **€169**

BRAMANTE > Vicolo delle Palline 24, Bus #40 ☎ 06 6880 6426, Ⓦ www .hotelbramante.com. MAP P.142–143, POCKET MAP A3. This little hotel, located right next to the ancient wall running from the Vatican to Castel Sant'Angelo, has charming rooms with original wood-beamed ceilings and antiques. **€200**

COLORS > Via Boezio 31
Ⓜ Ottaviano, ☎ 06 687 4030, Ⓦ www
.colorshotel.com. MAP P.142–143,
POCKET MAP C3. This hostel/hotel in a
quiet neighbourhood near the Vatican
provides kitchen facilities, a lounge
with satellite TV and a small roof
terrace. Doubles are available both
en-suite and with shared facilities,
and there are sometimes dorm beds
available too. No breakfast. €78

DEI CONSOLI > Via Varrone 2d,
Ⓜ Ottaviano ☎ 06 6889 2972, Ⓦ www
.hoteldeiconsoli.com. MAP P.142–143,
POCKET MAP C3. From the elegantly
welcoming entrance to the thoughtfully
designed rooms, this is one of the best
moderately priced choices in the Vatican
area, with a lovely roof terrace and
excellent service. €250

FRANKLIN > Via Rodi 29 ☎ 06
39030165, Ⓦ www.franklinhotelrome
.it. MAP P.142–143, POCKET MAP B2.
The central theme here is music: don't be
surprised to find a snare drum for a night
table or a disco ball in the bathroom.
Rooms come equipped with Bang &
Olufsen stereos and you can choose from
a library of hundreds of CDs. €175

GIULIO CESARE > Via degli Scipioni
287 Ⓜ Lepanto ☎ 06 321 0751,
Ⓦ www.hotelgiuliocesare.com. MAP
P.142–143, POCKET MAP D2. This
charming hotel is no longer the home of
an Italian countess, but you may feel like
royalty once you step into the elegant
foyer. Friendly staff lead you down
mirror-lined hallways to elegant rooms
with lovely marble bathrooms. €235

HEARTH HOTEL > Via Santamaura 2,
M Ottaviano ☎ 06 3903 8383,
Ⓦ www .hearthhotel.com. MAP
P.142–143, POCKET MAP B3. About as
close as you can get to the Vatican – the
entrance to the museums is just across
the street – this renovated *palazzo*
has large, stylishly furnished rooms. If
you're a light sleeper request a room on
the quieter side of the building or you
might be woken by the early-morning
chatter from the museums' inevitable
queue. €144

ROME CAVALIERI > Via A Cadlolo 101
☎ 06 350 91, Ⓦ www.romecavalieri
.com. MAP P.142–143, POCKET MAP
B15. Arguably Rome's smartest hotel is
quite a way out of the city centre, but
it is worth staying here once, not only
to check out Heinz's Beck's ledgendary
three-Michelin-star rooftop restaurant
(although you have to book well in
advance for this) but also to enjoy its
curious mix of Sixties glamour and
old-fashioned style. The rooms are large
and comfortable, there are three lovely
pools and service that's impeccably
gracious and professional. The hotel
runs regular free shuttle buses to Piazza
Barberini. €390

LA ROVERE > Vicolo S. Onofrio 4–5,
Bus #64 ☎ 06 6880 6739, Ⓦ www
.hotellarovere.biz. MAP P.142–143,
POCKET MAP B15. Just across the
bridge from Piazza Navona, this attractive
hotel is tucked away from Rome's
bustle, and offers a terrace garden and
antique-filled setting for its guests to
relax in. €215

Hostels

For dorm accommodation, see also *Des Artistes* (p.169), *The Beehive* (see p.170) and *Colors* (see p.171).

ALESSANDRO PALACE HOSTEL > Via Vicenza 42, Ⓜ Termini ☎ 06 446 1958, Ⓦ www.hostelsalessandro .com. MAP P.92–93, POCKET MAP J3. This place has been voted one of the top hostels in Europe, and it sparkles with creative style. Pluses include no lock-out or curfew, a good bar with two nightly happy hours, and free internet access and satellite TV. Breakfast costs €4. **Dorms €26–35; doubles with shared bath €110**

LA CONTRORA > Via Umbria 7, M Repubblica ☎ 06 9893 7366, Ⓦ www .lacontrora.com. MAP P.76–77, POCKET MAP G3. In an excellent location near Piazza Barberini, this new hostel has a relaxed, arty feel, funky decor and friendly staff. The spacious lounge has a big-screen TV and free wi-fi, and there's a large communal kitchen. **Dorms around €30, en-suite doubles €95**

OTTAVIANO > Via Ottaviano 6 Ⓜ Ottaviano ☎ 06 3973 8138, Ⓦ www.pensioneottaviano.com. MAP P.142–143, POCKET MAP B3. A simple pensione-cum-hostel near the Vatican that is very popular with backpackers; book well in advance. **Dorms €27–33, doubles €78**

YELLOW > Via Palestro 44 Ⓜ Termini ☎ 06 4938 2682, Ⓦ www.the-yellow .com. MAP P.92–93, POCKET MAP J4. Yellow is hands-down Rome's best hostel. Self-conciously cool, it encourages a lively scene in the downstairs bar (with drinks from €1) and club (open till 4am), so if you're after somewhere quiet it's probably not for you. **Dorms €26–35, en-suite doubles €95**

Arrival

Arriving in Rome is a painless experience if you're travelling by air, by train or even by bus, although negotiating the city's outskirts by car is something you might want to avoid.

By air

Rome has two airports: Leonardo da Vinci, better known simply as Fiumicino, which handles most scheduled flights, and Ciampino, where you'll arrive if you're travelling on a charter or with one of the low-cost European airlines. Information on both airports is available at ☏06 65951, ⓦwww.adr.it.

Fiumicino airport

Fiumicino is connected to the centre of Rome by direct trains, which make the 30min ride to Termini for €14; services run at 8min and 38min past the hour (first train at 6.38am, last train at 11.38pm). In the other direction, trains run at 20min and 50min past the hour (first train 5.50am, last train at 10.50pm). Be aware when leaving Rome, that the Fiumicino platform at Termini station is a good 5min schlep from the main part of the station. Alternatively, there are trains every 15min to Ostiense and Tiburtina stations, each on the edge of the city centre; tickets to these stations cost less (€8) and Tiburtina and Ostiense are just a short (€1.50) metro ride from Termini. You can also catch bus #175 from Ostiense, or #492 or #649 from Tiburtina, to the town centre (again €1.50). Taxis for the 30–40min journey to and from the airport cost a fixed-rate €48. Several buses go from the airport to Termini. COTRAL have 8 services a day from 1.15am to 7.05pm to Piazza dei Cinquecento (€5 one way; ⓦwww.cotralspa.it), while SIT bus services run every half hour from 8.30am to 12.30am to Via

Marsala and Via Crescenzio in the Vatican(€5 online, €6 on board one way; ⓦwww.sitbusshuttle.com). Both take 45min–1hr.

Ciampino airport

Several companies, including Terravision (ⓦwww.terravision.eu) and SIT bus (ⓦwww.sitbusshuttle.com) run shuttle services to Termini, which leave roughly every 30min and cost €4 one way. They pull up on Via Marsala, right by the station (journey time around 45min). Otherwise ATRAL buses (ⓦwww.atral-lazio.com) run to Via Giolitti, on the south side of Termini, every 50min–1hr (€3.90). If you don't want to get off at Termini, and are staying near a metro stop on the A line (near the Spanish Steps or Via Veneto areas, for example), you could take an ATRAL bus (€1.20 plus €1.20 per suitcase) from the airport to Anagnina metro station at the end of metro Line A (every 40min; 15min), and take a metro from there to your destination (€1.50). Taxis to and from the airport cost a fixed-rate €30 and take 30–40min.

By train

Most Italian and international trains arrive in Rome at Termini station, centrally placed for all parts of the city and the meeting point of the two metro lines and many city bus routes. Tiburtina (see below) is a stop for some north–south intercity trains. For general enquiries about schedules and prices, call ☏892 021 (24hr), or check ⓦwww.trenitalia.com.

By bus

Most national and international services stop at Tiburtina, Rome's second railway terminal after Termini, which is connected to the city centre by metro line B or buses #492 or #649. Other bus stations, mainly serving the Lazio region, include Ponte Mammolo (trains from Tivoli and Subiaco), Cornelia (Cerveteri, Civitavecchia, Bracciano area), Laurentina (Nettuno, Anzio, southern Lazio coast) and Anagnina (Castelli Romani); buses are run by Cotral (wwww.cotralspa.it) and all of these stations are on a metro line.

By car

Driving into Rome can be quite confusing and is best avoided unless you're used to driving in Italy and know where to park (see p.180). Note that non-residents aren't allowed to drive in the centro storico area. It's usually best to get on the Grande Raccordo Anulare (GRA), which circles Rome and is connected with all of the major arteries into the city centre – the Via Cassia from the north, Via Salaria from the northeast, Via Tiburtina or Via Nomentana from the east, Via Prenestina and Via Casilina or Via Cristoforo Colombo from the southeast, Via Appia Nuova and the Pontina from the south, and Via Aurelia from the northwest. From Ciampino, either follow Via Appia Nuova into the centre or join the GRA at junction 23 and follow signs to the centre. From Fiumicino, follow the A12 motorway into the city centre; it crosses the river just north of EUR, from where it's a short drive north up Via Cristoforo Colombo to the city walls and, beyond, to the Baths of Caracalla.

Getting around

The best way to get around is to walk – you'll see more and will better appreciate the city. However, you may need to take public transport to get around quickly or reach the more outlying attractions, and the network is good – a largely efficient blend of buses, a two-line metro and a few trams. ATAC runs the city's bus, tram and metro service. There's an information office in the centre of Piazza dei Cinquecento outside Termini station; their website, wwww.atac. roma.it, has information in English and a route planner.

Buses and trams

Buses are cheap, reliable and as quick as the clogged streets allow with several routes for visitors (see box on p.179). Remember to board through the rear doors and punch your ticket as you enter if it's the first time you're using it. There is also a small network of electric minibuses that negotiate the narrow backstreets of the old centre and a few trams, mainly serving outlying areas. After midnight, night buses (*bus notturni*) serve most parts of the city through to about 5.30am (see box, p.178); some have ticket machines on board but it's best to buy one before boarding.

GETTING AROUND

Tickets and travel cards

Flat-fare **tickets** (BIT) cost €1.50 each and are good for any number of bus and tram rides and one metro ride within 100 minutes of validation. Buy them from tobacconists, newsstands and ticket machines located in all metro stations and at major bus stops, and validate them in the yellow machines on buses, trams and at the entrance gates in metro stations. You can also get a **day pass** (BIG), valid on all city transport until midnight on the day purchased, for €6, a three-day pass (BTI) for €16.50, or a seven-day pass (CIS) for €24. Alternatively, you can travel on public transport for free with the **Roma Pass** (see p.183). A warning: there are hefty spot fines (€50–117) for fare-dodging, and pleading a foreigner's ignorance will get you nowhere.

Metro

Rome's metro runs from 5.30am to 11.30pm (1.30am Fri & Sat), and although its two lines – A (red) and B (blue) – don't cover large parts of the city centre, there are a few useful city-centre stations: Termini is the hub of both lines, and there are stops at the Colosseum, Piazza Barberini, Piazza di Spagna and Ottaviano (for the Vatican). A new line – C – will cross line A at San Giovanni and Ottaviano and line B at Colosseo; the first section is due to open in 2015 but the city-centre stations not for years after that.

Tourist buses

Many tourist buses circle Rome and its major sights – see the three best options below. All start from outside Termini, and combined tickets are available for the first two.

Bus #110 ☎06 684 0901, ⓦwww .trambusopen.com. Good for a quick glance at the sights, this ATAC-run open-top bus has a guided commentary. It leaves from Piazza dei Cinquecento outside Termini station and stops at all the major sights. The trip takes two hours, and in summer departures are every 15min from 8.30am until 7.30pm daily (including hols & Sun). Tickets cost €20 and allow you to get on wherever you like and hop on and off during a 48-hour period. Combined #110 and Archeobus (see below) tickets cost €25 for 72 hours. Tickets can be bought on board, before you get on at Piazza dei Cinquecento, or discounted fares are available online and for Roma Pass holders.

Archeobus ☎06 684 0901, ⓦwww .trambusopen.com. A hop-on-hop-off service, linking the most compelling monuments on and around the Via Appia Antica. It starts at Piazza dei Cinquecento, before heading to the Colosseum, Baths of Caracalla and the Porta San Sebastiano. On Via Appia,

there are stops at Domine Quo Vadis, the Catacombs of San Callisto and San Sebastiano and Tomb of Cecilia Metella; on the way back the bus stops at the Bocca della Verità and Piazza Venezia.. Buses run Friday to Sunday every 30min 9am–12.30pm & 1.30–4.30pm. Forty-eight hour tickets cost €12 (€40 family ticket), and an integrated ticket is available with the #110 bus (€25 for 72hr). Buy on board, at Piazza dei Cinquecento or online.

Roma Cristiana The Vatican's tourist bus service links Rome's major basilicas and other Christian sights, starting in Piazza dei Cinquecento. Services run daily every 30min between 9am and 6pm, and tickets cost €14 for a round trip, €20 for 24 hours, or €21 for 24 hours including public transport; buy on board, at Piazza dei Cinquecento or at PIT information kiosks.

Walking tours

Entrance fees are generally not included in the price of tours, so check costs before booking. Enjoy Rome (see p.183) is the best all-round operator, offering three-hour tours to groups (maximum 25 people). Most popular are the tours of the ancient sights and the highlights of the centro storico (€30). You may prefer the smaller-scale tours of Context Rome (☎06 9672 7371, ⓦwww.contexttravel.com), who run excellent small-group walking tours (maximum 6 people) of sights and neighbourhoods, led by engaging experts, on subjects ranging from architecture to gastronomic Rome. Eating Italy organize food tours of Testaccio and Trastevere (from €65; ⓦwww.eatingitalyfoodtours.com).

Nightbuses

#N1 follows metro line A; **#N2** calls at all stops along metro line B; and **#N8** runs from Trastevere to Termini station.

Useful bus and tram routes

#3 Tram Stazione Trastevere–Via Marmorata–Piramide–Circo Massimo–Colosseum–San Giovanni–San Lorenzo–Policlinico–Galleria d'Arte Moderna.

#8 Tram Piazza Venezia–Via Arenula–Piazza Sonnino–Viale Trastevere–Stazione Trastevere–Casaletto

#23 Piazzale Clodio–Piazza Risorgimento–Ponte Vittorio Emanuele II–Ponte Garibaldi–Via Marmorata–Piazzale Ostiense–Centrale Montemartini–Basilica di San Paolo.

#30 Express Piazzale Clodio–Piazza Mazzini–Piazza Cavour–Corso Rinascimento–Largo Argentina–Piazza Venezia–Lungotevere Aventino–Via Marmorata–Piramide–Via C.Colombo–EUR.

#40 Express Termini–Via Nazionale–Piazza Venezia–Largo Argentina–Borgo Sant'Angelo (Vatican).

#62 Piazza Bologna–Via Nomentana–Porta Pia–Piazza Barberini–Trevi Fountain–Via del Corso–Piazza Venezia– Corso V. Emanuele II–Largo Argentina–Piazza Pia (Vatican).

#64 Termini–Piazza della Repubblica–Via Nazionale–Piazza Venezia–Largo Argentina–Corso Vittorio Emanuele II–Stazione San Pietro.

#75 Via Poerio (Monteverde)–Porta Portese–Testaccio–Piramide–Circo Massimo–Colosseo–Via Cavour–Termini–Via XX Settembre.

#116 Porta Pinciana (Villa Borghese)–Via Veneto–Via del Tritone–Trevi Fountain–Campo de' Fiori–Piazza Farnese–Lungotevere Sangallo–Terminal Gianicolo.

#117 San Giovanni in Laterano–Colosseo–Cavour–Via Nazionale–Via del Corso–Piazza Venezia–Via dei Serpenti–Colosseo–San Giovanni in Laterano.

#119 Piazza del Popolo–Via del Corso–Piazza Cavour–Largo Argentina–Piazza Venezia–Via del Tritone–Via Due Macelli–Piazza di Spagna–Via del Babuino–Piazza del Popolo.

#175 Termini–Piazza Repubblica–Piazza Barberini–Via del Corso–Piazza Venezia–Colosseo–Circo Massimo–Aventine–Stazione Ostiense.

#271 S. Paolo–Via Ostiense–Piramide–Viale Aventino–Circo Massimo–Colosseo–Piazza Venezia–Ponte Sisto–Castel Sant'Angelo–Piazza Risorgimento–Ottaviano–Foro Italico.

#492 Stazione Tiburtina–Piazzale Verano (San Lorenzo)–Termini–Piazza Barberini–Via del Corso–Largo Argentina–Corso del Rinascimento–Piazza Cavour–Piazza Risorgimento–Cipro (Vatican Museums).

#590 Same route as metro line A but with access for disabled; runs every 90min.

#660 Largo Colli Albani–Arco di Travertino–Via Appia Antica–Tomb of Cecilia Metella.

#714 Termini–Santa Maria Maggiore–Via Merulana–San Giovanni in Laterano–Viale Terme di Caracalla–EUR.

#910 Termini–Piazza della Repubblica–Via Piemonte–Via Pinciana (Villa Borghese)–Piazza Euclide–Palazzetto dello Sport–Piazza Mancini (Stadio Olimpico).

M Termini–Piazzale Flaminio–Auditorium.

Bikes, mopeds and scooters

Renting a bike, moped or scooter can be the most efficient way of nipping around Rome's clogged city centre, and there are plenty of places offering this facility (see box, below). Some hotels – eg. *Locarno* (see p.168) – have bikes for guest-use. The best company for bike tours are TopBike Rental & Tours (☎06 488 2893, ⓦwww.topbikerental .com), whose small-group tours take interesting routes through the city, with options including a four-hour jaunt through the centre (€45) and a five-hour Panoramic Rome tour that takes in the best of Rome's views (€55). There's also a more challenging ride to the Via Appia Antica and Castelgandolfo lake (€99; 9hr).

Cycling along Rome's first highway and through the Caffarella Valley on a Sunday is a tranquil way of seeing the area. The Appia Antica visitor centre (see box below) also has good information in English about suggested routes.

Parking

It's generally safe to park your car in the centre, but you might prefer to pay a bit more to keep your car in one of the city's staffed car parks. You can park on the street for around €1.20/hr (8am–8pm), or there are garages in Villa Borghese (€2.20/hr) and in front of Termini station (€2/hr for the first two hours, then €1.50/hr). There are car parks next to the terminal metro stations, from where it's easy to get into the city centre.

Taxis

Central taxi stands (*fermata dei taxi)* include Termini, Piazza Venezia, Piazza San Silvestro, Piazza di Spagna, Piazza Navona, Largo Argentina, Piazza San Pietro and Piazza Barberini. Or, call a taxi (☎06 0609), but note you pay for the time it takes to get to you. Only take licensed white cabs with the "Comune di Roma" insignia on the door, and check the meter is on; a card in every official taxi explains the extra charges for luggage, late-night, Sundays and holidays, and airport journeys. Pick ups from Termini incur a supplement of €2. Journeys from Termini to the centre should cost around €10–15 and around €15–20 on Sunday or at night.

Renting cars, scooters and bicycles

Cars Avis (Termini ☎06 481 4373, Ciampino ☎06 7934 0195, Fiumicino ☎06 6501 1531); Europcar (Termini ☎06 488 2854, Ciampino ☎06 7934 0387, Fiumicino ☎06 6576 1211); Hertz (Termini ☎06 474 0389, Ciampino ☎06 7934 0616, Fiumicino ☎06 6501 1553); Maggiore (Termini ☎06 488 0049, Ciampino ☎06 7934 0368, Fiumicino ☎06 6501 0678); Sixt (Termini ☎06 4782 6000, Ciampino ☎06 7934 0802, Fiumicino ☎06 6595 3547).

Scooters Barberini (Via della Purificazione 84 ☎06 488 5485, ⓦwww .rentscooter.it) for €12/day for bikes, mopeds and scooters from €40/day. Treno e Scooter Rent, near Track 1 in Termini station (☎06 4890 5823, ⓦwww.trenoescooter.com. €10/day for bikes, €36–73/day for mopeds or scooters).

Bicycles Appia Antica Visitor Center (Via Appia Antica 58; ☎06 513 5316, ⓦwww.parcoappiaantica.it; €3/hr or €15/day for bicycles).

Directory A-Z

For the fire brigade, police or ambulance, call ☎113.

Cinema

Not many cinemas in Rome screen films in their original language, but the Nuovo Olimpia at Via in Lucina 16g (☎06 6861 1068), off Via del Corso, and Cinema Barberini on Piazza Barberini (☎06 8639 1361) are exceptions. Tickets cost around €7; ⓦ www.romeing.it has programme details.

Crime

To call the police, dial ☎112. Both the police (Polizia Statale) and the carabinieri (who wear military-style uniforms) have offices in Termini. Otherwise, the questura (main police office) is at Via San Vitale 15, off Via Nazionale; report any thefts to the police here.

Dress

The rules for visiting churches are much as they are all over Italy: dress modestly, which usually means no shorts, short skirts or bare shoulders.

Electricity

220 volts. Both UK and US adaptors are available to buy in Italy, but the latter can be expensive.

Embassies and consulates

Australia Via Bosio 5 (☎06 852 721; **Canada** Via Zara 30 ☎06 85444 3937; **Ireland** Villa Spada, Via G. Medici ☎06 585 2381; **New Zealand** Via Clitunno 44 ☎06 853 7501; **UK** Via XX Settembre 80a ☎06 4220 0001; **US** Via Veneto 121 ☎06 46 741.

Health

AlphaMed, Via Zanardelli 36 (☎06 6830 9493; Mon–Fri 9am–8pm), and Doctors in Rome ☎06 9028 7042; Mon–Sat 9am–7pm) are central medical practices with English-speaking doctors; Absolute Dentistry, Via G. Pisanelli 3, has a 24-hour emergency service (☎06 3600 3837).

The most central hospitals with emergency facilities are: Fatebenefratelli, Isola Tiberina (☎06 68371); Rome American Hospital, Via E. Longoni 69 (☎06 22 551), a private multi-speciality hospital with bilingual staff and a 24hr emergency line; San Giovanni at Via A. Aradam 9 (☎06 77051); Santo Spirito Lungotevere in Sassia 1, near the Vatican (☎6 68 351).

The following pharmacies are open 24hr, year-round: Internazionale, Piazza Barberini 49 ☎06 487 1195; Piram, Via Nazionale 228 ☎06 488 0754. The pharmacies in Termini station, including Farmacia Cristo Re on the lower level (☎06 488 0776) are open 7.30am–10pm.

Internet

Many of Rome's cafés and bars, and most of its hotels, now offer free wi-fi. If you need an internet café, try Bibli, Via dei Fienaroli 28 (Mon 5.30pm–midnight, Tues–Sun 11am–midnight); or Internet Train, Piazza Sant'Andrea della Valle 3 (Mon–Fri 10am–11pm, Sat 10am–8pm, Sun noon–8pm). There are also many internet cafés around Termini station. By law, internet cafés will ask you to show ID such as a passport before allowing you to access the internet. Free wireless hotspots in the city include the Circus Maximus, Villa Borghese, Piazza Navona, Largo Argentina, Trevi Fountain and the Spanish Steps. See ⓦ www.romawireless.com for other locations.

Left luggage

Termini station (daily 6am–11pm; €5 per piece for 5hr, then €0.70 for the sixth to the twelfth hour, then €0.30/hr; ☎ 06 474 4777).

Lost property

For lost property call ☎ 06 4730 6682 (daily 7am–10pm); the office is at Circonvallazione Ostiense 191 (Garbatella Metro).

Money

You'll find ATMs throughout the city. Nearly all hotels now accept credit cards, though many restaurants are still cash-only. To exchange money, post offices and banks tend to offer the best rates, or try American Express at both airports (daily 6am–10pm); or Travelex, Via della Conciliazione 23 (Mon–Sat 9am–7.30pm, Sun 9.30am–5pm). Post offices will exchange American Express travellers' cheques and cash commission-free.

For lost or stolen cards, call: American Express ☎ 800 914 912 or ☎ 06 7290 0347; MasterCard and Visa ☎ 800 819014.

Opening hours

Most museums and galleries are closed on Mondays. Opening hours for state-run museums are generally from 9am until 7pm, Tuesday to Sunday. Most other museums roughly follow this pattern too, although are likely to close for a couple of hours in the afternoon, and have shorter opening hours in winter. Some museums run late-night openings in summer (till 10pm or later Tues–Sat, or 8pm on Sun).

Opening times of ancient sites are more flexible: most are open daily, including Sunday, from 8.30am until the evening – usually one hour before sunset (changes according to the time of year). In winter, times are drastically cut; 4pm is a common closing time.

Most major Roman churches open in the early morning, at around 7am or 8am, and close around noon, opening up again at 4pm and closing at 6pm or 7pm.

Phones

If you have a GSM, dual- or tri-band phone which can be unlocked, consider investing in an Italian SIM card, which can be bought for about €10 from Italian providers TIM, Wind or Vodafone; ask for a "SIM prepagato". To use public telephones, you can buy telephone cards (*carta telefonica*) from *tabacchi* and newsstands in denominations of €5 and €10. You always need to dial the local code; ☎ 06 is the code for Rome and around. Numbers beginning ☎ 800 are free, ☎ 170 will get you through to an English-speaking operator, ☎ 176 to international directory enquiries. Any numbers that start with a 3 are mobile numbers. To make long-distance calls, it's cheaper to buy one of the international calling cards, also available from *tabacchi* for upwards of €5. You can make international reversed-charge or collect calls (*chiamata con addebito destinatario*) by dialling ☎ 170 and following the recorded instructions.

Post offices

The main post office is at Piazza San Silvestro 12 (☎ 06 6973 7205, Mon–Fri 8.20am–7.05pm, Sat 8.20am–12.35pm.

Smoking

Smoking is banned in all public indoor spaces in Italy, including restaurants, bars and clubs.

Time

Rome is one hour ahead of GMT, six hours ahead of Eastern Standard

Time, and nine hours ahead of Pacific Standard Time in North America.

Tourist information and passes

There are tourist information booths in Terminal 2 at Fiumicino (daily 9am–6.30pm; ☎ 06 0608), in the Arrivals Hall at Ciampino airport (daily 9am–6.30pm), in Termini station at Via Giolitti 34 (daily 8am–8pm; ☎ 06 0608), and on the Via dei Fori Imperiali (daily 9.30am–7pm; ☎ 06 0608) although you can also go to **Enjoy Rome** (Via Marghera 8a; Mon–Fri 9am–5.30pm, Sat 8.30am–2pm; ☎ 06 445 1843, ⓦ www.enjoyrome .com), an unofficial but reliable source of information whose English-speaking staff also run a free accommodation-finding service, organize walking and bus tours and can arrange shuttles to the airports. There are also green information kiosks (PIT; open 9.30am–7pm) near key locations around the city, such as Via Nazionale (Palazzo delle Esposizioni), Piazza Navona (Piazza delle Cinque Lune), Castel Sant'Angelo (Piazza Pia) and Trastevere (Piazza Sonnino). Rome's tourist information line ☎ 060608 is open daily 9am–7.30pm; calls are charged at the local rate.

For what's-on information, check out ⓦ romeing.it or the expat monthly, *Wanted in Rome* (€1; ⓦ wantedin rome.com), which is written entirely in English and is also useful if you're looking for an apartment or work. If you understand a bit of Italian, the daily arts pages of the Rome newspaper, *Il Messaggero*, lists movies, plays and major musical events, and can be found in most bars, or at newsstands for €1. The newspaper *La Repubblica* (€1.50) also includes the "TrovaRoma" section in its Thursday edition, another handy guide to current offerings.

Rome's main museum and transport pass is the **Roma Pass** (€34; ⓦ www.romapass.it), which gives you free admission to the first two participating museums or archeological sites visited, and discounts on visits elsewhere, plus full access to public transport for three days. Buy it from tourist offices, participating sights or online. It also allows you to skip the queue at sights such as the Colosseum and Forum – a huge bonus. The **Archeologia Card** (€23; valid seven days) covers the Colosseum, Roman Forum, Palatine Hill, Baths of Caracalla, Villa dei Quintili, Tomb of Cecilia Metella and Museo Nazionale Romano. Much of Rome's ancient sculpture, alongside other artefacts, has been gathered into the Museo Nazionale Romano, operating in four main sites: Palazzo Massimo, the Terme di Diocleziano, the Crypta Balbi and Palazzo Altemps. You can buy a ticket (at each branch) that grants entry to all for just €7 and is valid for three days. The Colosseum, Roman Forum and Palatine Hill are visitable on a combined ticket.

Travellers with disabilities

Although changes are in the works, Rome can be quite a challenge for those with disabilities. The city's hills, cobbles and steps can make getting around in a wheelchair a challenge, and little of the public transport network is accessible. See ⓦ www .sagetraveling.com for helpful tips on visiting the city. The state-funded Roma Per Tutti service (Mon–Fri 9am–5pm; ☎ 06 5717 7094, ⓦ www .romapertutti.it, in Italian only) provides information on accessible sights and transport. Dynamic Air (ⓔ info@dynamicair.it) offers the free loan of medical equipment to visitors in Italy, including wheelchairs, ventilators and oxygen tanks.

Festivals and events

Public holidays are denoted by **(PH)**; many sights and shops, and some bars and restaurants close.

NEW YEAR'S DAY (PH)

Jan 1

EPIPHANY (PH)

Jan 6
La Befana, or Epiphany, marks the end of a Christmas fair that fills Piazza Navona from mid-December.

CARNEVALE

Mid-Feb 10 days
Roman kids dress up and are paraded round the city by their proud parents, and clubs put on themed nights. Look out for the carnival delicacies sold throughout the city: *frappe* (deep-fried pastry strips) and *castagnole* (bite-sized pastries).

ROME MARATHON

Sunday in mid-March
ⓦwww.maratonadiroma.it
Thousands of runners take to the streets for Rome's annual marathon; the course takes in many of the major sights en route.

EASTER

During Holy Week, Catholics from across the world descend on Rome to witness the pope's address. On Good Friday, a solemn procession moves from the Colosseum to the Capitoline Hill, while on Easter Sunday the main event is the pope's blessing in St Peter's Square.

PASQUETTA (PH)

Easter Monday
Many Romans head out of town, traditionally for a picnic in the countryside.

NATALE DI ROMA

April 21
A spectacular fireworks display set off from the Campidoglio marks Rome's birthday.

FESTA DELLA PRIMAVERA

Late April
The Spanish Steps are lined with thousands of beautiful blooms.

SETTIMANA DELLA CULTURA

April ⓦwww.beniculturali.it
For nine days in April, you can enter all state-owned museums free of charge or at a discounted rate.

LIBERATION DAY (PH)

April 25

LABOUR DAY (PH)

May 1
"Primo Maggio" is celebrated with a free rock concert in Piazza San Giovanni.

ROME LITERATURE FESTIVAL

Late May–June
ⓦwww.festivaldelleletterature.it
Readings by well-known authors in one of the city's most atmospheric locations, the Basilica of Maxentius near the Roman Forum.

DAY OF THE REPUBLIC

June 2
The day is marked with a military parade along Via dei Fori Imperiali, and the gardens of the Quirinale palace are open to the public (expect long queues).

ESTATE ROMANA

Early June–late Sept

ⓦwww.estateromana.comune.roma.it

Rome's summer-long cultural extravaganza includes all sorts of events, from open-air film screenings to concerts in atmospheric surroundings. Many events are free.

ROMA INCONTRA IL MONDO

Mid-June to early Aug ⓦwww.villaada.org

An eclectic programme of pop, rock and indie concerts takes place in Villa Ada. Tickets €5–15.

TEATRO DELL'OPERA

Late June to mid-Aug

ⓦwww.operaroma.it

Teatro dell'Opera's summer season takes place in the floodlit setting of the Baths of Caracalla.

CONCERTI DEL TEMPIETTO

June–Oct ⓦwww.tempietto.it

Classical concerts with dramatic backdrops: the ancient Roman Teatro di Marcello and the Art Nouveau Casina delle Civette.

VILLA CELIMONTANA JAZZ

July–Aug

ⓦwww.villacelimontanajazzfestival.com

Open-air jazz performances in leafy Villa Celimontana, near the Colosseum. Tickets from €8.

FESTA DE' NOANTRI

Mid-July ⓦwww.festadenoantri.it

Two weeks of street performances and events in Trastevere culminate in a huge fireworks display.

FESTA DELLE CATENE

Aug 1

The chains of St Peter are displayed during a special Mass in the church of San Pietro in Vincoli.

FESTA DELLA MADONNA DELLA NEVE

Aug 5

The miracle of a summer snowfall (see p.91) is remembered in the Basilica of Santa Maria Maggiore with a shower of white petals on the congregation.

FERRAGOSTO (PH)

August 15

On the Feast of the Assumption, Rome empties as locals in search of cooling breezes head for the sea and mountains.

ROMAEUROPA FESTIVAL

Late Sept–Nov ⓦwww.romaeuropa.net

Rome's performing arts festival showcases international talents in music, theatre and dance, in venues around town.

ROME INTERNATIONAL FILM FESTIVAL

1 week mid-Oct ⓦwww.romacinemafest.it

Rome's film festival always draws Hollywood talent. The hub of the festival is Rome's Auditorium, but there are venues across town.

OGNISSANTI (PH)

Nov 1

On All Souls' Day, Romans visit family graves in the Verano cemetery in San Lorenzo.

IMMACOLATA CONCEZIONE (PH)

Dec 8

In honour of the Immaculate Conception of the Blessed Virgin Mary, a religious ceremony takes place in the Piazza di Spagna, often attended by the Pope.

NATALE/ SANTO STEFANO (PH)

Dec 25/Dec 26

Chronology

9th century BC > Iron Age village founded on the Palatine Hill.

753 BC > Romulus kills Remus and becomes the city's first ruler.

616–579 BC > Tarquinius Priscus is Rome's first Etruscan king.

509 BC > Tarquinius Superbus, the last Etruscan king, is deposed and the Roman Republic is established.

264–146 BC > Punic Wars against Carthage.

87 BC > Civil war breaks out between Marius and Sulla.

82 BC > Sulla becomes dictator of Rome.

65–63 BC > Marius' nephew, Julius Caesar, establishes a formidable military reputation.

60 BC > Triumvirate of Julius Caesar, Crassus and Pompey rules Rome.

58–51 BC > Caesar colonizes Gaul.

49–45 BC > Caesar marches on Rome, sparking off a civil war between him and Pompey.

44 BC > Caesar is assassinated in Pompey's Theatre on March 15.

43 BC > Leadership is assumed by a triumvirate of Antony, Octavian and Lepidus.

40 BC > Antony marries Octavian's sister, Octavia.

31 BC > Octavian defeats Antony and Cleopatra at the Battle of Actium.

27 BC > Octavian becomes sole ruler as Augustus.

14 AD > Tiberius, Augustus' stepson, assumes power and marries Augustus' daughter, Julia, who gives birth to Caligula, the next emperor.

41 AD > Caligula is assassinated after four years in power. His uncle, Claudius, proves to be a wiser successor.

54 AD > The reign of Claudius' stepson, Nero, is marred by corruption and excess.

69 AD > Emperor Vespasian restores order to Rome and builds the Colosseum in the grounds of Nero's Domus Aurea.

81 AD > Vespasian's son Titus is succeeded by Domitian, who builds the stadium that forms the foundations of today's Piazza Navona.

98 AD > Emperor Trajan expands the empire and Rome grows to a population of around a million.

117 > Trajan is succeeded by Hadrian, a wise and resourceful emperor, who ruled over the empire's golden age.

138–192 > Marcus Aurelius continues to rule a stable city and a rich empire but the Antonine line fizzles out when his son, Commodus, is strangled.

193 > Septimius Severus becomes the first emperor of the Severan dynasty.

211 > Severus' son, Caracalla, murders his brother and assumes power for himself.

275 > The emperor Aurelian builds a wall around the city to keep it safe from invaders.

284 > Diocletian stabilizes Rome and divides the empire into east and west.

306 > Constantine converts to Christianity and defeats his rival Maxentius to claim the Western Empire.

325 > Constantine shifts the seat of power east to Byzantium, renaming it Constantinople.

410 > Rome is captured by the Visigoths, the first time a foreign invader has held the city for 800 years.

5th century > The city declines to a population of around 30,000.

590 > Gregory I becomes pope, revitalizing the city with new basilicas and converting ancient Roman structures like the Pantheon and the Castel Sant'Angelo.

800 > Charlemagne visits Rome and is crowned ruler of the Holy Roman Empire.

850–1300 > Rome is the focus of struggles between the papacy, Holy Roman emperors and its own aristocracy.

1305 > Clement V transfers the papal court to Avignon, France.

1347 > Cola di Rienzo seizes power and re-establishes Rome's Republic for seven years.

1417 > Martin V consolidates papal power in Rome.

1475 > Pope Sixtus IV commissions the Sistine Chapel.

1503 > Julius II becomes pope and commissions frescoes for the Sistine Chapel from Michelangelo.

1513 > Leo X continues Julius's role as patron of the city's greatest artists and architects.

1527 > Holy Roman Emperor Charles V captures Rome and Clement VII flees to the Castel Sant'Angelo.

1534 > Alessandro Farnese is elected pope as Paul III and Michelangelo completes his Sistine Chapel painting of the *Last Judgement*.

1585 > Sixtus V undertakes widespread construction, creating grand vistas and squares.

1605 > St Peter's is completed under the Borghese pope, Paul V.

1623 > Urban VIII ascends the papal throne and becomes the greatest patron of the Baroque's most dominant figure, Gianlorenzo Bernini.

1700 > The city's population is now 150,000, and Rome becomes an essential stop on any traveller's Grand Tour.

1798 > French forces commanded by Napoleon occupy the city; Pius VI is taken as a prisoner to France.

1815 > Papal rule is restored under Pius VII.

1849 > Giuseppe Mazzini forces Pope Pius IX to leave Rome but the papacy is restored four months later by Napoleon III.

1859–64 > Unification forces gather strength and Florence becomes the capital of the new kingdom of Italy.

1870 > Italian forces take Rome and declare the city the capital of the new state under Vittorio Emanuele II. Pope Pius IX is confined to the Vatican.

1922–42 > Mussolini oversees the construction of numerous public works.

1929 > The Lateran Pact is signed by Italy and the Vatican, recognizing the sovereignty of the Vatican City.

1946 > King Vittorio Emanuele III is forced to abdicate and a republic is declared under Alcide de Gasperi.

1960 > Fellini releases *La Dolce Vita*, a film that would define the Sixties in Rome.

1970s > The *anni piombi*, or "years of lead", when Rome became a focus for terrorism, culminating in the murder of politician Aldo Moro.

1990s > Corruption scandals lead to a series of trials and the reconfiguration of the entire Italian political landscape.

2001 > Walter Veltroni is elected mayor of Rome, and oversees a series of prestigious public works.

2005 > Pope John Paul II is succeeded by Josef Ratzinger as Pope Benedict XVI.

2013 Following the resignation of Pope Benedict XVI, Pope Francis, the first pope from the Americas, is elected. Also this year, after years of scandal, Prime Minister Silvio Berlusconi resigns.

2014 Two modern-day popes, John Paul II and John XXIII, are canonized at St Peter's, drawing around a million pilgrims from all over the world.

Italian

Speaking some **Italian**, however tentatively, can mark you out from the hordes of tourists in Rome, and having a little more can open up the city no end. What follows is a brief pronunciation guide, some useful words and phrases, and a food and drink glossary. For more detail, *Italian: The Rough Guide Phrasebook* has a huge and accessible vocabulary, a detailed menu reader and conversational examples to get you through most situations.

Pronunciation

Italian **pronunciation** is very simple – generally words are stressed on the penultimate syllable unless an accent (` or ´) denotes otherwise. The only difficulties you're likely to encounter are the few consonants that are different from English:

c before e or i is pronounced as in **ch**urch, while **ch** before the same vowels is hard, as in **c**at.

The same goes with **g** – soft before e or i, as in **g**eranium; hard before h, as in **g**arlic.

sci or **sce** are pronounced as in **sh**eet and **sh**elter respectively.

gn has the ni sound of o**ni**on.

gl in Italian is softened to a sound similar to lyi, as in sta**lli**on.

h is not aspirated, as in **h**onour.

Words and phrases
BASICS

good morning	buongiorno
good afternoon/ evening	buonasera
good night	buonanotte
hello/goodbye	ciao (informal; to strangers use phrases above)
goodbye	arrivederci
yes	sì
no	no
please	per favore

thank you (very much)	grazie (molte/mille grazie)
you're welcome	prego
all right/OK	va bene
how are you? (informal/formal)	come stai/sta?
I'm fine	bene
Do you speak English?	parla inglese?
I don't understand	non ho capito
I don't know	non lo so
excuse me (to get attention)	mi scusi
excuse me (in a crowd)	permesso
I'm sorry	mi dispiace
I'm here on holiday	sono qui in vacanza
I'm English	sono inglese
Scottish	scozzese
Welsh	gallese
Irish	irlandese
American (m/f)	americano/a
Australian (m/f)	australiano/a
a New Zealander	neozelandese
today	oggi
tomorrow	domani
day after tomorrow	dopodomani
yesterday	ieri
now	adesso
later	più tardi
tonight	stasera
morning	mattina
afternoon	pomeriggio
evening	sera
wait!	aspetta!
let's go!	andiamo!
here/there	qui/là
good/bad	buono/cattivo
big/small	grande/piccolo
cheap/expensive	economico/caro
early/late	presto/tardi
hot/cold	caldo/freddo
near/far	vicino/lontano
quickly/slowly	velocemente/ lentamente
with/without	con/senza
more/less	più/meno
enough, no more	basta
Mr/Mrs/Miss	signore/signora/ signorina

ITALIAN

QUESTIONS AND DIRECTIONS

where?	dove?
Where is/where are...?	Dov'è/Dove sono ... ?
How do I get to ... ?	Per arrivare a ... ?
turn left/right	giri a sinistra/destra
go straight on	vai sempre diritto
How far is it to ... ?	Quant'è lontano a... ?
What time does it open/close?	A che ora apre/chiude?
What time is it?	Che ore sono?
when?	quando?
what? (what is it?)	cosa? (cos'è?)
How much/many?	Quanto/Quanti?
why?	perché?
It is/there is (is it/is there ...)?	C'è ... ?
How much does it/they cost?	Quanto costa/costano?
How do you say it in Italian?	Come si dice in italiano?

TRANSPORT

bus station	autostazione
train station	stazione ferroviaria
a ticket to ...	un biglietto a ...
one-way/return	solo andata/andata e ritorno
Can you tell me when to get off?	Mi può dire dove scendere?
What time does it leave/arrive?	A che ora parte/arriva?
Where does it leave from?	Da dove parte?

SIGNS

aperto	open
bagno/gabinetto	WC/bathroom
cassa	cash desk
chiuso	closed
chiuso per ferie	closed for holidays
chiuso per restauro	closed for restoration
entrata	entrance
ingresso libero	free entry
signori/signore	gentlemen/ladies
spingere	push
tirare	pull
uscita	exit
vietato fumare	no smoking

ACCOMMODATION

hotel	albergo
hostel	ostello
I'd like to book a room	Vorrei prenotare una camera
Is there a hotel nearby?	C'è un albergo qui vicino?
I have a booking	Ho una prenotazione
Do you have a room ...	Avete una camera
for one/two night/s	per una/due notte/i
for one/two week/s	per una/due settimana/e
with a double bed	con un letto matrimoniale
with twin beds	con due letti
with a shower/bath	con doccia/bagno
with a balcony	con balcone
How much is it?	Quanto costa?
It's expensive	È caro
Is breakfast included?	È compresa la colazione?
Do you have anything cheaper?	Ha qualcosa che costa di meno?
Full/half board	Pensione completa/mezza pensione
Can I see the room?	Posso vedere la camera?
I'll take it	La prendo

NUMBERS

uno	1
due	2
tre	3
quattro	4
cinque	5
sei	6
sette	7
otto	8
nove	9
dieci	10
undici	11
dodici	12
tredici	13
quattordici	14
quindici	15
sedici	16
diciassette	17

190

diciotto	18
diciannove	19
venti	20
ventuno	21
ventidue	22
trenta	30
quaranta	40
cinquanta	50
sessanta	60
settanta	70
ottanta	80
novanta	90
cento	100
centuno	101
centodieci	110
duecento	200
cinquecento	500
mille	1000
cinquemila	5000
diecimila	10,000

Food and drink terms
BASICS AND SNACKS

aceto	vinegar
aglio	garlic
biscotti	biscuits
burro	butter
caramelle	sweets
cioccolato	chocolate
formaggio	cheese
frittata	omelette
marmellata	jam
olio	oil
olive	olives
pane	bread
pepe	pepper
riso	rice
sale	salt
uova	eggs
zucchero	sugar
zuppa	soup

STARTERS (ANTIPASTI) AND FRIED SNACKS (FRITTI)

antipasto misto mixed cold meats and cheese (and a selection of other things in this list)

arancini fried rice balls with mozzarella and tomato

caponata mixed aubergine, olives, tomatoes and celery

caprese tomato and mozzarella salad

insalata di mare seafood salad

insalata di riso rice salad

melanzane alla parmigiana layers of aubergine, tomato and parmesan

mortadella salami-type cured meat

pancetta bacon

peperonata grilled green, red or yellow peppers stewed in olive oil

pomodori ripieni stuffed tomatoes

prosciutto ham

salame salami

suppli fried rice balls with mozzarella

SOUP (ZUPPA)

brodo clear broth

minestrina any light soup

minestrone thick vegetable soup

pasta e fagioli pasta soup with beans

pastina in brodo pasta in clear broth

stracciatella broth with egg

PASTA

bucatini thick, hollow spaghetti-type pasta.

cannelloni large, stuffed pasta tubes

farfalle literally "bow"- shaped pasta; the word also means "butterflies"

fettuccine flat ribbon egg pasta

paccheri large tubes of pasta

pasta al forno pasta baked with minced meat, eggs, tomato and cheese

penne tubed pasta

rigatoni Large, curved and ridged tubes of pasta – bigger than penne but smaller than paccheri

spaghettini thin spaghetti

strozzapreti literally "strangled priests" – twisted flat noodles

tagliatelle flat ribbon egg noodles, slightly thinner than fettuccine

vermicelli thin strand pasta often served in soup – literally "little worms"

PASTA SAUCES

aglio e olio with garlic and oil

amatriciana With tomato and *guanciale* (similar to bacon)

arrabbiata ("angry") spicy tomato sauce, with chillies

alla carbonara pasta with beaten egg, pan-fried guanciale or bacon, and pecorino cheese

alla gricia with pecorino and guanciale

cacio e pepe with pecorino and ground black pepper

con vongole with clams

panna cream

parmigiano parmesan

pasta alla pajata with calf's intestines – a very Roman dish

peperoncino chilli

pomodoro tomato

puttanesca ("whorish") Tomato, anchovy, olive oil and oregano

ragù (or Bolognese) meat sauce

MEAT (CARNE)

abbacchio milk-fed lamb roasted with rosemary and garlic

agnello lamb

bistecca steak

carpaccio slices of raw beef

cervello brain, usually calves'

cinghiale wild boar

coda alla vaccinara oxtail stewed in a rich sauce of tomato and celery

coniglio rabbit

costolette cutlet, chop

coratella lamb's heart, liver, lungs and spleen cooked in olive oil with lots of black pepper and onions

fegato liver

guanciale unsmoked bacon made from pigs' cheeks

maiale pork

manzo beef

milza spleen – sometimes served as a pâté on toasted bread

ossobuco shin of veal

pajata the intestines of a unweaned calf

pancetta bacon

pollo chicken

polpette meatballs

porchetta pork stuffed with herbs and roasted on a spit

rognoni kidneys

salsiccia sausage

saltimbocca alla romana veal cooked with a slice of prosciutto and sage on top, served plain or with a Marsala sauce

scottadito grilled lamb chops, eaten with the fingers

spezzatino stew

trippa tripe

vitello veal

FISH (PESCE) AND SHELLFISH (CROSTACEI)

acciughe anchovies

anguilla eel

aragosta lobster

baccalà cod, best eaten Jewish-style, deep-fried

calamari squid

cozze mussels

dentice sea bream

gamberetti shrimps

gamberi prawns

granchio crab

merluzzo cod

ostriche oysters

pesce spada swordfish

polpo octopus

rospo monkfish

sampiero John Dory

sarde sardines

sogliola sole

tonno tuna

trota trout

vongole clams

VEGETABLES (CONTORNI) AND SALAD (INSALATA)

carciofi... artichokes

   ...alla romana stuffed with garlic, mint and parsley and stewed in wine

   ...alla guidia flattened and deep fried in olive oil

carciofini artichoke hearts

cavolfiore cauliflower

cavolo cabbage

cipolla onion

fagioli beans

fagiolini green beans

fiori di zucca batter-fried courgette (zucchini) blossom stuffed with mozzarella and sometimes a sliver of marinated anchovy

finocchio fennel
funghi mushrooms
insalata verde /mista green/mixed salad
melanzane aubergine (eggplant)
patate potatoes
peperoni peppers
piselli peas
pomodori tomatoes
radicchio red salad leaves
spinaci spinach

COOKING TERMS

ai ferri grilled without oil
alla brace barbecued
alla griglia grilled
alla milanese fried in egg and
   breadcrumbs
alla pizzaiola cooked with tomato sauce
allo spiedo on the spit
al dente firm, not overcooked
al forno baked
al sangue rare
arrosto roast
ben cotto well done
bollito/lesso boiled
cotto cooked (not raw)
crudo raw
fritto fried
in umido stewed
ripieno stuffed
stracotto braised, stewed

CHEESE (FORMAGGI)

dolcelatte creamy blue cheese
fontina northern Italian cheese
pecorino strong, hard sheep's cheese
provola/provolone smooth, round mild
   cheese, made from buffalo's or sheep's
   milk, sometimes smoked

FRUIT (FRUTTA) AND NUTS (NOCI)

ananas pineapple
anguria/cocomero watermelon
arance oranges
banane bananas
ciliegie cherries
fichi figs

fichi d'India prickly pears
fragole strawberries
limone lemon
mandorle almonds
mele apples
melone melon
pere pears
pesche peaches
pinoli pine nuts
uva grapes

DESSERTS (DOLCI)

cassata ice-cream cake with candied fruit
crostata pastry tart with fruit, chocolate or
   ricotta topping
gelato ice cream
macedonia fruit salad
torta cake, tart
zabaglione dessert made with eggs, sugar
   and Marsala wine
zuppa inglese trifle

DRINKS (BEVANDE)

acqua minerale mineral water
acqua naturale/frizzante still/sparkling
   water
acqua del rubinetto tap water
bicchiere glass
birra beer
bottiglia bottle
caffè coffee
cioccolato caldo hot chocolate
ghiaccio ice
granita iced drink, with coffee or fruit
latte milk
limonata lemonade
spremuta fresh fruit juice
succo concentrated fruit juice with sugar
tè tea
vino wine
vino rosso/bianco/rosato red/white/
   rose wine
vino secco/dolce dry/sweet wine
litro litre
mezzo half
quarto quarter
salute! cheers!

PUBLISHING INFORMATION

This third edition published February 2015 by **Rough Guides Ltd**.

80 Strand, London WC2R 0RL

11, Community Centre, Panchsheel Park, New Delhi 110017, India

Distributed by Penguin Random House

Penguin Books Ltd, 80 Strand, London WC2R 0RL

Penguin Group (USA) 345 Hudson Street, NY 10014, USA

Penguin Group (Australia) 250 Camberwell Road, Camberwell, Victoria 3124, Australia

Penguin Group (NZ) 67 Apollo Drive, Mairangi Bay, Auckland 1310, New Zealand

Rough Guides is represented in Canada by

Tourmaline Editions Inc., 662 King Street West, Suite 304, Toronto, Ontario, M5V 1M7

Typeset in Minion and Din to an original design by Henry Iles and Dan May.

Printed and bound in China

© Rough Guides 2015

Maps © Rough Guides

No part of this book may be reproduced in any form without permission from the publisher except for the quotation of brief passages in reviews.

208pp includes index

A catalogue record for this book is available from the British Library

ISBN 978-1-4093-6953-0

The publishers and authors have done their best to ensure the accuracy and currency of all the information in the **Pocket Rough Guide Rome**, however, they can accept no responsibility for any loss, injury, or inconvenience sustained by any traveller as a result of information or advice contained in the guide.

1 3 5 7 9 8 6 4 2

MIX
Paper from responsible sources
FSC www.fsc.org FSC™ C018179

ROUGH GUIDES CREDITS

Text editors: Olivia Rawes, Lucy Kane
Layout: Anita Singh, Pradeep Thapliyal, Dan May
Photography: James McConnachie, Natascha Sturny
Cartography: Katie Bennett
Picture editor: Marta Bescos, Mark Thomas
Proofreader: Jennifer Speake
Production: Emma Sparks
Cover design: Nicole Newman, Pradeep Thapliyal

THE AUTHOR

Natasha Foges packed her bags and moved to Rome on a whim, and stayed for four years. Now based in London, she misses the food, the sun and the scooter rides, but escapes back to Rome as often as she can to revisit old haunts and overindulge on ice cream.

ACKNOWLEDGEMENTS

Natasha Foges would like to thank Olivia Rawes, for sharp-eyed editing; Lorenzo Zanasi, *padrino numero uno*; Richard, Chiara, Lesley and Antonio, for great Roman nights out; and Will and Joe Widén, for being the perfect Rome-mates.

HELP US UPDATE

We've gone to a lot of effort to ensure that the third edition of the **Pocket Rough Guide Rome** is accurate and up-to-date. However, things change – places get "discovered", opening hours are notoriously fickle, restaurants and rooms raise prices or lower standards. If you feel we've got it wrong or left something out, we'd like to know, and if you can remember the address, the price, the hours, the phone number, so much the better.

Please send your comments with the subject line "**Pocket Rough Guide Rome Update**" to ⊜ mail@roughguides.com. We'll credit all contributions and send a copy of the next edition (or any other Rough Guide if you prefer) for the very best emails.

Have your questions answered and tell others about your trip at ⊚ www.roughguides.com

PHOTO CREDITS

p.118 Tomb of Cecilia Metella © Glyn Thomas Photography

p.119 EUR © Masci/Tips Images

p.126 Corsini Palace © Gaertner/Alamy

p.127 View from the Janiculum Hill © imageBROKER/Alamy

p.128 Porta Portese Market © Susan Wright/Alamy

p.130 Interior of *Glass Hostaria* © Glass Hostaria

p.131 Interior of *Freni e Frizioni* © Freni e Frizioni

p.133 Galleria Borghese © The Bridgeman Art Library

p.144 Michelangelo's Pieta © Reinhard Dirscherl/Photolibrary

p.145 Interior of St Peter's Basilica © Mark Thomas

p.149 Sistine Chapel © Russell Mountford/Photolibrary

p.151 Vatican Gardens © Mark Thomas

p.155 Temple of Vesta and Tiburnus © Yannick Luthy/Alamy

p.157 Anzio © Bruce Bean/iStock

p.158 Sperlonga © Juergen Sack/iStock

p.159 Terracina © Fabio Franco Mancino/Alamy

p.160 Amphitheatre, Ostia Antica © imagebroker/Alamy

p.174–175 View from the Spanish Steps © Mark Thomas

Index

Map entries are in **bold**.

A ROUGH GUIDE TO ROUGH GUIDES

ROUGH GUIDES

Published in 1982, the first Rough Guide – to Greece – was a student scheme that became a publishing phenomenon. Mark Ellingham, a recent graduate in English from Bristol University, had been travelling in Greece the previous summer and couldn't find the right guidebook. With a small group of friends he wrote his own guide, combining a highly contemporary, journalistic style with a thoroughly practical approach to travellers' needs.

The immediate success of the book spawned a series that rapidly covered dozens of destinations. And, in addition to impecunious backpackers, Rough Guides soon acquired a much broader and older readership that relished the guides' wit and inquisitiveness as much as their enthusiastic, critical approach and value-for-money ethos.

These days, Rough Guides feature recommendations from shoestring to luxury and cover more than 200 destinations around the globe. Our ever-growing team of authors and photographers is spread all over the world, particularly in Europe, the US and Australia.

Rough Guides now number around 200 titles, including Pocket city guides, inspirational coffee-table books and comprehensive country and regional titles, plus technology guides from iPods to Android. As well as print books, we publish groundbreaking apps and eBooks for every major digital device.

Visit Ⓦ roughguides.com to see our latest publications.

Rough Guide travel images are available for commercial licensing at Ⓦ roughguidespictures.com.

SO NOW WE'VE TOLD YOU
ABOUT THE THINGS NOT TO
MISS, THE BEST PLACES TO
STAY, THE TOP RESTAURANTS,
THE LIVELIEST BARS AND THE
MOST SPECTACULAR SIGHTS,
IT ONLY SEEMS FAIR TO
TELL YOU ABOUT THE BEST
TRAVEL INSURANCE AROUND

WorldNomads.com
keep travelling safely

RECOMMENDED BY ROUGH GUIDES